INSTRUCTOR'S MANUAL

HARBRACE COLLEGE HANDBOOK

ELEVENTH EDITION

INSTRUCTOR'S MANUAL

HARBRACE COLLEGE HANDBOOK
ELEVENTH EDITION

ROBERT K. MILLER
University of Wisconsin, Stevens Point

HARCOURT BRACE JOVANOVICH, PUBLISHERS
San Diego   New York   Chicago   Austin   Washington, D.C.
London   Sydney   Tokyo   Toronto

Acknowledgments

AMERICAN MEDICAL ASSOCIATION For "It's Over, Debbie." Reprinted by permission. *Journal of the American Medical Association*, January 8, 1988, Vol. 259, No. 2, p. 272. Copyright © 1988, American Medical Association.

HARPER & ROW For "Tulips" from *The Collected Poems of Sylvia Plath*, edited by Ted Hughes. Copyright © by Ted Hughes. Reprinted by permission of Harper & Row, Publishers, Inc.

MCGRAW-HILL For the three definitions from *Concise Dictionary of Literary Terms* by Harry Shaw. Copyright © 1976. Reprinted by permission of McGraw-Hill Publishing Company.

ISBN: 0-15-531866-7

Printed in the United States of America

PREFACE

For many teachers of writing, a handbook has become a symbol rather than a tool. On the one hand are traditionalists who believe that writing is a skill that can be learned through mastering rules. Concerned with mechanical correctness, they see the handbook as a rock upon which they can defend the sanctity of language from the assaults of an aggressive illiteracy that threatens to engulf their world. On the other hand are instructors for whom writing is a romantic act of self-discovery. Believing that writing is a process and that communication is more important than grammatical correctness, they see the handbook as a relic of nineteenth-century pedagogy—a type of giant ruler used to smash the knuckles of aspiring writers, leaving hands crippled and creativity thwarted.

Fortunately, an increasing number of composition specialists are coming to recognize that the effective teaching of writing requires both instruction in rhetorical strategies that can inspire meaningful communication and enforcement of standards of mechanical correctness, including grammar. Instructors using the Eleventh Edition of the *Harbrace College Handbook* are well placed to teach writing in a manner that reflects this growing consensus.

Where you choose to put your emphasis should be determined by the most pressing needs of your students. The Handbook is flexible enough to be used in different ways in different courses. You can teach the book sequentially from one section to the next, beginning with lessons in basic sentence structure and asking students to write essays only after you have helped them master more modest assignments. Or you can ask your students to start writing at the onset of your course by beginning with the sections on paragraph development and the whole composition and then turning to lessons drawn from earlier sections as the need arises. Numerous cross-references contribute to the book's flexibility. (Sample syllabi provided in the appendix of this manual lend themselves to variations determined by your own interests and by the nature of the course you are teaching.)

Because they are not interested in teaching rules but recognize that a handbook is a valuable reference tool, many instructors require their students to buy a handbook and to use it on their own as they need it. This approach may benefit well-motivated students but may fail to help others. Although experienced writers like to keep a handbook nearby for resolving the numerous questions of usage that few people can keep constantly in mind, students are not likely to use their handbooks until they have been taught to do so. A handbook is not a dictionary. Many of the principles set forth in the handbook require elaboration and discussion in class. And although the general table of contents that appears inside the front cover of the *Harbrace College Handbook* can be easily mastered, it may never be used by students whose instructors have not encouraged the habit of consultation or helped them to acquire practice in looking things up.

Once students discover that this Handbook provides answers to most of the puzzling questions that occur when they are revising and editing their work, they are likely to refer to it on their own. But you need to help them reach this point. Although the extent to which the book is used in class will vary from course to course, the Handbook should be specifically incorporated into any course that has required its purchase. Your students will not thank you if you make them buy a book and then seem to ignore it.

One way you can encourage students to use their Handbooks is to respond to their work by using lettered references that direct the students to specific sections of the book. This system is illustrated in **8e** and **8f** of the Handbook, pages **96–99**. (Note that all page or section references to the Handbook are set in boldface.) Once you have learned the book's reference keys, you can often provide a fast and specific response to the pile of papers before you. Writing "12a" is easier than writing a comment explaining why a comma is needed, and a "20c" in the margin can sound less judgmental than "cliché!" Recognizing that many instructors use this system, the authors of the *Harbrace College Handbook* have been careful to preserve its well-established sequence of numbered and lettered sections. Unfortunately, there is no reason to assume students will automatically turn to their Handbooks to decipher a comment that looks suspiciously like a shoe size. And a paper that is returned with nothing but numbers and letters upon it can make students feel as if they are being taught by a machine. Those of you who use a system of numbered references when responding to student prose should frequently check to see that students understand these references and should try to combine them with written comments. Additional advice on evaluating student writing can be found in the essays on Part One.

The *Instructor's Manual* includes many activities designed to help you incorporate the Handbook into your course. It includes the following:

- Answers to all exercises in the Eleventh Edition except those that call for original work
- Brief, practical discussions of the thirty-five sections in the Handbook, emphasizing strategies for teaching them
- Explanatory comments augmenting the text
- References to pertinent professional literature
- Quotations about writing that can enliven class discussion
- Supplemental class activities, arranged by Handbook section, intended to stimulate student interest in various aspects of language and to encourage their proficient use of the Handbook
- Supplementary examples
- Bibliographical notes on selected authors who have been excerpted in the Handbook

In addition, this manual includes five specially commissioned essays on the teaching of writing by nationally recognized authorities in rhetoric and composition. Each of these essays is accompanied by an annotated bibliography that can help instructors identify additional sources that will be of use to them. The first essay provides an overview of major issues confronting teachers of writing. The remaining four suggest strategies for helping speaking lead to writing, evaluating student writing, using computers to help teach writing, and teaching writing across the curriculum.

The *Harbrace College Handbook*, Eleventh Edition, has an extensive ancillary package:

- *The Resourceful Writer*, Second Edition (and its Instructor's Manual), by Suzanne S. Webb—readings to accompany the Handbook
- *Harbrace College Workbooks* (and their accompanying Instructor's Editions): Form 11A, "Exploring the Cosmos," by Larry G. Mapp; Form 11B (available in 1991) by Larry G. Mapp; Form 11C, "Writing for the World of Work," by Melissa E. Barth; and *Harbrace ESL Workbook* by Sheila Graham and Wynn J. Curtis
- *The Harbrace Tutor: Self-Correcting Lessons* by J. N. Hook, William H. Evans, and Sally B. Reagan—programmed exercises
- Correction Chart
- Transparency Masters
- Test Package (also available on disk) by Alice T. Gasque
- *The Caret Patch* by Sheila Graham and Eileen Evans—a study disk
- *The Writing Tutor* by Laurence G. Avery, Erika C. Lindemann, and Joseph S. Wittig—word-processing software with prewriting tutorial
- PC-Write Lite—word-processing software
- *GramPop* and *DocuPop* by T. David Cowart—online reference software

Acknowledgments   Substantial portions of this manual have been retained from earlier editions by Eileen B. Evans, Suzanne S. Webb, and Mary E. Whitten. In preparing this edition, I had the good fortune to be able to consult with Winifred B. Horner and Suzanne S. Webb, both of whom generously gave me their valuable advice and support. For contributing essays to the manual, I also want to thank Gary Tate, Barry Kroll, Vivian Davis, Hugh Burns, and Toby Fulwiler. Finally, I owe many thanks to the Harbrace team at Harcourt Brace Jovanovich: Stuart Miller, acquisitions editor; Sarah Helyar Smith, manuscript editor; Lisa L. Werries, production editor; Don Fujimoto and Jamie Fidler, designers; and Lynne Bush, production manager.

Robert K. Miller

CONTENTS

PREFACE   v

Part One
ESSAYS ON TEACHING WRITING   1
   "An Introduction to Teaching Composition," Gary Tate   1
   "Speaking and Writing: Help or Hindrance?" Barry Kroll   8
   "Evaluating Student Writing," Vivian Davis   14
   "'CLASS' Acts: On Teaching Computer-Assisted Writing,"
   Hugh Burns   20
   "Writing across the Curriculum and the Writing Teacher,"
   Toby Fulwiler   29

Part Two
SECTIONS 1–35: DISCUSSIONS, ACTIVITIES, AND
ANSWERS TO EXERCISES   37

Part Three
BIOGRAPHICAL DATA ON WRITERS CITED IN THE
HARBRACE COLLEGE HANDBOOK: A PARTIAL
LISTING   219

Appendix: Sample Syllabi   223

PART ONE
ESSAYS ON TEACHING WRITING

An Introduction to Teaching Composition

Gary Tate,
Texas Christian University

Although the teaching of composition in American colleges has changed dramatically in the past three decades, many of the basic problems that confront the teacher of writing on an almost daily basis have remained the same. How are writing students motivated? What kinds of writing assignments should they be given? How should student writing be evaluated? What should go on during the hour or so of class? In addition to these seemingly timeless questions, new questions, which cannot be avoided by the conscientious teacher who pays attention to what is going on in the profession, appear with increasing frequency: Is collaborative learning helpful in the writing class? What is the "process" approach to the teaching of composition? Should teachers attempt to introduce students to the writing of various discourse communities? and so on.

Although the questions seem endless, they raise important issues which every teacher is obligated to confront. In this brief essay, I will say a few words about only three such topics, chosen because I think they have been either neglected or misunderstood.

Not totally neglected by writers in Composition Studies, but often lost sight of in the hectic day-to-day teaching of college composition is the extremely important issue of purpose: Am I teaching with a purpose? Do I have an overarching sense of *why* I do what I do each day in class? Do I have a clear and detailed vision of what I am attempting to achieve? I am not prepared to argue for the superiority of this or that particular purpose. There are many legitimate reasons for teaching composition, and these reasons or purposes will often vary from college to college and from teacher to teacher. That is probably not only inevitable but desirable. What I *do* want to suggest is that a clear-cut sense of purpose is necessary. Without it, for example, I cannot possibly make intelligent decisions about most of the issues mentioned at the beginning of this essay. How can I decide what kinds of writing assignments to give my students unless I know clearly what it is the students

1

and I are trying to accomplish in this class? If my primary goal is to help them become intelligent critics of their own ideas and the ideas of others, then one kind of writing and evaluation will be in order. If my primary goal is to introduce students to the traditions and standards of academic discourse, then another kind of writing and evaluation will necessarily be called for.

Every aspect of the course is—or *should* be—affected by the context of purpose. Unless the teacher has what might be called a "philosophy of composition" that guides her as she moves through the course, she will make decisions in isolation, decisions which, as a consequence, will often send contradictory signals to her students. What should be avoided, I think, is the "patchwork" course, the course made up of a collection of unrelated "good ideas": an interesting assignment described by a colleague in the faculty lounge, an exercise on transitions recommended by a textbook, a "new" method of marking papers discovered in a recent journal article, and so forth. The teacher should be concerned not only about the usefulness of each new idea but also about how that idea is related to her philosophy of composition.

Although I have said that there are many valuable goals, many commendable philosophies of composition, I would not argue that all goals are equally valuable. A basic rule, I believe, is this: the attention should always be on the writing—the act of writing and the results of that act. It is fine to want to "teach students to think," but that thinking must be made manifest in prose. It is fine to help students question their beliefs and the beliefs of others, but that questioning must be done in writing. The quality of the students' thinking and questioning can be seen only in the quality of their prose. As a general rule, any purpose that moves the class away from a focus on the craft of writing should be viewed with suspicion.

Finally, a word about the individual teacher's relationship to the general goals of the department and college. I have often heard teachers argue that they cannot teach as they wish because of the restrictions placed on them by others. This may sometimes be the case, but the goals of many departments and colleges are so general that resourceful teachers not only *can* shape their courses as they wish, but *must* do so if the course is to be effective. Such commonly proclaimed goals as "teaching students to write better" or "helping students improve their writing" leave almost all the important questions unanswered: Write *what* better? What is "improved" writing? and so on. It is as we attempt to answer such questions as these that we begin to create for ourselves a set of goals and purposes, a truly useful philosophy of composition.

But the development of a carefully articulated philosophy is just a beginning. A multitude of problems remain, although now they can be dealt with within the context of a clearly defined purpose. One of the most important of these problems, strangely enough, has been almost completely ignored by the profession: motivating the student writer. One searches the journals and books in the field in vain for helpful discussions of motivation. Specialists in composition have, so far as I can tell, spent the last twenty or thirty years discussing in print almost every topic even distantly related to the teaching of writing—except motivation. This situation exists in spite of every teacher's knowledge that the uncaring student, the unmotivated student will not improve as a writer. Any tennis coach or ballet teacher will tell the same story. Performance improves only as a result of effort, and effort is the result of the desire to improve.

The situation is especially critical in most college composition classes because the majority of students are in these classes not because they want to be but because the classes are required, whether it is a college Freshman English requirement or, in the case of upper-level writing courses, a requirement of the student's major field of study. To make matters worse, many students come into our writing classes with a long history of problems in English courses. They have often not been successful in their high school English classes, and they see no reason why their college English classes will be different. Finally, many of them have never had the opportunity to take a full-blown writing course. They may have written in high school only occasionally and as a part of a course devoted primarily to literature or some other subject. Is it any wonder, then, that motivation is an issue we cannot avoid?

So few helpful discussions of motivating the composition student exist because the life of each writing class is complex. Each student's history as a writer is unique, and what motivates one will often not work with others. Consequently, generalizations can easily be inaccurate. But let me make two or three.

We can make a beginning by bringing the whole business of motivation out into the open so that it becomes an issue recognized by students as a topic worthy of serious discussion. Each student will have a checkered history of successes and failures in writing, and most will be able to see the relationship between these successes and failures and the degree of motivation that was involved in each instance. Students, when approached openly, when not put on their guard, are rich sources of information about what motivates them and what turns them off. Teachers need to draw on this valuable knowledge, asking students to discuss the topic in writing as well as orally in class. Early in each writing course, I ask students to write accounts of their lives as writers. Who has influenced them? What have been their successes and failures? About what aspects of writing do they feel insecure? Confident? What has motivated them in the past? What has failed to motivate them? What kinds of specific help do they most want from me this semester?

Students will provide an enormous amount of valuable information about many aspects of their lives or half-lives as writers if they are not intimidated by the teacher or fearful of the teacher. They will be less fearful and intimidated if they see the teacher as a fellow writer who struggles with the same problems that they struggle with every time writing must be done. Teachers not only should show drafts of their own writing to students but also should invite students to comment on these drafts, pointing out weaknesses, suggesting improvements, and so on. Teachers might also occasionally try to do the writing assignments they give their students. The results could then be treated in class in the same way that student writing is treated.

Anything that helps to demystify writing and the process of writing is helpful as we try to motivate students. When I first began teaching, we gave students assignments that we had made up in secret. Students would then go away and, in secret, write their papers, which they would then turn in so that we could go away and mark them, again in secret. Quite understandably, the entire process remained, for most students, a great mystery. It is this debilitating mystery that the composition teacher who writes can dispel by involving students in realistic discussions of motivation and the entire process of writing. For example, I have recently had some modest success motivating students by asking them to try writing their papers not late at night as many college writers do, but early in the morning as many professional writers do. Those who have tried morning writing testify that they feel much more secure about what they are writing. This promising first step was made possible by realistic class discussions of such nitty-gritty matters as when students write, where they write, and so forth.

A realistic view of what is involved in the process of composing is one ingredient that must not be missing from the writing class. But teachers can help create a realistic view only if they themselves struggle to write on a fairly regular basis. If they do not—as many have not over the years—they will, for instance, almost always underestimate the difficulty of a writing task. They will often suggest, at least by implication, that students need only follow a set of straightforward procedures and guidelines to be successful writers. As a result of this kind of instruction, many students feel that writing is much like arithmetic. Once you learn that 2 plus 2 equals 4, you need never worry about it again. Teachers who do not write often seem to suggest that once you learn to write an introduction or revise a paper, you should then be able to perform these tasks any time it is necessary. They never need be worried about it again. Teachers who write know that this is not true, that every encounter with a blank sheet of paper is a new experience. Consequently, the teacher who writes is better able to motivate students by talking with them—and writing with them—in a way that provides a realistic context for learning.

Finally, we should not underestimate the motivating force of success. Even the student who struggles to compose a few sentences can be praised. I remember vividly my first encounter with college composition. On the first day of my college career, my freshman composition teacher, a tough-talking woman just back from several years' teaching in Paris, told us to write a paper in class—about anything we chose. I moved to the back of the room and during the class hour wrote a single sentence. Nothing more would come. When I handed the paper in, I muttered something about its being only one sentence long, to which the teacher replied, after looking at it, "Yes. But my God, kid, what a sentence!" I have long ago forgotten what that sentence was; I'm certain it was undistinguished. But I will never forget the surge of enthusiasm I felt when I heard those encouraging words. I was energized for the rest of the semester as I worked to produce other worthy sentences. We can and should energize our students in similar ways.

Responding to student work in positive and energizing ways is possible, however, only if we avoid the most dangerous trap that confronts the writing teacher: negativism. Faced day after day, month after month, year after year with the awkward, benumbing prose of our students, we are threatened by cynicism and downright despair every semester. We must fight this threat in every way possible because cynicism and despair lead inevitably to failure in the teaching of writing. We must fight this threat because we know that the best writing teachers are optimists who see possibilities in the writing of students that others, even the students themselves, do not see. And it is this optimism, this belief in students, that can provide much of the motivating force that is so essential in the writing class.

Finally, there is the vexing issue of grammar in the composition class. The research in our field has for many years supported the belief that teaching grammar does not help students write better. And yet every teacher of writing is faced with the very real problem of "error" in student writing. What can be done? As I have been suggesting throughout this essay, the first step we must take when facing any issue is to find a way of thinking about the issue, a context in which we can place the problem so that we can examine it fruitfully. I'll mention here only two or three ideas that might help us think about the problem of error in student writing.

We must begin by distinguishing carefully among the kinds of errors that students make as they write. Probably more errors than we would guess are the results of haste and carelessness. Some teachers deal effectively with this problem by refusing to read beyond a first paragraph or a first page filled with errors. They merely hand the offending papers back to students as unacceptable. A large percentage of these papers will come back containing far fewer mistakes.

But this rather hard-nosed approach will not work for all papers and with all students because many errors are not the results of haste and carelessness. What teachers must do at this point is to distinguish more carefully than we often have between two kinds of errors: those resulting from the student's lack of control over the conventions of writing—problems with commas, apostrophes, spelling, and so forth—and those resulting from the student's use of a dialect that deviates from so-called standard English, which is, after all, more a symbol than a real dialect of our language. Students can often be helped to observe the conventions of writing much more easily than they can be helped with problems created by the speaking of a nonstandard dialect. Thirty years ago we talked about these latter problems as "bad habits" which needed to be replaced by "good habits." We know now that the problem goes much deeper. Rather than trying to eliminate a bad habit, the student and teacher must deal with linguistic rules—phonological, syntactic, semantic, and so on—that have been deeply internalized by the student as a very young child learning the language, rules that have been "performed" by the student for at least seventeen years. Furthermore, these rules exist, in most instances, below the level of consciousness. What all of this suggests is that the teacher is attempting to help the student alter something much more deeply ingrained than a bad habit. Is it any wonder, then, that many students find traditional grammar drills unhelpful?

Must we despair? I think not, although we should not be surprised by many failures in this area of our teaching. We might begin by referring students to a handbook, but we cannot leave teaching to the resources we employ. No matter what strategies we devise, two things are essential as we try to help student writers with usage and grammar problems. One is individual attention. Many college writing programs today try to confront these problems not in the classroom but in tutorial sessions at writing centers or labs. Classroom teachers, especially if they are teaching more than one writing class, do not have the time to give each student the kind of individual attention necessary to try to help the student solve serious grammar problems. (Where writing centers do not exist, the classroom teacher often tries to give individual help in conferences, but this is seldom an ideal solution.) But before even the best tutorial help can work, the other essential requirement takes us back to our earlier discussion: students will not improve unless they are motivated. In no other area of writing instruction is motivation more important than our attempts to help students write grammatically and observe the conventions of edited American English. What we are doing is not unlike asking them to walk differently or to breathe differently—asking them, in other words, to change something that they have been doing without conscious thought for all or almost all their lives. It can be done, but we must be realistic about what we are asking the student to do. We should also be optimistic in the knowledge that it takes as much intelligence to acquire a nonstandard dialect as it does to acquire a dialect that is prestigious. But change will occur only if the student desires such change—only, that is, if the student is motivated.

Suggested Readings

The following reading suggestions are intended for the busy composition teacher who, when faced with the latest extensive bibliography of "essential" readings in the field, says, "What a wonderful list! I'll read everything on it . . . next summer." So, if you have time to read only a few articles and books, I recommend these.

Berlin, James A. *Rhetoric and Reality: Writing Instruction in American Colleges, 1900–1985.* Carbondale, IL: Southern Illinois UP, 1987. • Much of what we do today in composition classes can be understood only if we know something about our history. Berlin helps us begin to understand.

Elbow, Peter. *Embracing Contraries: Explorations in Learning and Teaching.* New York: Oxford UP, 1986. • The most consistently interesting writer about the teaching of writing, Elbow here examines the many forces that pull us, as writing teachers, in different directions.

Knoblach, C. H., and Lil Brannon. "The Development of Writing Ability." *Rhetorical Traditions and the Teaching of Writing.* Upper Montclair, NJ: Boynton/Cook, 1984. • In this chapter of their controversial book, the authors discuss, among other topics, the fascinating proposition that "the growth of students as writers is not the same as the improvement of texts."

Larson, Richard L. "The 'Research Paper' in the Writing Course: A Non-Form of Writing." *College English* 44 (1982): 811–16. • Larson gives a perceptive and convincing critique of the traditional research paper.

Lees, Elaine O. "Evaluating Student Writing." *College Composition and Communication* 30 (1979): 370–74. • Lees provides a helpful anatomy of the kinds of commentary that teachers can make on student papers.

Murray, Donald M. *Learning by Teaching.* Montclair, NJ: Boynton/Cook, 1982. • As a writer teaching writing, Murray speaks to us of our many concerns in a voice that is difficult to resist.

Ohmann, Richard. "Use Definite, Specific, Concrete Language." *College English* 41 (1979): 390–97. • Ohmann argues that our traditional emphasis on definite, specific, and concrete language may end up increasing the powerlessness of our students.

Reither, James A. "Writing and Knowing: Toward Redefining the Writing Process." *College English* 47 (1985): 620–28. • Arguing that the traditional view of the "writing process" is too narrow, Reither urges us to "broaden our concept of what happens when people write."

Speaking and Writing: Help or Hindrance?

Barry M. Kroll,
Indiana University

The freshmen who arrive in our composition classes each semester come to us, with few exceptions, as proficient talkers. And yet some of those same effervescent and verbally creative students turn awkward or mute when they put pen to paper. The contrast can be striking—and perplexing. Most students have not, of course, had the same immersion in written language that they have had in talk. Some of them have neither read very much nor written very often, and for such students the requirements of writing—especially college writing—are often laborious and troublesome, whereas conversation seems easy and spontaneous. Still, the contrast can raise questions about the relationship between students' speaking and writing abilities. Can students' facility as talkers help them as writers? Or does the language of everyday talk interfere with writing? Is students' oral language a help or a hindrance in the composition class?

One view is that students' habits of speech are a source of many of the errors that mar their essays, and that students' proficiencies as talkers can create difficulties for them as writers. Everyday speech is full of structures and locutions that, if transferred directly to writing, will produce inappropriate forms—especially colloquialisms and usage errors. According to this "interference" view, it follows that because students' talk is often different from the language of written essays, composition teachers must work against students' tendencies to draw on the processes, skills, and forms of spoken language when they write essays for Freshman English.

This view is not so much wrong as it is misleading. To begin with, students are surely not mistaken to draw on the language they know—the language of the communities that have nurtured them—when they try to say something in writing. Students who have limited experience as readers and writers must tap the skills and strategies of speech to produce written texts. (They will also, of course, draw on their best sense of the ways in which written texts differ from talk, sometimes resulting in hypercorrections, inflated diction, and overly complex and tangled syntax.) Drawing on oral language competence is surely reasonable and often appropriate. Sometimes, however, that tactic will result in errors—forms or expressions that are acceptable in many speech communities, perhaps, but either incorrect (according to the standards of edited American English) or inappropriate for written essays.

If students are making many errors, the teacher has to decide where to begin and how to proceed. And the first step, surely, is to take a close look at the *kinds* of errors students are making, engaging in "error analysis." An analysis might show us, for example, that we have too hastily assumed that the errors in a student's writing reflect habits of speech. Errors often have multiple sources and complex roots, and they are not always as straightforwardly traceable to oral language patterns as one might assume. The error analysis approach is helpful because it is based on the idea that not all errors are equally serious or equally stigmatized. The teacher's task is to find out which errors in a student's essay are infrequent and relatively unobtrusive (and so can be ignored for the time being) and which errors are pervasive, systematic, and disruptive for a reader (and thus need immediate attention).

Once such decisions have been made, there is still the question of how much attention to pay to certain errors, as well as the question of what instructional approaches are likely to prove most productive. A "let's start with errors" orientation often teaches students that writing is primarily an act of avoiding mistakes, rather than an act of communicating with readers. And an early preoccupation with correctness often leads students to adopt unproductive composing strategies, such as trying to identify and fix each mistake as it occurs, leading them to focus on words rather than meanings, on forms rather than messages. The kind of practice that promises to foster growth in written language is, finally, sustained practice in reading, writing, and revising texts. Increasingly, then, writing teachers have concluded that composition courses at all levels must focus primarily on writing—on the production of discourse with a variety of aims and audiences.

This is not to say that it is inappropriate to work on frequent and highly stigmatized errors. And a clear explanation of principles of usage or grammar—the kind of explanation found in *The Harbrace College Handbook* and other guides to writing—will help some students. But a composition teacher must be careful to keep the focus on composing, seeing error reduction as part of the writing process rather than a goal in itself. One way to keep the focus on composing without ignoring correctness is to employ multiple drafts. We should expect initial drafts to contain errors and infelicities: because we know that even experienced writers do not produce perfect first drafts, it is simply unreasonable—as well as counterproductive—to expect inexperienced writers to do so. But we can teach them how to work with drafts, showing them what kinds of problems to anticipate and training them to be better revisers and editors of their own work. Once we realize that first drafts are preliminary or "working" versions of a text, we are not going to be so troubled by the presence of "oral interference" errors in those drafts.

But there is another kind of "interference" that I have not yet considered: those difficulties with writing that can be traced to students' familiarity with—and hence reliance on—an oral or conversational style of communication. According to this view, students are accustomed to the circumstances of everyday conversation, circumstances in which they have a familiar context, a concrete and responsive audience, and a set of reliable expectations about their listeners' interests and perspectives. Because of such circumstances, oral exchanges can be quite effective even when the messages seem (to an outsider) to be cryptic, unelaborated, or disconnected. Essay writing, on the other hand, involves the production of messages that must be explicit and well focused, with elaborated arguments and supporting details—texts that seem relatively autonomous from the situations in which they were produced. Students who lack experience with written texts will rely on conversational assumptions and strategies when they compose their essays, and the result will be texts that do not have the features—especially tight structure and full elaboration of ideas—that most readers expect and need in expository prose.

For most composition teachers, the solution is to explain how expository prose works. Traditionally, composition teachers have emphasized principles of organization and development, such as the principle of always stating a general topic or thesis early in an essay, or the principle of using transitional devices between major subtopics. Also, because essays typically elaborate and qualify ideas in ways that are less common in everyday talk, teachers usually emphasize methods for developing and supporting ideas (sometimes using prose models to teach development by comparison, illustration, analogy, and so forth). And many composition instructors use exercises in audience analysis to teach students how to imagine the needs and responses of their readers.

Principles, examples, exercises—I don't discount their usefulness. But the emphasis should always be on practice, with instructors creating situations in which students learn about expository texts by writing (and reading) them. Some students may benefit from activities that integrate talk and writing. For example, some teachers use oral monologues—short presentations—to bridge the gap between students' skills as talkers and as writers. In these monologues, students are freed from the burdens of transcription. They have an audience of peers. And yet they are composing, rather than conversing, and thus getting practice with sustained discourse. Other teachers have gone in a different direction, using interactive activities—sometimes a kind of "collaborative, conversational composing"—to produce texts. By drawing on students' conversational skills and affinities for interaction and discussion, such activities provide a comfortable step toward independent composing.

Discussions of examples or model texts can be useful, but they should be augmented by pieces written by the students in the class. What students need—but too rarely get—is a chance to see how other people read and interpret their texts. For example, when members of the class respond to a student's draft, the teacher can point to ways in which features of the text guide readers' responses, shaping their expectations or contributing to their confusions. For a novice writer, the experience of discovering why his or her text did or did not work for readers (and figuring out how to make it work better) is worth more than analysis of professional writing. Peer discussions are effective, too, if they are structured so that writers learn how readers understand and interpret their texts.

If there are ways in which students' oral competencies and conversational strategies can be said to interfere with their writing, there are also ways in which talk strengthens writing and enhances composing. Most of us prefer the qualities of conversation—concreteness, involvement, natural rhythm, unpretentious diction—to the abstraction and indirection of a good deal of bureaucratic and academic writing. At its best, contemporary prose style has become increasingly informal and conversational, capturing in print many of the features of oral exchanges. We surely do not want our students to abandon, in their writing, all of the qualities that make their conversations so lively and engaging.

Finally, talking need not be seen as antithetical to composing. In fact, talk is often central to composing, and there are many ways to employ oral activities in a writing course. For example, in any rhetoric course we will certainly teach invention (or the discovery of ideas). Many familiar prewriting activities can be done orally and in group settings: brainstorming, shifting perspectives, or asking a series of questions about a topic. Some writers benefit from talking out their ideas—perhaps with a good listener, perhaps with a tape recorder (dictation), or perhaps on a walk—before they put them in print. Debates can help students explore the reasons for a particular position on an issue, as well as expose them to different viewpoints. And even a research assignment can include oral communication skills, if students conduct interviews, survey people's opinions, or talk with experts about a topic.

Most contemporary writing courses emphasize revision, and here, too, talk can be important. Some writers need to read their work aloud—engaging in something like an oral performance—in order to hear what is wrong and discover how to get it right. Others profit from hearing someone else read their words. And all of the talk that goes on between writers and their readers— whether a conversation with another student, a conference with the teacher, a response from a peer-critique group, or a discussion involving the whole class—can be an occasion to discover how texts work on readers and how readers work on texts.

My discussion has moved from a view in which oral language presents obstacles and interferences for writers to a view in which talk enriches writing and facilitates composing. While we should not ignore the insights of the first view—especially when it shows us the logic of our students' errors—we will be more successful, I believe, if we look for ways to take advantage of students' conversational experiences and oral competencies, using them as bridges into reading and writing.

Suggested Readings

Ede, Lisa. "New Perspectives on the Speaking-Writing Relationship: Implications for Teachers of Basic Writing." *A Sourcebook for Basic Writing Teachers.* Ed. Theresa Enos. New York: Random. 318–27. • This essay provides an overview of recent discussions of speaking-writing relationships, with special emphasis on implications for teaching college-level composition. Ede recognizes that the dichotomy between conversing and composing oversimplifies the multiple and complex connections between speaking and writing.

Enos, Theresa, ed. *A Sourcebook for Basic Writing Teachers.* New York: Random, 1987. • This collection contains a number of relevant essays, some addressed specifically to speaking-writing relationships, others concerned with broader issues involved in teaching students who have had limited experience with expository writing.

Hartwell, Patrick. "Dialect Interference in Writing: A Critical View." *Research in the Teaching of English* 14 (1980): 101–18. • Although I do not deal with the issue of dialect interference, the topic is certainly part of a broader consideration of speaking-writing relationships. Hartwell argues that dialect speakers do not need to learn new forms or structures; rather, like all inexperienced writers, they need to acquire a "print code" by being immersed in written language. (For a different view, see Daniel Morrow, "Dialect Interference in Writing: Another Critical View." *Research in the Teaching of English* 19 (1985): 154–80.)

———. "Grammar, Grammars, and the Teaching of Grammar." *College English* 47 (1985): 105–27. Rpt. in *A Sourcebook for Basic Writing Teachers*. Ed. Theresa Enos. New York: Random, 1987. 348–72. • Hartwell reviews the evidence against grammar teaching as a solution to the errors students make when they write essays.

Hull, Glynda. "Acts of Wonderment: Fixing Mistakes and Correcting Errors." *Facts, Artifacts, and Counterfacts*. Ed. David Bartholomae and Anthony Petrosky. Upper Montclair, NJ: Boynton/Cook, 1986. 199–226. • This essay presents an excellent overview of the strengths and limitations of error analysis. Hull is particularly insightful about the problems students face when they edit their work.

Kroll, Barry M., and Roberta J. Vann, eds. *Exploring Speaking-Writing Relationships: Connections and Contrasts*. Urbana, IL: NCTE, 1981. • This is a collection of original essays about various relationships between speaking and writing, including essays that take linguistic, psychological, and pedagogical perspectives on orality and literacy.

Liggett, Sarah. "The Relationship Between Speaking and Writing: An Annotated Bibliography." *College Composition and Communication* 35 (1984): 334–44. • This bibliography contains many useful references for anyone who wants to pursue the issue of speaking-writing relationships in greater depth.

Olson, David. "From Utterance to Text: The Bias of Language in Speaking and Writing." *Harvard Educational Review* 47 (1977): 257–81. • Olson argues that in written texts the author's meaning is explicit and autonomous, residing in the text alone, whereas in spoken utterance meaning depends on shared experiences—the interaction among speaker, listener, utterance, and context. Writing performs "ideational" functions, whereas speaking performs primarily "interpersonal" ones. Olson's views have been quite influential. (But for an opposing view, see Martin Nystrand, "The Role of Context in Written Communication." *Comprehending Oral and Written Language*. Ed. Rosalind Horowitz and S. Jay Samuels. San Diego: Academic, 1987. 197–214.)

Robinson, Jay L. "Basic Writing and its Basis in Talk: The Influence of Speech on Writing." *Fforum: Essays on Theory and Practice in the Teaching of Writing*. Ed. Patricia L. Stock. Upper Montclair, NJ: Boynton/Cook, 1983. 116–28. • Robinson discusses some of the ways in which inexperienced writers use the linguistic forms and discourse rules of their talk when they compose essays. He argues for an emphasis on revision.

Rubin, Donald L., and William M. Dodd. *Talking Into Writing: Exercises for Basic Writers*. Urbana, IL: NCTE, 1987. • The authors discuss a number of oral-based exercises that can support and facilitate composition instruction, focusing on role switching, peer questioning, "topic-sculpting," and "forensic- discussion" (debate) activities.

Shaughnessy, Mina P. *Errors and Expectations: A Guide for the Teacher of Basic Writing.* New York: Oxford, 1977. • This is the essential text for anyone interested in error analysis. Shaughnessy considers punctuation, syntax, common errors, spelling, vocabulary, and problems beyond the sentence. (Excerpts from chapters on "Vocabulary" and "Beyond the Sentence" are reprinted in *A Sourcebook for Basic Writing Teachers.* Ed. Theresa Enos. New York: Random, 1987. 507–34.)

Spear, Karen. *Sharing Writing: Peer Response Groups in English Classes.* Portsmouth, NH: Boynton/Cook, Heinemann, 1988. • Spear provides both a rationale for peer response groups and many practical suggestions for how to implement such groups in a writing class.

Stotsky, Sandra. "A Meaningful Model of Written Language Development for Teachers." *Fforum: Essays on Theory and Practice in the Teaching of Writing.* Ed. Patricia L. Stock. Upper Montclair, NJ: Boynton/Cook, 1983. 194–201. • Stotsky argues that because written language is qualitatively different, in structure and substance, from spoken language, it is through experiences with written language—especially the experience of reading progressively more difficult texts—that students learn how to produce mature writing.

Evaluating Student Writing

Vivian I. Davis,
Eastfield College

Teachers who understand that writing is best learned through practice cannot always read everything students write during a course. But it is impossible to teach composition without carefully reading and evaluating a number of student papers, and it is often necessary for the teacher to read and respond to different drafts of the same paper. Since each writing assignment requires its own tasks, which may be very different from the tasks required by other assignments preceding or following it, the evaluation of each piece of writing has to consider the purpose of that assignment and its context within the course.

Traditionally, the evaluation of all student writing has been *analytic,* which requires breaking the writing into the smallest units and examining each unit carefully for errors in mechanics, grammar, structure, paragraph development, sentence structure, word usage, cohesion, sense of audience, and whatever other features the individual teacher may choose. Instructors usually write comments in the margins and sometimes at the end of the papers about mechanical errors and/or different kinds of changes the student should make to improve the writing. Theoretically, analytic assessment helps students improve their writing by calling their attention to all *errors* they make in each paper. The assumption is that once students are aware of their errors, they will be able to correct them, thereby improving the quality of their writing.

Some English departments develop scales or other guides to objectify analytic evaluation. However, what individual teachers mark often represents their own personal biases about certain types of mechanical errors, particular dialects, or the appropriateness of certain writing conventions, strategies, and subjects. Many errors are not marked at all. Apparently, it is not possible to standardize analytic evaluation, but even if it were possible, analytic evaluation still could diagnose only surface errors in writing. Identifying writing errors, however, does not assure that students will understand what caused the errors or what to do to correct them. Moreover, when mechanical errors are not the only or most significant flaws in a piece of writing, analytic evaluation cannot provide students all the information they need to improve their writing.

Good pedagogy demands that methods for evaluating student writing involve the whole composing process and be keyed directly to classroom instruction. A good evaluation process demands at least three important conditions: (1) carefully crafted writing assignments, (2) clear consensus between students and teacher about what is expected from each writing assignment and about the writing strategies necessary to complete the assignment, and (3) a clear understanding between students and teacher about how each writing assignment will be evaluated.

The type of writing assignments students receive affect both the quality of their writing and the teacher's response to their writing. Writing assignments should thus be carefully developed and reflective of the criteria to be used to evaluate the writing they generate. The assignments should be interesting to both students and teacher, not abstract, biased, offensive to the writers or evocative of strong emotion. Topics that limit writing to special audiences or to modes or situations that are unfamiliar to students can lead to writing that is unclear or meaningless. As they develop writing assignments, teachers should consider the purpose of the assignments, the method by which the writing will be assessed, the scope of the assignments, what prior knowledge students will need, the context in which the writing is to be done, the rhetorical specifications, and the amount of time students will need to compose and revise.

If students and teacher do not have the same understanding of assignments, the writing will reflect that, and the teacher's response to the writing will mean very little to the student. Some assignments that seem perfect do not work for a particular class or a group within a class—for example, students whose first language is other than English, minority students, or students of a certain geographical area of the country. Sometimes it is impossible to know if an assignment will work until it is actually tried in the classroom. But the time spent refining assignments pays off by reducing the number of papers not written to the purpose and specifications of the assignment. After designing an assignment, it is wise, as part of their preparation for writing and as a final test of the appropriateness of the assignment, for the teacher to lead the students through several discovery questions about that assignment: (1) What does this assignment ask the writer to do? (2) What information is needed to complete this assignment, and where can that information be found? (3) For what audience should this paper be written? (4) What ideas or information must be communicated in this piece of writing? (5) What is the best way to begin to compose this assignment? (6) What will a good paper for this assignment have in it? As the students share their answers with the whole class, asking questions and making comments, consensus will develop, clarifying the writing assignment for students and teacher alike.

Other teaching strategies increase the likelihood that students will write better papers and decrease the likelihood that teachers will have to respond to large numbers of errors in student papers. Before they begin to write, students can benefit from reviewing models of good student writing done earlier in response to a similar assignment. Peer revision before first drafts are handed in is another good way to help students improve the quality of the writing their instructor will subsequently read. Both activities require the teacher to provide the students with clear guidelines and careful training. The teacher and students must also take the necessary class time to examine models carefully and to do individual and peer revision as part of the process for completing each writing assignment.

Students should be led to understand what specific features must appear in a piece of writing to meet the demands of a particular assignment, to recognize those features in models and in their own writing, and to use appropriate writing strategies to create the required features before they write an assignment. Students will then understand more about how to start to write their papers, and important groundwork will be laid for evaluating what they write. Students and teacher will have developed common expectations, a common language, and common descriptors for responding to the writing. Such commonalities will make the evaluation of the writing meaningful to the students and easier for the teacher.

Students can also be taught to develop scoring guides for evaluating their writing assignments. They can learn to reach a consensus about how to categorize sample papers written to a specific assignment along a six-point scale: excellent writing (6-5); good but not excellent writing (4-3); very flawed writing (2-1). (For examples of models I use in my own classes for this exercise, see pages 183–84 of this manual.) After determining, with the teacher's guidance, the proper category for each paper, students can work collaboratively in small groups to develop descriptions of features that would place any piece of writing to that assignment into one of the categories. It is good practice to involve students in the development of scoring guides before they begin an assignment as a means of helping them understand how to approach that assignment, what writing strategies to use to compose the piece of writing, and what decisions to make as they revise their writing. When the basis of the teacher's response to student papers is a scoring guide that students have shared in developing and have internalized, teacher and students have a common vocabulary to talk about writing, and the teacher is then able to respond to student papers with brief but meaningful comments.

From classroom strategies such as those discussed above, a teacher can develop a careful, useful process for evaluating student writing. Every piece of writing should first be read *holistically*, or impressionistically as a whole piece, from the perspective of a reader who reads to discover the writer's message and its effect on the intended audience. The teacher's first response should simply affirm the writer as an author by some positive comment, "I enjoyed reading about your work in Kansas." "You give convincing reasons for using credit cards." Second, the teacher should let the author know, in a simple statement, that the paper did or did not communicate the author's message, or that the message was or was not communicated clearly. Third, the teacher should simply tell the student if the paper is well written or suggest what the student might do to improve the paper, which may include a range of options: going to the learning center, revising the paper on the word processor, or meeting with the teacher. If the student is making jarring errors or has other writing problems, the first time such errors or problems appear in the paper, the teacher should identify them perhaps by circling or highlighting. A note on the paper should explain the error or problem if it is recurrent. For reappearing mechanical errors, students may be referred to appropriate information in a handbook, but being referred to a handbook is no guarantee that the student will learn what to do; therefore, the student should be asked to talk with the teacher so the errors can be clarified and some heuristics can be developed for the individual student.

Criteria for grading papers should be as objective as possible. Ideally, the teacher would grade only *finished* pieces of writing—that is, those pieces that have gone through the whole composing process, including having been revised to the satisfaction of the student authors. This means that students must be taught and retaught skills for self-revision and collaborative peer revision. Revision should be structured into each writing assignment as a part of the process of completing the final drafts of papers. Students also need opportunities to learn proofreading skills and time to proofread before their papers are graded.

Teachers must be very clear about the criteria they use to grade papers and to assess student progress in writing. If the criteria are issued by the department, teachers should understand exactly what those criteria mean pedagogically, and how they apply in individual classes. The teacher's own grading criteria must be concrete and definable, not impressionistic. It should be clear if grades are determined by comparing the work of individual students with that of their peers, or if students are graded according to the progress they make individually during the course.

Some teachers ask students to choose only their best writing for grading at intervals during and/or at the end of the course. Others have students maintain and present portfolios of all their writing for grading at both mid-term and the end of the course. Still other teachers meet with each student in an assessment conference to review the student's writing and discuss what the student has learned about the composing process based on change or the lack of change in his or her writing throughout the course.

Teachers have to be able to choose what works best in their own situations. At the same time they must guard against a number of variables that often negatively affect the evaluation of student writing: trying to read too many papers at once, or attempting to evaluate writing when fatigued; penalizing writing because of difficult-to-read handwriting or rewarding typing or word processing; and responding with personal biases about particular subjects. Whatever method of evaluation a teacher uses must be as objective as possible and must not penalize any group of students, including minority group members and those whose first languages are other than English.

Suggested Readings

This bibliography presents additional information for teachers interested in learning more about teacher response to student writing.

Catano, James V. "Computer-Based Writing: Navigating the Fluid Text." *College Composition and Communication* 36 (1985): 309–15. • Catano provides insights about use of computers in revision from observations of two published authors and a student project.

Conners, Robert J., and Andrea A. Lunsford. "Frequency of Formal Errors in Current College Writing, or Ma and Pa Kettle Do Research." *College Composition and Communication* 39 (1988): 395–409. • This article reports types and numbers of college freshman errors which teachers marked in 300 student papers randomly chosen from a sample of 21,000 papers. It shows what errors are common and that students have historically made the same errors.

Davis, Barbara Gross, Michael Scriven, and Susan Thomas. *The Evaluation of Composition Instruction.* 2nd ed. New York: Teachers College, Columbia UP, 1987. • This book reviews methods for large-scale assessment; discusses current issues in composition instruction, including evaluation of writing assignments, and students' self and peer assessment; and provides select bibliography.

Elbow, Peter, and Pat Belanoff. "Portfolios as a Substitute for Proficiency Examinations." *College Composition and Communication* 37 (1986): 336–39. • The authors detail the use of a portfolio system at State University of New York Stony Brook.

Faigley, Roger G., et al. *Assessing Writers' Knowledge and Processes of Composing.* Norwood, NJ: Ablex, 1985. • Faigley et al. review research on theories and practices in composition; discuss and evaluate methods for assessing writing and composing in classrooms; and advance performative assessment. Bibliography.

Flower, Linda, et al. "Detection, Diagnosis, and the Strategies of Revision." *College Composition and Communication* 37 (1986): 16–53. • The article reports on a study defining the revision process and problems that students encounter upon revising. Extensive bibliography.

Greenberg, Karen, Harvey S. Wiener, and Richard A. Donovan, eds. *Writing Assessment: Issues and Strategies.* Longman Series in College Composition and Communication. New York: Longman, 1986. • This collection of articles on large-scale assessment includes testing African-American and ESL writers. Annotated bibliography.

Grimm, Nancy. "Improving Students' Responses to their Peers' Essays." *College Composition and Communication* 37 (1986): 91–96. • Grimm makes suggestions and illustrates activities for improving peer evaluation.

Harris, Jeanette. "Student Writers and Word Processing: A Preliminary Evaluation." *College Composition and Communication* 37 (1986): 323–30. • Harris reports from case studies of six students using computers to revise essays.

Hillocks, George, Jr. *Research on Written Composition: New Directions for Teaching.* Urbana, IL: ERIC Clearinghouse on Reading and Communication Skills, 1986. • Hillocks widely reviews composition research and discusses findings in terms of their impact on classroom practice. Extensive bibliography.

Newkirk, Thomas. "Direction and Misdirection in Peer Response." *College Composition and Communication* 35 (1984): 301–11. • This article reports on the study of differences in teacher and student evaluations of writing and suggests reasons for the differences.

Reid, Joy M. "ESL Composition: The Linear Product of American Thought." *College Composition and Communication* 35 (1984): 449–52. • Reid explains the linearity of essay writing in America and suggests some ways of teaching it to ESL students.

Robertson, Michael. "Is Anybody Listening? Responding to Student Writing." *College Composition and Communication* 37 (1986): 87–91. • The article analyzes the tone of many common teacher comments on student essays and suggests different perspective for responding.

Ruth, Leo, and Sandra Murphy. *Designing Writing Tasks for the Assessment of Writing.* Norwood, NJ: Ablex, 1988. • This book discusses in depth the multifaceted issues involved in large-scale writing assessment and makes suggestions for improvement of assessment and the teaching of writing.

Schwalm, David E. "Degree of Difficulty in Basic Writing Courses: Insights from the Oral Proficiency Interview Testing Program" *College English* 47 (1985): 629–40. • Schwalm explains the Oral Proficiency Interview Testing Program used in CIA language school and the Interagency Language Roundtable, its outgrowth, as implications for determining levels of the writing tasks students must perform.

Shaughnessy, Mina P. *Errors and Expectations: A Guide for the Teacher of Basic Writing.* New York: Oxford, 1977. • This seminal work in the analysis of student writing errors explains the logic behind errors and many reasons why immature writers do not recognize and correct their errors without help.

White, Edward M. *Teaching and Assessing Writing.* San Francisco: Jossey-Bass, 1986. • White examines problems in the large-scale assessment of writing and classroom composition instruction and makes practical suggestions for improving both. He includes examples from a composition course that suggest ways of teaching writing and responding to student writing.

"CLASS" Acts: On Teaching Computer-Assisted Writing

Hugh Burns,
University of Texas, Austin

Teaching computer-assisted writing is not so much a strategic matter (what things to do) as a tactical enterprise (how to do things). Writing teachers must still give students a sense of purpose and audience, still encourage them to arrange ideas appropriately, still coach them to compose efficiently, and still have them recognize effective sentences, paragraphs, and essays. With or without a computer, nurturing these strategic senses is an essential part of a writing teacher's job.

Now what do writing teachers stand to gain tactically if they use computers? For me, they at least gain this set of "CLASS" acts:

- *C*redibility
- *L*earning
- *A*ctivity
- *S*tyle
- *S*urprise

Acts of Credibility

A teacher's professional credibility depends in part on how well he or she keeps up with the complex world of educational technology. Staying abreast of technology is a challenge, and many writing teachers question if they need to take the trouble. Instructors trained in the humanities are often particularly wary of the computer, which they perceive as a symbol of all that threatens the individual. This bias is unfortunate. Plainly stated, writing teachers cannot afford computer illiteracy in this day and age. They cannot afford it for their professional lives; they certainly cannot afford it for their students' futures. The computer is clearly here to stay, and writing teachers need to be able to exploit it.

In education, using efficient tools should promote instructional effectiveness. That efficient computers may be used inefficiently means that users must be effectively trained. The credibility writing teachers need, therefore, is the credibility that being a competent, efficient user of computer-assisted writing tools can help establish.

Teachers should understand that computers have operating systems which are sets of instructions that computers use to manage their own operations, to "read" and "write" data, and to "communicate" with human users. Next, teachers should understand that computer programs, or "applications," can be used for specific purposes: word processing, spreadsheets, page layouts, communications, computer-assisted instruction, spelling checkers, and even games. Finally, teachers should understand that they can create, modify, save, delete, and use files in such applications as the following: drafting an article for *College Composition and Communication* in their word-processing application; managing a gradebook for English 101 in their spreadsheet application; laying out a literary magazine in their desktop publishing application; or automatically dialing a computerized bulletin board of English faculty in their communication application. Understanding applications and files is basic competence, and writing teachers should be moving toward a principled management of applications for their students.

Beyond the basic computer operation, applications, and personal files, teachers may want to learn something about hardware, networks, and remote access. Modern-minded teachers may eventually wish to advise administrators about word processing, interactive prewriting, interactive style analysis, interactive mechanics and usage analysis, as well as evaluation and security matters.

These roles represent quite a responsibility for composition teachers. But in the next few years, such responsibilities will seem more and more natural.

Acts of Learning

The computer can be an electronic mirror, reflecting what writers want to say and allowing them to think more about their choices and still meet the writer's commitment to produce a polished product. Whichever way a writing teacher perceives the art of teaching writing, a computer allows more opportunities for teachers to intervene precisely in the writing process.

Trends in teaching composition today suggest a balanced view of products and processes. Teachers are articulate about the product they wish to see demonstrated. They are concerned about the rhetorical processes student writers use to master various writing skills. If such trends continue, then the computer can be a valuable ally. Computers provide writing teachers increased capability for evaluating an individual writer's work in progress.

A computer can help a teacher teach more efficiently, but a huge question remains: Can computers help students learn how to write more effectively? The honest, intuitive answer is "It depends." A more honest, intellectual answer is "We do not have enough empirical data to cite a significant difference." However, if both students and teachers use computer applications appropriately, then students will learn to write more effectively. Most of today's computers provide sophisticated tools for efficient word processing, outlining, notetaking, spelling, and on-line researching. Some reasonable computer-assisted instruction applications may tutor a writer effectively in specific subjects, such as grammar, usage, punctuation, and sentence structure.

But teachers must intervene to suggest better tactics for encouraging more proficiency in their students' uses of the various applications. Researchers such as Helen Schwartz, Lillian Bridwell, Colette Daiute, and William Wresch point out that students need to be taught revision in overall structure. Some preliminary evidence suggests that composition teachers have not developed an adequate sense of how word processing can help in this larger task and so have not been able to pass that knowledge on to students.

How long does it take to learn to use a word-processing or a computer-assisted writing application? Again, it depends, but most of us tend to underestimate how long. We tend to speak in terms of hours when, in fact, it may be days or weeks. What the user needs to master to do efficient word processing includes (1) opening a file, (2) loading text, (3) typing text, (4) deleting text, (5) moving text, (6) searching text, (7) formatting text, (8) saving text, (9) printing text, and (10) closing a file. This seems a lot to master in eight hours.

Why learn it then? The single, major advantage of teaching computer-assisted writing is simply achieving a more favorable teacher-student ratio. One-on-one tutoring of writing is not new. Any teacher or coach who is trying to improve a student's performance of a skill can attest that the more time he or she can spend one-on-one, the greater the likelihood that a student's performance will improve. So, computer-assisted instruction potentially allows more one-on-one instructional efficiency and, thereby, leverages more instructional effectiveness. But there are complications.

Most writing teachers feel that today's inflexible or brittle software does not significantly help them meet their specific student's needs. Many writing teachers are not convinced that the computers reach individual students with individual help. A lot of this brittle software sits on the shelf in the writing laboratory, waiting to be prescribed. The solution is to create flexible software that permits teacher-controlled modifications. Teachers want more control over supplementary materials; they want to have authority over software prescriptions. Since they want the capability to reinforce their students personally, teachers should be able to customize software. And these programs are coming. Be alert for them.

Another related complication is cost, both in terms of time to become well enough acquainted with the various software packages and in terms of the funds required to purchase and maintain computer-assisted writing software. Teachers need to be given time to learn about specific operating systems, to survey the diverse applications, to read the documentation, and to plan potential computer-assisted activities. Consequently, teachers need training and training support—just like anyone else from whom expertise is expected. Very few colleges or school districts are promoting adequate training for their faculties and staffs, assuming instead that faculty will train themselves if they care enough. Writing labs with thirty computers and only one printer are inadequate, especially when the printer breaks or when the department has no planned funding to purchase ribbons. In plain language, a school cannot profit from computers without investing wisely and well—in hands-on training, in reliable equipment, in flexible software, and in adequate support. Demand that your school acquire these resources if it does not already have them.

Computers help teachers teach only if wise investments of time, money, and personnel are made. For instance, well-integrated and easy-to-use software can be found in computer-assisted writing, but you will have to look for it and adapt it to your students' needs. When writing teachers witness the synergy of teacher-student-computer collaborations, then the odds are that writing processes will be more efficient and written products will be more effective.

Acts of Activity

What activities should be available for teaching computer-assisted writing? Interactivity is undoubtedly the real strength of and hope for computer-assisted writing instruction. It provides a forum for investigating, exploring, and stimulating the processes of writing. Activities are numerous—for example, taking notes, "first" drafting, cutting and pasting, revising sentences, reorganizing whole documents, polishing text, beginning with headstart files, collaborating with writers on a single dynamic text, planning what's next, creating an interactive short story, troubleshooting a friend's paper, researching on-line. Overall, depending on the teacher's strategic goals for individualizing writing instruction, computer applications can generally be viewed as tutors or tools.

The computer as tutor involves computer-assisted instruction (CAI). Here, explicit products are achieved through implicit processes. As a tutor, a CAI lesson often takes the form of a twenty- or thirty-minute activity in which a specific outcome can be scored or evaluated with feedback provided to the user. The interaction between student and CAI application usually depends more on what the computers "know." Simply put, information flows from the computer to the user, and applications software supports the cognitive workload of mastering specific aspects of writing. Drill and practice CAI supplements those curriculums in basic writing, English as a second language, standard grammar and usage, typing skills, and even GRE test preparation.

Computer-assisted instruction is controversial because it must take an explicit instructional point of view, and its value is determined by how well it reflects the using teacher's own point of view.

Since teaching writing is poorly codified and hotly debated in professional circles, reaching a consensus about a specific CAI lesson's effectiveness would be difficult if not impossible. This situation, however, means that computers are generally more likely to be appreciated widely as tools rather than as tutors.

As tools, computers are used most for word processing. The "knowledge burden" is obviously within the user. If teachers can assign practical activities, students will have more opportunities to master the word-processing features while actually producing the necessary "products." For instance, if a teacher wishes to have the students learn to write an effective business letter, some of the activities which could be assigned to allow a student writer to use a word-processing application efficiently and effectively are (1) brainstorming about the reader, (2) deciding on the tone, (3) listing the main points, (4) compiling the questions to be asked, (5) summarizing the questions to be answered, (6) recalling effective models from the class discussions, (7) identifying key problems in openings and closings, (8) reviewing motivations, (9) outlining the linear flow, (10) deciding on the personality to be projected, (11) deciding how much background to provide, (12) deciding on the most appropriate business words, and (13) selecting among several business formats. Such a business letter composed on a word-processing application might have the completed assignment in the following format: the final letter; the draft letters; the notes regarding the facts, the opinions, the general ideas; and a commentary or evaluation which reflects what the student feels he or she has accomplished as an interactive writer. All of this could be "saved" on the same document, printed, and turned in. And, if electronically submitted, the teacher could comment right on the electronic text.

Teachers' assignments and expectations should thus reflect an awareness of the tutor-tool continuum as well as of the flow of information when student writers have access to computers. Among the better references for these "acts of activity" are Helen Schwartz's *Interactive Writing,* Colette Daiute's *Writing and Computers,* and Cynthia Selfe's *Computer-Assisted Instruction in Composition.*

Acts of Style

Can a computer help a student become a better rhetorician, a writer more in touch with the processes of invention, arrangement, and style? Yes, and writing teachers must lead novice writers to this realization.

Writing clearly is risk-taking work because thinking clearly is risk-taking work. The tools for rewriting—now standard fare in most word-processing applications—give the writer the ability to put the right word in the right place at the right time, provided the writer keeps on thinking and searching. Without drudgery, the act of revision is made more achievable. Without drudgery, writers can be guided to the grammar checkers, spelling programs, and even textual analysis programs.

Prewriting, organizing, and editing features are found in the best computer-assisted writing applications. Some of the better integrated word-processing applications can help writers brainstorm, provide organization windows, or facilitate proofreading. Prewriting or invention software may include timed free writing, "invisible" writing, question dialogues, graphic mapping, listing, analogy brainstorming, audience analysis, and rhetorical stance questions. Arrangement applications may include paragraph templates, graphic paragraph models, and short essay models. In the 1970s, much of the computer-assisted instruction in English composition was of the drill and practice variety. Later, prewriting software, question-asking applications, outliners, and "think tank" software tools emerged, which prompted writers to use the computer as a place to assemble, organize, collect, brainstorm, and rearrange the information they wished to write about. By trying to help writers find and think about topics which interest them and by offering a place for these topics to be explored, such computer programs have been most helpful.

Some applications for developing style include sentence-combining exercises, sentence-level syntactic models, cohesion lessons, grammar checkers, or a passive-voice identification routine. By striving for more exactness in computer-assisted writing, writing teachers can focus and refocus a student's thinking. Imagine writers actually applying dictums such as "sharpen your thoughts" or "be precise." Listen to the writer's inner tactical voice: "This word should be placed here; let's use this one instead. That sentence is in the wrong place, isn't it? Let's try it later on page six. This quotation is not as persuasive here; move it to the next-to-last paragraph." The likelihood of such stylistic revision is improved if the task of managing a changing text is simple.

The issue is not just whether students have improved individual essays, but, more importantly, whether or not they have developed and internalized more effective ways of writing.

Acts of Surprise

Experienced writers produce discourses, not sentences. They seem more likely to think of a writing project as a purposeful crafting activity rather than inspiration spontaneously combusting on the page. When writing with a computer, they seem more willing to engage the screen as an experimental easel rather than as a threatening blank page. Thus, they benefit greatly from the electronic manipulation of ideas. They may spend more time in the process, but they spend less time just staring at blank paper. Not only are they willing to be surprised, they are trying to surprise themselves.

William Zinsser writes, "Writing is a deeply personal process, full of mystery and surprise. . . . The word processor is God's gift, or at least science's gift, to the tinkerers and the refiners and the neatness freaks" (96, 98). Add creativity freaks, for touring the human imagination, corresponding with the page or screen, toying around with text—this is a machine Lewis Carroll and James Joyce would have loved.

More surprises are ahead for writers using computer-assisted writing tutors and tools. In the short term, computers will provide recordings of a writer's problem-solving processes so that writers may observe their own performances as well as the performance of experts. Such writing experiences will offer a time-compressed view of the tactics involved in writing a text. The compression of process will allow for past habits to inform future writing decisions more fully. Imagine seeing writing expertise in motion. In the long term, some computers will be designed with artificial intelligence. Applications then will be *truly* individualized. These trends are unmistakable. Yet until such hardware and software matures and until such computing power can be made widely available both in our culture and in our schools, computers still foster fruitful activity and furious creativity. When we better perceive how humans write and learn, computers may surprise us even more.

CLASS Acts: In Perspective

The outlook for teaching computer-assisted writing is bright. But understand one thing: computers do what we ask and program them to do. As professional educators, we therefore must be wise about what we ask computers to do. Individual teachers should strive to be wise about achieving a balanced perspective when using computers. No English teacher wants to teach word processing rather than writing. We must all guard against letting machines and powerful word-processing features become more important than our students' coming to know ideas through the processes and products of good writing. Let them discover ideas which are well created, well arranged, well worded, well edited, and well delivered. If this discovery is made on a cathode-ray tube or a liquid crystal display, instructors trained in the humanities should be just as pleased as if it were made on paper.

Now, can all of these strategic outcomes be achieved with tactical computing technologies? Yes, I believe so.

If teachers have computational *credibility,* then they can use operating systems and computer applications masterfully. If teachers better understand the nature of human *learning,* then they can teach wisely. If teachers better understand the dynamic features of *activity,* then they can individualize instruction efficiently. If teachers are committed to revealing processes of *style,* then they can encourage simplicity and clarity effectively. If teachers are open to *surprise,* then they can model the writing and learning advantage enthusiastically.

Computers—tools for the twenty-first century, machines improving and evolving—with them or without them, the language arts will be taught. But with wise decisions, teaching computer-assisted writing will be more efficient, more effective, and much more fun.

Suggested Readings

Burns, Hugh. "Computers and Composition." *Teaching Composition: Twelve Bibliographical Essays.* Ed. Gary Tate. Fort Worth: Texas Christian, 1987. • This article reviews the historical context through 1986 for using computers in composition, examines where word-processing pedagogies are moving the teaching of composition, summarizes the state-of-the-art computer-assisted instruction in teaching composition, and foreshadows future intellectual and practical issues of using computers to teach writing.

———. "The Promise of Artificial-Intelligence Research for Composition." *Perspectives on Research and Scholarship in Composition.* Eds. Ben W.

McClelland and Timothy R. Donovan. New York: MLA, 1985. • A future-looking perspective on composition, cognition, and computers, it defines artificial-intelligence research as a way for writers to investigate how we operate as writers, thinkers, arrangers, and editors; introduces expert systems; and speculates about intelligent computer-assisted instruction in the composition classroom. Future computer programs will have more and more intelligence "designed. in."

Collins, James L., and Elizabeth A. Sommers, eds. *Writing On-Line: Using Computers in the Teaching of Writing.* Upper Montclair, NJ: Boynton/Cook, 1985. • The book is a collection of practical essays on teaching writing with word processors. Lots of experience here.

Daiute, Colette. *Writing and Computers.* Reading, MA: Addison-Wesley, 1985. • Daiute stimulates us to think about computers and writing in fresh ways, stressing the social, physical, and cognitive processes of computer-assisted writing; well grounded on research. Excellent bibliography and resource directory.

Halpern, Jeanne W., and Sarah Liggett. *Computers and Composing: How the New Technologies Are Changing Writing.* Carbondale, IL: Southern Illinois, 1984. • This discusses how word processing, interactive television, audio mail, electronic mail, and dictating equipment are changing the way writers write; specifically focuses on how dictation/word-processing systems have affected business writing; argues that composition teachers should establish better connections between the classroom and the business world by attending more to the technological settings writers will work in.

Hofstadter, Douglas R. *Godel, Escher, Bach: An Eternal Golden Braid.* New York: Vintage, 1980. • "A metaphorical fugue on minds and machines in the spirit of Lewis Carroll" which won the 1980 Pulitzer Prize for "General Nonfiction." Several levels of exploring and articulating how our minds develop formal systems to explain, only to realize that the system itself cannot explain itself. Rich examples for teachers bent on stimulating creativity in their classrooms.

Olsen, Solveig. *Computer-Assisted Instruction in the Humanities.* New York: MLA, 1985. • Olsen reports the findings of the Modern Language Association's conference on the instructional uses of computers in the high school and undergraduate humanities curriculum. Cautious optimism is reflected in the twelve essays of Part One. Part Two, "Sources and Resources," is extensive, over seventy-five pages of people, programs, and print sources. Invaluable.

Papert, Seymour. *Mindstorms: Children, Computers, and Powerful Ideas.* New York: Basic, 1980. • Papert views computers in education as having tremendous power to stimulate ideas, as tools for discovery and self-enrichment; is upbeat about human-computer communication as a natural process; tells the story of the LOGO environment, the computer language which gave us the "turtle—a computer object to think with."

Schank, Roger C., with Peter G. Childers. *The Cognitive Computer: On Language, Learning, and Artificial Intelligence.* Reading, MA: Addison-Wesley, 1984. • A manifesto on computers as tools to investigate better human understanding, especially the complexities of human intelligence, this book probes the basic issues of linguistics, learning, and even philosophy in artificial intelligence research. It contains readable and common-sense descriptions of computer literacy, natural language understanding, knowledge structures, and educational implications for using computers in schools.

Schwartz, Helen J. *Interactive Writing: Composing with a Word Processor.* New York: Holt, Rinehart, & Winston, 1985. • This textbook is excellent for teaching writing with computers; keeps the rhetorical strategies center stage; lets the word processor stay in the tactical background; suggests many useful activities for incorporating computers in a writing class.

———— and Lillian S. Bridwell. "A Selected Bibliography on Computers in Composition." *College Composition and Communication* 35 (1984): 71–77. • An important compilation of articles, books, and software on computer-assisted instruction in composition, the article is good for composition programs based on word processing.

Selfe, Cynthia L. *Computer-Assisted Instruction in Composition: Create Your Own!* Urbana, IL: NCTE, 1986. • Selfe describes the process of creating computer-assisted instruction: identifying assumptions about writing, selecting topics, planning the interaction, designing, lesson development, developing appropriate feedback, developing screen displays, field testing, and communicating the results. Workbook format. Well illustrated.

Turkle, Sherry. *The Second Self: Computers and the Human Spirit.* New York: Simon & Schuster, 1984. • A fascinating account of how computers are affecting culture: a computer is a psychological machine because it makes us think about our own processes; a computer becomes a second self.

Wresch, William, ed. *The Computer in Composition Instruction: A Writer's Tool.* Urbana, IL: NCTE, 1984. • This is a collection of thirteen essays by composition teachers who have attempted to harness computers to their own purposes—prewriting, editing and grammar instruction, word-processing research, and integrated writing processors; emphasizes software design, development, and classroom applications.

Zinsser, William. *Writing with a Word Processor.* New York: Harper & Row, 1983. • The book depicts how useful and usable computers can be after one breaks through the fear and trembling. If word processors are servants, they can help writers achieve clarity, simplicity, and humanity. Use this book to introduce word processing to huddled masses yearning to write free.

Writing across the Curriculum and the Writing Teacher

Toby Fulwiler,
University of Vermont

Since 1970 a number of leading writers and scholars have advocated that college instructors pay more attention to the variety of roles writing can play in the academic curriculum (Britton 1970; Kinneavy 1973; Moffett 1982). In fact, programs have emerged at all grade levels to promote writing across the curriculum (Britton 1975) in an effort to "*balance* the basics" (Graves 1978) and get away from simplistic slogans about "*back* to the basics."

These writing across the curriculum programs vary widely in scope and method, but most attempt to accomplish essentially the same thing: to improve student learning and writing by encouraging faculty in all disciplines to use writing more often and more thoughtfully in their classrooms (Maimon 1979). While some colleges have developed placement instruments or initiated junior-year competency examinations—primarily English Department projects—most schools require the cooperation or direct action of large numbers of teachers in areas such as history, business, biology, social studies, and engineering—teachers who have never been trained formally to teach writing and who do not, in many cases, know where to start or what to do.

Basic to any program which aims to exercise students more often in various modes of written language is the premise that writing is inextricably interlocked with learning, thinking and knowing (Emig 1977). More writing in other disciplines, to put it another way, means more thinking in and about the subject matter of those disciplines. Teachers who ask students to explore, through writing, all the subject matter of their course must necessarily slow down, cover less, and look more closely at the student expression of course knowledge (Gere 1985). At the same time, schools which opt to write across the curriculum begin to promote a critical and inductive mode of inquiry rather than a passive or didactic one. And, by extension, when whole districts, K–college, adapt such an approach, a revolution in education will have occurred.

A comprehensive writing across the curriculum program at the college level asks students to work on their writing in all disciplines and at all grade levels, and it places some responsibility for assigning and evaluating writing with every teacher; language instruction becomes the business of all teachers who use language. As a consequence, students cannot view English teachers alone as concerned about good writing. Nor can faculty view the teaching of writing as the responsibility of the English department alone. Students and faculty alike must view good writing as closely related to good reasoning. At every turn of the curriculum someone must pay the serious attention to writing that his or her fundamental and reflective learning mode requires.

The most common means of introducing college instructors to the ideas which inform writing across the curriculum is through intensive, multiday faculty workshops, where participants are introduced to ideas for teaching with writing in a variety of classroom settings (Fulwiler 1981). Often, these workshops are led by composition instructors who translate what they know about *teaching* writing to content area teachers to enable them to teach *with* writing. But what, exactly are we talking about?

In the remainder of this essay I want to describe both the relationship between "teaching writing"—which is the business of the composition instructor who is using the *Harbrace College Handbook—and* "teaching with writing"— which is the business of everyone, including composition teachers—in the curriculum and the appropriate strategies for accomplishing each.

Teaching with Writing

Writing can be used as a tool to help students learn better in any discipline. Once teachers accept that premise, the next thing they need to do is figure out how, exactly, to make this tool work in their classrooms. I'll give one specific example of the use of writing to promote learning in discipline-specific classrooms (which also works in composition classrooms): journals.

If teachers want students to think daily about the issues addressed in their classes, no other assignment works as well as the journal (Fulwiler 1979). Unlike many other assignments, students write journals primarily for themselves and only secondarily for instructors—which means that journals cannot be graded in a conventional sense, but must still count. Journals allow students to explore ideas, ask questions, and try out theories without being penalized for doing so. For example, I commonly start every class session I teach with a five-minute journal entry, asking my students in "American Literature" to write about their first reaction to reading *Moby Dick* or their ideas about a passage from Whitman that I write on the blackboard. Once students write in response to such simple yet open questions, the ensuing classroom discussion is commonly more animated and informed. (Journal writing to start class works equally well in history, chemistry, political science, and the like.) Here are some specific guidelines that help journal assignments succeed, regardless of discipline or class size:

1. Ask students to buy loose-leaf notebooks. Make two distinct sections, one academic (your course) and the other personal (for whatever private writing they want to do).

2. Ask students to write in their most comfortable language, paying little attention to precision or correctness. I ask them to use their "letter-writing voice."

3. Ask open-ended content questions to start or conclude class. Also ask that they write on their own outside of class in response to assigned readings or in preparation for doing more formal writing assignments.

4. Keep a class journal along with your students. When they write, you write too—which both models and validates the exercise.

5. Use journals actively in class by asking students to read voluntarily from them to the whole class or to share insights from them in smaller groups. (This validates them—again without grades—as students see that class discussion is easier and more engaged if preceded by private writing.)

6. Collect "ten good pages" (student selected) three or four times during the term. Browse through them, and respond personally and positively in your letter writing voice to what interests you. (What are "good" pages? Full and at least tangentially about your subject area.)

7. Grade journals quantitatively by allowing a certain number of points for simply turning them in. (It's important that in these notebooks students be allowed to write personal impressions, dumb questions, and wrong hypotheses without being penalized for doing so—as I do in my own journal.)

These guidelines should work equally well for teachers of composition classes as well as for teachers of so-called content classes. In composition classes, I believe the journal has two especially useful purposes: as a place for students (1) to find and try out ideas for more formal paper topics ("Write about what you would like to write about in the next few months") and (2) to promote self-consciousness about each writer's own voice and writing process ("How did you learn to write in the first place?").

Teaching Writing

It is no secret how serious writers make their writing better: they revise and edit it until it pleases them or until a deadline makes them stop (Murray 1978). That's also how my own writing gets better. And that's how my students' writing gets better. The most profound advice I have to give to teachers who want to help students learn to write better is to remember their own struggles as writers when they make writing assignments and respond to them. (What difficulties have I had starting a writing task? What kind of response helps my own writing get better?)

Teachers of history, engineering, or botany seldom have the luxury of being able to spend very much time on rewriting activities in class itself, though such time, if found, may reward them handsomely in both better learning and improved writing. The major change these instructors may make will be to provide for revision and editing opportunities before final grades are given out. For example, instead of assigning a single term paper due at the end of the term, instructors might ask for one-page proposals, require a research log, schedule conferences, create in-class writing response groups, and make sure that students write more than one last-minute draft of the paper.

The luxury of the writing teacher is the luxury of being able to teach a rewriting class. Instead of sneaking time away from content to pay attention to the process by which writing gets done, it is the writing teacher's primary business to pay attention to that process. What this means for me is fewer formal papers and more opportunities for revision. For example, in the last freshman writing class I taught, I asked my students to write only three formal papers in fifteen weeks. However, the first paper, a narrative of a personal experience, I asked them to work on for six weeks. At first, many students thought the paper was finished after one draft; I made it my role as a teacher to keep suggesting other possibilities for that paper: new directions, more detail, a compressed or expanded time frame, more data, a variant perspective, and so on. And each time I asked students to read these papers to each other in writing groups and revise in light of requests for more information or explanation.

Class time is devoted primarily to looking at student texts on overhead projection transparencies, talking about positive examples of leads, transitions, descriptions, etc. In such classes I seldom use an anthology or reader, as the students' own texts provide most of the models and variety of subjects that we need. I do use a handbook on an individualized basis, referring students (as needed) to this section on commas or that section on analytical strategies.

The other two multiple-draft assignments usually include an analytical paper requiring some research (on-site observations and interviews as well as library searching) and a set piece such as a two-page book review, on which we spend less time. Throughout the term we are talking about the kinds of things that real writers talk about to make their writing better, most of which revolve around creating belief among readers, whether from memory, as in narrative, or from external sources, as in much informational or referential writing.

What has this got to do with writing across the curriculum? Well, the best anchor for a schoolwide writing program is a first-year writing course in which students learn the self-conscious techniques and strategies of experienced writers and have an opportunity to internalize them. In such courses I try hard to put grades in the background by using a portfolio system, grading the portfolio as a whole just twice, at mid-term and at finals. This allows us to concentrate on the process of change rather than on final drafts. Students well grounded in revision and editing strategies will keep using those strategies as long as other teachers in the rest of the curriculum seem to value them also.

Here are some guidelines for making portfolios work in a writing class— these work equally well in small process-oriented content classes across the curriculum:

1. Ask students to buy pocket folders and to keep *all* drafts of their papers in these folders all term long.

2. Every time you collect a draft of student writing, ask that the prior draft be clipped behind; this allows you to see the process of revision in action.

3. Comment extensively on drafts to be further revised, but do not put letter grades on these drafts. Students will then read your comments, not your short-hand grade, and revise accordingly.

4. Tell students that you will be willing to give them an approximate grade any time during the semester, if they will simply show you their whole portfolio to date. (They will seldom take you up on this; they always think the portfolio will be better *next* week; but this does put grades in the background.)

5. At the end of the term, ask for the complete portfolio containing all finished papers (these should be close to "perfect" I tell them), with all prior drafts clipped behind each.

6. Ask students to attach a self-assessment of their writing abilities at this time (one page, typed) as a cover sheet.

7. Grade the portfolio as a whole, taking into account both the quality of the final drafts and the amount of serious revision work demonstrated in the earlier drafts. This allows you to give a combined process/product grade: "A" folders must demonstrate both strong final products plus substantial efforts at serious revision.

8. Finally, write each student an assessment letter on a separate sheet of letterhead stationery, commenting on both their finished pieces and their self-assessments. Return the folders intact to the students.

Collaborative Learning and Writing

Both writing and learning get better when they take place in a community of people who talk over and explore ideas, provide feedback and motivational help for each other (Bruffee 1975). These are the principles at work when teachers form on-going writing groups in their classes. In the second week of my composition classes, for instance, I divide my students into permanent groups (five each) and provide weekly opportunities for these groups to meet and become comfortable with each other: these are the groups that will read each other's papers (five copies of each paper, writer reads aloud, group mates respond gently but honestly to what they hear, about ten minutes apiece on short papers).

I often use these and even smaller ad hoc groups in my class to share journal entries or solve brief problems that will help advance the business of the class. For example, handing out some sample pages for editing exercises, or asking for short reports on various aspects of writing (for example, introductions, conclusions, transitions, active versus passive voice, documentation). In fact, a common rhythm in my writing class is five minutes of private writing, five minutes of small-group talk, five minutes for me to collect ideas from the whole class and put them on the chalkboard.

I consider these group activities an essential part of any writing across the curriculum program, as the small-group talk is one of the strongest motivators of writing and learning that we have. In fact, I especially like journals because they do a close approximation of small-group talk, allowing the writers in this case to talk to themselves. Again, if I can spend some extra time on groups and how they work in my writing class, then when teachers across the curriculum use groups, the students will have more experience with them.

Of all the techniques mentioned here, the use of groups will be the hardest. Most groups do not work especially well the first time; students are simply too polite or do not yet trust themselves to be honest with each other. In order to guarantee success you must provide regular opportunities for the groups to meet and become comfortable with each other (and you). When they are finally able to give each other helpful critical feedback about papers, exercises, or problems, then you'll see a new kind of active energy in your class—a motivation to write and learn for each other as well as for themselves or the teacher. Recently, I asked my writing classes to brainstorm a list of guidelines for students to keep in mind when they read and respond to each other in writing groups. Here is a slightly edited version of their suggestions:

1. Listen critically and courteously to each reader and speaker. Make time for each person in the group to speak, one student at a time.

2. Ask for the kind of response you want on this particular piece of writing. ("I'm having trouble with the introduction; what do you think?" or "Can you give me your overall impression?")

3. Try to give the author the kind of response that he or she asks for. ("I think your introduction actually works . . . " or "I hear your voice strongly, but I'm not sure your examples support your argument.")

4. Tell the writer what he or she is doing right! Be positive. ("Good examples on page 3" or "Your conclusion raises a really good question.")

5. Be honest about problems you see. And be gentle. ("I could not follow your idea on the second page; could you explain it another way?" or "It seems to me that your paper really starts at the bottom of the first page; do you really need that long introduction?")

6. Raise questions rather than give commands. ("What did you mean here?" or "Would some examples help?")

7. Respect and listen for the author's intention. ("I was really trying to describe what it's like to be alone in Ecuador when you don't speak Spanish" or "Who is really your audience for this?")

8. Comment on a few important things rather than everything. Try not to overwhelm the author by pointing out everything that you would do differently.

9. Comment on the larger issues (purpose, theme, content, argument) first; the smaller stuff (punctuation, spelling, grammar, documentation) later. Or mark these smaller considerations on the paper in pencil and return at the end. That will allow the writer to consider your suggestions later, and you won't waste valuable group time on trivia.

10. Budget time carefully so each writer gets a fair share. (Elect a timekeeper; start with a new writer each session; don't waste time on small matters such as commas.)

Observations

It should be obvious by now that I consider language to be the medium of *active* learning in all subjects (Freire 1970). We need to look at how we talk, write, and listen to our students as well as how we ask them to talk, write, and listen to us. As composition teachers, we have the chance to focus on student *processes* that teachers in other disciplines will seldom have the time to do. Those students who enter into a serious relationship with you and their writing classmates will, in fact, grow as writers in your class. What you hope is that when your students participate in the rest of the curriculum, their other teachers will respond to their writing in a way that will reinforce, not diminish, your writing lessons. If your college or university does not now have such a comprehensive writing program in place, maybe it's time to talk about starting one.

Works Cited, Annotated

Britton, J. 1970. *Language and Learning.* Harmondsworth, England: Penguin. • This is Britton's original formulation of the relationship between language and cognitive growth and development.

Britton, J., et al. 1975. *The Development of Writing Abilities 11-18.* London: MacMillan. • This report surveys the kind of writing required of British secondary students and makes the case for more variety in both audience and purpose in school writing.

Bruffee, K. 1984. "Collaborative Learning and the Conversation of Mankind." *College Composition and Communication* 46: 635–52. • Bruffee succinctly articulates the role of collaboration in the promotion of thinking and learning within classroom discourse communities.

Emig, J. 1977. "Writing as a Mode of Learning." *College Composition and Communication* 28: 2. • Emig articulates the differences between writing and the other language modes, arguing that writing is the most powerful mode of learning in many situations.

Freire, P. 1970. *Pedagogy of the Oppressed.* New York: Herder. • Brazilian educator Paulo Freire describes the difference between "banking" and "liberatory" education, making a strong case for the role of self-generated language in promoting autonomous learning and critical thinking.

Fulwiler, T. 1984. "How Well Does Writing across the Curriculum Work?" *College English* 46: 113–25. • Fulwiler assesses the impact of five years of a program in writing across the curriculum at Michigan Tech and discusses both the advantages and problems associated with the program.

———. 1979. "Journal Writing across the Curriculum." *Classroom Practices in Teaching English, 1979–1980: How to Handle the Paper Load.* Ed. G. Stanford. Urbana, IL: NCTE. 15–22. • Fulwiler makes a case for using journals to promote critical thinking, active learning, and better writing in all classrooms, grade levels, and disciplines.

————. 1981. "Showing, Not Telling, at a Writing Workshop." *College English* 43: 55–63. • Fulwiler describes the theory and practice of conducting two-day, off-campus, interdisciplinary writing workshops, including step by step plans for conducting such workshops.

Gere, A. R., ed. 1985. *Roots in the Sawdust: Writing to Learn across the Disciplines.* Urbana, IL: NCTE. • Gere edits a collection of essays written by secondary teachers describing specific writing assignments in disciplines from history and social studies to music, art, and biology.

Graves, D. 1978. *Balance the Basics: Let Them Write.* New York: Ford Foundation. • Graves makes the case that children's writing will improve when teachers let them spend time in supportive environments writing about things that matter to them.

Kinneavy, J. L. 1971. *A Theory of Discourse.* Englewood Cliffs, NJ: Prentice-Hall. • A major theoretical discussion of the major modes of discourse (referential, persuasive, literary, and expressive); includes rationale, examples, and characteristics of each mode.

Maimon, E. Dec. 1979. "Writing in the Total Curriculum at Beaver College." *CEA Forum:* 7–10. • Maimon describes the writing across the ourriculum program at Beaver College, including freshman writing courses, the writing center, and advanced writing courses tailored to specific disciplinary needs.

Moffett, J. 1981. *Active Voice.* Upper Montclair, NJ: Boynton/Cook. • Moffett presents a collection of student writing in a variety of modes, including informal, persuasive, and imaginative, to suggest what is possible when students write across the disciplines in secondary school settings.

Murray, D. 1978. "Internal Revision: A Process of Discovery." *Research on Composing: Points of Departure.* Ed. C. Cooper and L. Odell. Urbana, IL: NCTE. • Murray explains the principles of revision in terms of acts of discovery on the writer's part; he concludes with suggestions for further research and investigation.

Thaiss, C., ed. 1982. *Writing to Learn: Essays and Reflections by College Teachers across the Curriculum.* The George Mason Faculty Writing Program. Fairfax, VA: George Mason UP. • Thaiss's collection of essays written by college teachers in various disciplines makes a strong argument that writing has many places in higher education classrooms.

Zinsser, W. 1988. *Writing to Learn.* New York: Harper & Row. • Writing for the lay public, Zinsser makes a compelling and well-written case that writing across the curriculum ideas are in fact useful to all thinkers and learners, inside the academy and out; includes chapters on math, art, science writing.

PART TWO
SECTIONS 1–35:
DISCUSSIONS, ACTIVITIES,
AND ANSWERS TO EXERCISES

1

SENTENCE SENSE

Grammar instruction shows the patterns of English and provides part of the common vocabulary students and instructors use in discussing the strategies of effective sentences and paragraphs. Unfortunately, students who are unfamiliar with the material covered in this section may be intimidated by it. Consider a partial list of the terms introduced in this section: *auxiliary, helping verbs, verb markers, phrasal verbs, particle, direct objects, indirect objects, active voice, passive voice, subject complements, object complements, intransitive linking verbs, verbals, suffixes, noun phrases, verbal phrases, subordinate clauses, gerund phrases, appositive phrases, relative clauses, adjective clauses,* and *adverb clauses.* Teaching this material too quickly can undermine students' confidence by leaving them convinced that grammar is complex and that their knowledge is incomplete. On the other hand, lingering over this material at the beginning of a writing course can reinforce common misconceptions about composition: that good writing is "correct writing" and that a thorough understanding of grammar is essential before anyone can take pen to paper.

Teachers of writing should recognize that mastering English grammar does not necessarily lead to good prose and that good prose can come from writers unable to explain the difference between a phrasal verb and a verb phrase. This recognition does not mean that instruction in grammar can be dispensed with; on the contrary, such instruction remains of great importance, and teachers may be doing their students a serious misservice if they overlook grammar and focus entirely upon other concerns. The question is how much emphasis should grammar have within a writing course and at what point is it best introduced.

37

As a courtesy to instructors familiar with the numbered and lettered sections in earlier editions of *Harbrace*, this edition retains the arrangement first established by John Hodges many years ago. But teaching this Handbook has never required instructors to assign sections in the exact sequence in which they appear. Much of the research in composition in recent years has emphasized that writing is not a linear act, proceeding orderly from one clearly defined stage to another. One of the implications of this research has been to encourage instructors to reexamine such traditional assumptions as the belief that students need to be able to write good sentences before they can write good paragraphs and good paragraphs before they can write good essays. Your students may profit more from the lessons of section **1** after they have already done some writing and, in so doing, have discovered that they need this instruction as part of what makes writing successful.

To lessen the risk of putting either too much or too little emphasis upon the material covered in section **1**, consider assigning parts of it at different times. You can defer the discussion of verbs in **1a** until you are ready to assign section **7** for a lesson focused on verb forms. Because it offers a self-contained series of examples illustrating the function of different parts of speech, **1c** can be assigned separately at almost any time (although doing so early in the semester may help build students' confidence about grammar, since they are likely to recognize a term like "pronoun" more readily than a term like "object complement"). The other parts of section **1** (**1b**, **1d**, and **1e**) introduce fundamentals of sentence structure that may be more meaningful if tied to the discussion of emphasis and variety found in sections **29** and **30**. When students perceive that structure helps determine emphasis and that varied sentence structure helps make writing read easily, they can then perceive important reasons for understanding the various types of phrases, clauses, and sentences.

Of course, you can also teach all of section **1** before turning to any other concerns. Doing so can work with sophisticated students for whom this material will simply be a review of lessons long learned. The systematic study of section **1** may also be appropriate in a developmental writing class if the material is tied to exercises in one of the workbooks that accompany the Handbook. The book provides you with enough flexibility to choose the approach that works best with any one class.

But whether you choose to teach this material early or late, in full or in part, try to keep terminology from making students feel grammatically illiterate. Although student writing often includes fragments and fused sentences (which are discussed in sections **2** and **3**), most students already have a great deal of sentence sense. It is a rare essay that does not include many examples of complete sentences, the word order of which—while occasionally awkward—is nevertheless adequate for communicating meaning. You may be able to reassure your own students by pointing out that they already know more grammar than they may realize; they may simply lack the vocabulary to explain why they have arranged words in a particular pattern and why altering that pattern may change the meaning conveyed by those words. You can also reassure your students by pointing out that the **Glossary of Grammatical and Rhetorical Terms** at the back of the Handbook contains definitions of the many terms first introduced in section **1**. Reminding students that this glossary is available to them should help keep them from becoming discouraged if—like most people—they cannot keep all of these terms permanently in mind.

Because grammar is frequently confused with usage, you might share with your students the three meanings of grammar defined by W. Nelson Francis in "Revolution in Grammar" (*Quarterly Journal of Speech* 40[1954]: 299–312):

> The first thing we mean by "grammar" is "the set of formal patterns in which the words of a language are arranged in order to convey larger meanings." It is not necessary that we be able to discuss these patterns self-consciously in order to be able to use them. In fact, all speakers of a language above the age of five or six know how to use its complex forms of organization with considerable skill; in this sense of the word—call it "Grammar 1"—they are thoroughly familiar with its grammar.
>
> The second meaning of "grammar"—call it "Grammar 2"—is "the branch of linguistic science which is concerned with the description, analysis, and formulization of formal language patterns." Just as gravity was in full operation before Newton's apple fell, so grammar in the first sense was in full operation before anyone formulated the first rule that began the history of grammar as a study.
>
> The third sense in which people use the word "grammar" is "linguistic etiquette." This we may call "Grammar 3." The word in this sense is often coupled with a derogatory adjective: we say that the expression "he ain't here" is "bad grammar." What we mean is that such expression is bad linguistic manner in certain circles.

This division is useful not only in making the distinction between grammar and usage (which is what Nelson means by Grammar 3) but also in helping students realize that they already know more "grammar" than they probably realize. Nelson went on to question the teaching of Grammar 2, suggesting that the study of formal language patterns "is of highly questionable value in improving a person's ability to handle the structural patterns of . . . language" (301). During the last three decades, debate over the value of grammar instruction has continued without interruption. For an article providing an overview of this debate, see Patrick Hartwell, "Grammar, Grammars, and the Teaching of Grammar" (*College English* 47 [1985]: 105–27). Hartwell assumes that grammarians are "rigidly skills-centered and rigidly sequential" whereas instructors who question the value of grammar are committed to "a rich and complex interaction of learner and environment" (108). But his essay is nevertheless both lively and provocative.

ACTIVITIES

1. Show students that they already understand grammar even if they can't explain it by writing the following words on the board: *German* *the* *new*

teachers three. Ask them to arrange these words in the order that seems natural (*the three new German teachers*). Almost any student should be able to succeed with this task (which is adapted from an exercise by Patrick Hartwell), and it can help inspire interest in why words must often be arranged in a particular sequence before they make sense.

2. Students may not be familiar with the term *expanded verb*, which refers to the fifty or more combinations of the verb with auxiliaries: *auxiliary + tense + verb*. If you wish to give students practice in forming expanded verbs, write a subject such as *I* or *Jack* on the board and then list several auxiliaries and verbs that students can combine to make expanded verbs. (It is probably best to put the tense marker after the verb rather than before it as is usual in stating the formula. Students tend to get confused if they have to make too many adjustments of this sort.)

Jack be + eat + -ing = is eating
      have + walk + -ed = has walked
      have + be + -en + think + -ing = has been thinking

3. The patterns for subject and object complements are explained in **4b**. You may wish to include a discussion of intransitive verbs and of subject and object complements:

Subject + Intransitive verb (+ adverb).
Jack   walked   (slowly).

Subject + Linking verb + Noun [subject complement].
Jack   became   an engineer.
Jack   was   an engineer.

Subject + Linking verb + Adjective [predicate adjective].
Jack   felt   sleepy.
Jack   was   angry.

Subject + Verb +   Object +   Object complement
Jack   painted   the fence   white.

4. Ask students to form two sentences, using the words below. Use the results to discuss the importance of word order in English.

Sentence 1: camping, gear, handing, is, Kate, Marcia, the
Sentence 2: and, beside, forlorn, fountain, Jennifer, lost, sitting, studied, terrier, the, the

Possibilities for Sentence 1:

Kate is handing Marcia the camping gear.
Marcia is handing Kate the camping gear.
Is Marcia handing Kate the camping gear?
Is Kate handing Marcia the camping gear?

Possibilities for Sentence 2:

Jennifer, lost and forlorn, studied the terrier sitting beside the fountain.
Sitting beside the fountain, Jennifer, lost and forlorn, studied the terrier.
Jennifer studied the lost and forlorn terrier sitting beside the fountain.
Lost and forlorn, the terrier sitting beside the fountain studied Jennifer.

5. Students who can readily identify subjects and verbs in exercise sentences may still have difficulty finding them in their own sentences. A useful activity is to have students find the subjects and verbs of the sentences they wrote in activity 4.

6. Ask students to identify any objects in these two sentences:

The witness told a *lie* to the jury.
The witness told the jury a *lie*.

Students who equate function and meaning may identify the italicized words as indirect objects. To clarify the difference here, point out the presence of *to* in the prepositional phrase and the position of *jury* as indirect object. Omitting *to* from the first sentence without shifting the word order produces *The witness told a lie the jury*; adding *to* to the second without shifting word order creates a prepositional phrase awkwardly placed after the verb: *The witness told to the jury a lie.*

7. Have students eliminate prepositional phrases from the following sentences and then identify subjects and verbs. Deleting prepositional phrases reduces the number of nouns and, thus, the number of possible choices for subject.

   a. Among my collection of houseplants over the past five years, strawberry begonias remain a favorite above all others.
   b. According to horticulturists, the strawberry begonia is neither a strawberry nor a begonia in spite of its name.
   c. In its natural habitat the plant produces runners which creep across the ground in search of a place to anchor miniature plants.
   d. With the exception of overwatering and overfertilizing, an indoor gardener past the age of reason can make few mistakes in the tending of these plants with hairy, variegated leaves.
   e. Once, however, I did uproot an entire plant during an attempt to remove a dead leaf near the edge of the pot; because of that unfortunate mistake, I've been more cautious about grooming plants since then.

8. A word's part of speech is determined by its use in the sentence. Have students write sentences following the patterns on page **9** to show

   down as adverb, adjective, preposition, verb
   well as noun, verb, adverb, adjective, interjection

outside as noun, adjective, adverb, preposition
near as adverb, adjective, verb, preposition
like as verb, noun, preposition, adjective, adverb
that as adjective, pronoun (demonstrative and relative), adverb, conjunction

Suggest that students keep their Handbooks open to the lists of prepositions (pages **14–15**).

9. Have students identify each word according to function and/or part of speech:

    a. If Kris has been a Steeler's fan for years, why does she want to see the Eagles play?
    b. Selecting a most unusual name for her cat, Rachel called him Zeus, but when Zeus had kittens, Rachel chose another name—Zenobia.
    c. Really! That's a likely excuse coming from such conspicuous consumers.
    d. Planning a holiday party becomes more exhausting every year; but as soon as our guests leave, we will probably begin to plan another one.
    e. Heavens! If your cheese soufflé flops, we can always eat cauliflower or some extremely tasty muffins that were baked yesterday.

10. Some suffixes that signal nouns are *-ation, -hood, -acy, -ism, - ence, -ance, -ness, -ment, -ship, -ity, -age, -dom.* Some suffixes that signal verbs are *-ize, -ify.* After introducing some of these suffixes, ask students to supply suffixes for the following words and make any necessary changes in spelling:

foot (footage)	code (codify)
incline (inclination)	secrete (secretion)
liquid (liquidate, liquify)	rely (reliance)
bright (brightness, brighten)	public (publicize, publicity)
lunar (lunacy)	note (notation, notify)
lively (liveliness, livelihood)	kin (kinship)
opportune (opportunity, opportunism)	
plural (pluralism, plurality, pluralize)	

▲ **Note**: *-er* to signal nouns (*teacher, driver, baker*) carries the meaning "one who"; *-er* to signal verbs (*glimmer, flutter*) carries the meaning "recurrent or frequent action."

Ask students to think of other suffixes that signal verbs and/or nouns, to invent nouns and verbs using these suffixes, and to provide definitions for these made-up words. For a useful treatment of suffixes, see Norman C. Stageberg's *An Introductory English Grammar* (4th ed. New York: Holt, 1981). Stageberg discusses source verbs with derived nouns, source nouns with derived verbs and adjectives, and source adjectives with derived verbs and nouns.

11. Have students use the present-participle form (the *-ing* form of verbs) as a verb in a verb phrase, as an adjectival (participle), and as a noun (gerund):

He was *playing* the villain. [verb in verb phrase]
The man *playing* the villain is Joe. [participle in adjective phrase]
His role is *playing* the villain. [gerund in noun phrase]
Suggested verbs: *dive, press*, and *babbling*.

12. Ask students to provide past participles (adjectives) describing their reactions when

   a. a two-hundred-dollar tax refund arrives in the mail [*relieved sigh, elated squeal*]
   b. an instructor asks a question on material that the student has not read yet [*embarrassed mumble, fabricated excuse*]
   c. a personnel director calls to offer a job interview
   d. inclement weather forces the university to close for a week
   e. the last parking space in the lot is taken by someone on a moped

13. Ask students to compose a sentence with three infinitives that name activities or goals for the year after graduation, goals or activities within five years of graduation, and reasons the goals may not be achieved.

14. Ask students to identify main and subordinate clauses in the following sentences:

   a. It is the tale of a young scientist named Frankenstein who discovers a means of animating a composite corpse. —GARY GOSHGARIAN [main clause + adjective clause]
   b. If a motion is too swift for the human eye to see it in detail, it can be captured and artificially slowed down by means of a slow-motion camera. —JAMES C. RETTIE [introductory adverb clause + main clause]
   c. The nuclear tests revealed how little we knew about the environmental network. —BARRY COMMONER [main clause + noun clause]
   d. I was in the theater district once, sitting on a stoop, enjoying the stream of life, when a brisk, well-preserved man with custom-fitted pants, a cane and good coloring halted in front of me. —EDWARD HOAGLAND [main clause + adverb clause]
   e. If it were not for the capacity of ambiguity, for the sensing of strangeness, that words in all languages provide, we would have no way of recognizing the layers of counterpoint in meaning, and we might be spending all our time sitting on stone fences, staring into the sun.

—LEWIS THOMAS [introductory adverb clause + adjective clause + main clause + main clause]

Although several of these sentences are quite difficult, some students will be able to identify not only main and subordinate clauses, but also the kinds of subordinate clauses (see section **24**). Others will do well simply to identify which are main clauses and which are subordinate. Students will also benefit considerably from writing their own sentences, following these basic patterns:

a. Main clause + *who* or *which* + subordinate clause.
b. *If* + subordinate clause, main clause.
c. Main clause (subject + verb) + noun clause (direct object).
d. Main clause + adverb clause.
e. *If* + subordinate clause + subordinate clause, main clause, *and* main clause.

15. To review the various forms of sentences (simple, compound, complex, compound-complex), have students spend a class period writing a paragraph on the board. The amount of board space will determine the number of paragraphs. Hand pieces of chalk to the first group of volunteers and ask each of them to create a simple sentence. Make no comment. As they finish, have them hand the chalk to their replacements, who should continue the paragraph (usually, but not always narrative) with a compound sentence. Repeat the process until sentences of all types are written for each paragraph. Then read each paragraph aloud, asking students to check the sentences for correct form and to revise when necessary. This approach relieves the routine of exercises and promotes camaraderie, especially when done on a Friday as a review of sentence types.

16. Have students compose sentences that contain the elements specified below:

a. adjective clause; noun clause   [*She knew that this woman who sat before her had tried many criminal cases.*]
b. adverb clause modifying verb; noun clause as direct object   [*As Margaret listened to the witness, she realized that her client had not divulged all the facts.*]
c. adverb clause modifying adverb; adjective clause   [*Margaret's calm reaction, which surprised me, was more restrained than even I had expected.*]
d. noun clause as indirect object; adverb clause modifying verb   [*Send whoever is treasurer this bill from the caterer before we are charged a late fee.*]

e. noun clause as direct object; noun clause as appositive   [*The fact that the landlord has doubled the rent means we must look for another apartment.*]

Because sentences for this exercise are time-consuming to write and to grade, many instructors prefer to conduct this activity in class, asking students to bring their completed sentences to class for discussion and evaluation.

ANSWERS TO EXERCISES

■ **Exercise 1** (p. 5)　　　**Underlining verbs**

1. are facing
2. descended
3. gobbled up
4. may be found
5. has given
6. Is
7. are
8. makes
9. invade, pollinate
10. pushed, grasped, swung

■ **Exercise 2** (p. 7)　　　**Identifying subjects and objects**

	Subjects	*Objects*
1.	nations	difficulties
2.	flock	—
3.	fire	real estate
4.	parts	—
5.	manner	statements (i.o.), force
6.	exercise	—
7.	students	—
8.	history	attitude
9.	gnats, flies	sheath, blossoms
10.	he	bike, handlebars, leg

■ **Exercise 3** (p. 10)　　　**Identifying subjects, objects, and complements**

	Subjects	*Objects and Complements*
1.	idea	nation (d.o.)
2.	Inventions	hallmark (s.c.)
3.	Art, games	rules, conventions, spectators (d.o.)
4.	people	nothing (d.o.)
5.	Homer	us (i.o.), information

6. We   tasks, tasks (d.o.)
7. enemy   —
8. multitude   us (d.o.), ignorant (o.c.)
9. American   kind (s.c.)
10. English, which,   full (s.c.)
     which, one

■ Exercise 4 (p. 16)   Classifying words according to part of speech

   pron. v. prep. art. n. prep. art. adj.   n.
1.   He struts with the gravity of   a frozen penguin.

    conj.   n.   conj. n. v. v. v. prep. n.
2.   Neither intelligence nor integrity can be imposed by   law.

    pron. v. art.   n.   conj. adv. prep. adj.   n.   pron. v.
3.   They pick a President and then for four years they pick

   +particle pron.
     on   him.

   prep. adj.   n.   n.   v. art. adv.   adv.   n.
4.   Of   all persons, adolescents are the   most intensely personal;

   pron./adj. n.   v. adv.   adj.   prep. n
    their intensity is often uncomfortable to adults.

   pron. v.   v.   adv. conj.   adv. adv. art. n. pron.
5.   We can remember minutely and precisely only the things which

   adv. adv. v.   prep. pron.
    never really happened to   us.

■ Exercise 5 (p. 19)   Identifying gerund and infinitive phrases

	Gerund	*Infinitive*
1.	Taking criticism from others	—
2.	—	to fight back
3.	No gerund phrase; "Running . . . sidewalk" is a participial phrase; "a danger to everyone" is an appositive.	—
4.	—	Merely to argue for the preservation of park land
5.	"even . . . drowning" "donating . . . " are also appositivies	—

■ **Exercise 6** (p. 21)   **Identifying and labeling phrases**

1. like that one   [adjective]
2. Dazzled by Baryshnikov's speed and grace   [adjective]
   _____ [adverb]
3. Crawling through the thicket   [adjective]
   _____ [adverb]
   of shells left on top of the truck   [adjective]
   _____ [adjective]
   _____ [adverb]
   _____ [adjective]
4. to watch closely   [adjective]
   ruling behind the political scene   [adjective]
   _____ [adverb]
5. one man sawing logs   [adverb—absolute phrase]
   _____ [adjective]
   the other loading the truck   [adverb—absolute phrase]
   _____ [adjective]
6. curling over the surfer   [adjective]
   _____ [adverb]
   for a moment   [adverb]
7. a slender blond woman   [appositive]
   to the right   [adverb]
8. Not wanting to wait for the rest of us   [adjective]
   _____ [noun]
   _____ [adjective]
   _____ [adjective]
   in a cab   [adverb]
9. to get a better salary   [adverb]
   to move to a more pleasant area of the country   [adverb]
   _____ [adverb]
   _____ [adjective]
10. small but fuel-efficient   [adjective]

■ **Exercise 7** (p. 24)   **Identifying and labeling subordinate clauses**

1. that threatens the first use of nuclear weapons [adjective]
2. As the days grew shorter [adverb]
3. which immediately became a symbol of the stalemated global war [adjective]
4. What excited scientists most [noun]
5. If, like a musical Rip Van Winkle, a nineteenth-century man awoke today in a concert hall [adverb]
   that things had hardly changed [noun]

■ **Exercise 8** (p. 26)   **Identifying main and subordinate clauses**

1. <u>Practice never really makes perfect</u>, and <u>a great deal of frustration invariably accompanies juggling</u>.

2. Nature is his passion in life, and colleagues say [he is a skilled naturalist and outdoorsman].
3. The two clouds have a common envelope of atomic hydrogen gas, [which ties them firmly together].
4. Transportation comes to a halt [as the steadily falling snow, accumulating faster [than snowplows can clear it away], is blown into deep drifts along the highways].
5. Agriculture is the world's most basic industry; its success depends in large part on an adequate supply of water.
6. [Probably because their whirling sails were new and strange to Cervantes], windmills outraged the gallant Don Quixote.
7. There have been several attempts to explain this rhythm, but [when each hypothesis was experimentally explored], it had to be discarded.
8. Allegiance to a group may be confirmed or denied by the use or disuse of a particular handshake, [as Carl's experience indicates].
9. Some black stem rust of wheat has been controlled by elimination of barberry, a plant [that harbored the rust].
10. We know [that innocent victims have been executed]; fortunately, others condemned to death have been found innocent prior to execution.

■ Exercise 9 (p. 26) Classifying sentences

1. compound
2. compound-complex
3. complex
4. complex
5. compound
6. complex
7. compound-complex
8. complex
9. complex
10. compound-complex

■ Exercise 10 (p. 27) Identifying clauses, classifying sentences

1. *Main clause:* Jim angrily called himself a fool
   Subordinate clause: as he had been doing . . . swamp
   Complex
2. *Simple*
3. *Simple*
4. *Main clause:* He had enough mysteries . . . sort
   Subordinate clause: which involved . . . values
   Complex
5. *Main clause:* now he was chasing down ghosts
   Main clause: this chase . . . was absurd
   Compound
6. *Simple*
7. *Main clause:* The legends had horrified him as a child
   Subordinate clause: that surrounded the ghosts
   Main clause: they were a horror still
   Compound-complex

8. *Subordinate clause:* As he approached the dark trail
   Subordinate clause: that would lead him to . . . mansion
   Main clause: he felt almost sick
   Complex
9. *Simple*
10. *Main clause:* Only this grotesque night seemed . . . real
    Subordinate clause: whatever ghosts might be . . . shadows
    Complex

2

SENTENCE FRAGMENTS

Unintentional fragments are considered serious errors in formal writing because they violate the reader's expectations and may hamper communication. Overworked instructors may be tempted to simplify this issue and insist that students avoid all fragments. But anyone who takes a rigid position on fragments is both teaching the potentially demoralizing lesson that student writers must honor rules that can be ignored by professionals and depriving students of a means of introducing variety into their prose. Any discussion of fragments should recognize that there are occasions in which a fragment can be more effective than a sentence.

Rather than teaching that the fragment is an error, many instructors subordinate the discussion of fragments to the overall discussion of sentence structure, including such concerns as emphasis and variety which are addressed later in the Handbook. These teachers are still able to discourage the use of unintentional fragments, but they send a more appealing message to students: to use sentence fragments effectively, writers must be able to recognize one when they see it; only writers who understand the difference between complete and incomplete sentences know how and when to use a fragment for special effect.

As Mina P. Shaughnessy has observed in *Errors and Expectations* (New York: Oxford UP, 1977), students often write fragments out of "caution about losing control of the sentence by allowing it to become too long—too full—too full, that is, of embedded structures." As a result, helping students practice with embedding structures may be effective in reducing sentence fragments (28–29). Students who unintentionally write fragments may also be poor readers of their own writing. They mentally supply omitted words or punctuate without actually seeing the problem. Generally the fragments these students write are parts of preceding or following sentences punctuated as if they are complete thoughts. For these students, identifying and understanding fragments in contexts (blocks of writing) seems to help more than working with isolated fragments. Encouraging such students to read their own prose aloud may help them identify those fragments that are the most disruptive to communication.

Other students use fragments because they write quickly and informally, as if an essay were the same as a journal entry or a letter to a friend. Although such students often understand the difference between a sentence and a fragment, they may believe that fragments can be used routinely, whatever the audience or writing occasion. These students need to learn that fragments lose their effectiveness when overused or used for no apparent reason. If such students are already good writers, they may respond best to criticism that shows them that using fragments too regularly makes their prose too predictable.

For a useful discussion of sentence fragments, see Charles R. Kline, Jr., and W. Dean Memering, "Formal Fragments: The English Minor Sentence" (*Research in the Teaching of English* 11 [1977]: 97–110), and Muriel Harris, "Mending the Fragmented Free Modifier" (*College Composition and Communication* 32 [1981]: 175–182).

ACTIVITIES

1. Discuss the use of fragments in the following passage, the introduction to an article in the *Wall Street Journal*:

> Columbus, Ohio, is embarking on a year-long campaign to become the capital of truth. Honest.
> And who has been tapped to oversee the effort? Jeb Stuart Magruder, the former Nixon White House aide who spent seven months in jail for his role as a Watergate conspirator. Really. Scout's honor.   CLARE ANSBERRY

2. Use the following excerpt from "The Right to Arms" by Edward Abbey to demonstrate how the use of fragments can become a stylistic mannerism. Ask students if they think Abbey uses too many fragments.

> If guns are outlawed, only the government will have guns. Only the police, the secret police, the military. The hired servants of our rules. Only the government—and a few outlaws. I intend to be among the outlaws.

3. Have students distinguish fragments from sentences by using ads found in popular magazines, such as the following (from an issue of *Ladies' Home Journal*):

   a. Set yourself free. With Stouffer's.
   b. Save a Lettuce's Life. (General Electric)
   c. Improving on the French. (Stouffer's)
   d. California Avocados. Only 17 calories a slice.
   e. And you thought Ethan Allen just made great furniture.
   f. The Benson's "new" Faribo wool blankets are still in use. One Great Depression, one World War and One Golden Anniversary later.
   g. Less is More. (Ivory Liquid)
   h. Why No-Wax Floors Need Help. (Brite)
   i. The first dry dog food that's like a home-made meal. (Gravy Train)
   j. Introducing Cutex Nailcare. Because great-looking nails don't just grow that way.
   k. Wonderfully flavorful vegetable combinations, in a special light sauce that lets each unique taste come through. (Green Giant)
   l. The Fisher-Price Riding Toys. Because your kids have more energy than you know what to do with.

Discuss what reasons might justify the use of fragments in ads (discourse aim, limits of space, need to attract interest quickly, and so on) or how the use of fragments affects a reader. In the items above, have students identify the grammatical structures used as fragments (if necessary, suggest the categories: prepositional phrase, verbal phrase, dependent clause, adjective, appositive, adverb). Finally, have students collect fragments from their favorite magazine ads and label the grammatical structures of those fragments.

4. Have students number from 1 to 20 on a piece of paper. Then dictate ten short sentences mixed with ten fragments. Students should write down each word group and write S or F after each. Then have students check their answers and revise any fragments to make sentences.

5. Give each student a copy of the following collection of fragments. Caution students to read the entire passage before they begin to rewrite it. Doing so will help them to plan their strategy for including all of the ideas as smoothly as possible.

> Celebrating birthdays as an occasion for a family get-together. A summer barbecue or a winter buffet at Aunt Leah's. The oldest child and only daughter in a family of eight. Because planning a meal for forty-seven relatives requires the cooperation of every family involved. Certain relatives bringing their traditional specialities. To be sure. Potato salad from Aunt Catherine and corn relish from Aunt Meg. With Uncle Frank's contribution being the favorite. Pecan pie for dessert. Although there is no birthday cake and no one ever sings "Happy Birthday." To celebrate birthdays just the same.

6. Ask students to attach each fragment below to an existing sentence or make it into an independent sentence. (Follow-up for Exercise 3.)

a. [1]As a weather watcher, I am often amused by official forecasts. [2]Or, rather, by occasional prophecies made by weathermen who seldom bother to look out the window. [3]For example, one day late last spring when heavy rain and large hail lashed the city. [4]I promptly telephoned the weather bureau. [5]To ask about the possibility of a tornado. [6]A confident voice replied glibly, "Oh, don't worry about a tornado; we're not even in an alert area."
[7]Relieved, I turned on the radio, found a chair near a window, and watched the angry clouds. [8]To my amazement, I soon saw a swirling funnel emerge from a black cloud and strike toward the ground. [9]Just north of the city, about five miles away. [10]Of course, I immediately notified the weather bureau.
[11]A Short time later. [12]An important message interrupted the rock music on the radio: \"The weather bureau has issued a warning that a tornado may strike north of here." [13]I smiled as I repeated the words "may strike." [14]Knowing that the official prophets were busily rushing about their work. [15]As they tried to repair their radar and kept an eye on falling barometers and erratic wind gauges instead of paying attention to the turbulent weather itself.

b. [1]Very late in *The Merry Wives of Windsor*, Shakespeare introduces an incident which is altogether extraneous to either of the plot lines in the play.

[2]And which advances the action in no way whatsoever. [3]Bardolph in a very brief scene with the Host announces that "the Germans" desire three of the Host's horses. [4]So that they may go to meet "the Duke," who is to be at court on the next day. [5]The Host seems to know so little of these Germans that he must ask if they speak English. [6]A highly improbable ignorance on his part, for in his next lines he states that they have been already a week at his tavern. [7]But he lets them have the horses. [8]Insisting, however, that they must pay for them. [9]Two scenes later Bardolph returns to the tavern with the report that the villainous Germans have handled him roughly on the road. [10]Thrown him into a puddle, and run off with the horses. [11]Immediately on his heels, in come first Sir Hugh and then Dr. Caius. [12]With rumors confirming Bardolph's assurance of the evil character of the Germans. [13]So that the Host is at last alarmed. [14]He is convinced now that the Germans have indeed cozened him of a week's board bill. [15]And stolen his horses in the bargain.

ANSWERS TO EXERCISES

■ Exercise 1 (p. 31)   Eliminating sentence fragments

1. home, earnestly seeking
2. Constitution, a single issue dividing voters.
3. His beard was gone and his hair was cut.
4. effect, not only on
5. swat—against the law of averages

■ Exercise 2 (p. 32)   Eliminating sentence fragments

1. a try after I had grown tired
2. to college and that all tests
3. spring fever, which
4. blood and whenever
5. advertisements that use

■ Exercise 3 (pp. 32–33) Revising sentence fragments

Answers may vary. The following is a possibility.

The little paperback almanac I found at the newsstand has given me some fascinating information. Not just about the weather and changes in the moon, the almanac contains intriguing statistics. A tub bath, for example, requires more water than a shower—in all probability, ten or twelve gallons more, depending on how dirty the bather is. And one of the Montezumas downed fifty jars of cocoa every day, which seems a bit exaggerated to me, to say the least. I also learned that an average beard has thirteen thousand whiskers. In the course of a lifetime, a man could shave off more than nine yards of whiskers, over twenty-seven feet if my math is correct. Another interesting fact is that a person born on Sunday, February 29, 1976, will not celebrate another birthday on Sunday until the year 2004 because February 29 falls on weekdays till then—twenty-eight birthdays later. As I laid the almanac aside, I remembered that line in *Slaughter-house- Five*: "So it goes."

3

COMMA SPLICE AND FUSED SENTENCE

Students who frequently write comma splices or fused sentences are so busy trying to get their ideas down while simultaneously modifying or clarifying them that they lose sight of the strategy for a particular sentence. Failure to remember the structure at the beginning of the sentence may result in a fused sentence; an afterthought may result in a comma splice.

Drawing examples from students' writing and explaining why the errors might have happened will help students see how the process has gone awry and which of their composing habits they must watch in the future. Students need to pay attention to structural details—to understand how planning sentences, selecting ideas for emphasis, ordering ideas, and revising can help them avoid these errors. Once students have this understanding, they can correct the comma splices or fused sentences more effectively. As attention to structure increases, the number of comma splices and fused sentences should decrease.

Teaching punctuation alone does not correct the practice of writing a comma splice or a fused sentence, but because punctuation remains the means through which both errors are corrected, you may want to refer students ahead to rules **12a** and **14a**. Doing so would enable you to demonstrate how rules governing structure overlap with rules governing punctuation—a reassuring message for students who fear that English involves a bewildering number of rules. Tying these lessons together will also address the needs of students for whom the comma splice and fused sentence are more likely to be performance errors than conceptual errors.

ACTIVITIES

1. Have students replace the coordinating conjunctions between main clauses first with conjunctive adverbs and then with transitional phrases, making any necessary changes in punctuation. Encourage students to vary the placement of conjunctive adverbs and transitional phrases. Refer students to rule **23a**, to a list of conjunctive adverbs in **3b**, and to the list of transitional expressions in **32b(4)**.

   a. Kelly likes playing basketball, and she is a good sport when she loses.
   b. Last month she got a part-time job, and she now has less time for sports.
   c. She hates working on weekends, but she needs the money she is earning.

d. Kelly solved her problem by asking her boss for different hours, and she is now working after school on weekday afternoons.

e. To hear Kelly's stories about work is a pleasure, for she is as good in her storytelling as she is in her ball playing.

2. Ask students to correct the faulty punctuation between main clauses in the following sentences:

a. In high school Laura decided that she would become a research physicist, in fact, she even knew what area of research—cryogenics. [physicist. In fact, OR physicist; in fact,]

b. She excelled in her physics class; yet her trigonometry and algebra teachers kept telling her that her math skills would never be strong enough for her career. [class, yet]

c. She listened attentively to their warnings because she assumed that teachers were expert judges of a student's potential in all fields, the fact that she always had the highest grades in physics did not influence her as much as the opinions of two teachers. [fields; OR fields. The]

d. Laura abandoned her career in physics and chose another career equally demanding now she is excelling in her study of econometrics. [demanding. Now OR demanding;]

3. Have students punctuate the following paragraph (adapted from Sheila Tobias, "Who's Afraid of Math, and Why?"):

> A common myth about the nature of mathematical ability holds that one either has or does not have a mathematical mind mathematical principles may well be needed to do advanced research but why should people who can do college-level work in other subjects not be able to do college-level math as well rates of learning may vary competency under time pressure may differ certainly low self-esteem will get in the way but where is the evidence that a student needs a "mathematical mind" in order to succeed at learning math?

ANSWERS TO EXERCISES

■ **Exercise 1** (p. 37)   **Linking sentences**

Answers may vary in the choice of the coordinator.

1. pond; I
   pond, for I
2. nonsense; others
   nonsense, but (or and) others
3. hunting; he
   hunting, and (or but) he
4. details; he
   details, but he

■ **Exercise 2** (p. 37)   **Using a subordinating conjunction**

Answers will vary in the choice of the subordinating conjunction and in the position of the subordinate clause.
1. . . . pond because I remember seeing them when I was a child.
2. Even if some call his theory nonsense, others think . . .
3. When Dexter goes hunting, he carries . . .
4. Although he may haggle fiercely over details, he also . . .

■ **Exercise 3** (pp. 37–38) **Marking comma splices and fused sentences**

A check mark should follow sentences 1, 5, 7, 8, 10.
An *X* should follow sentences 2, 4, 6, 9.

■ **Exercise 4** (p. 38)   **Various methods of revision**

Since various methods of revision are called for, answers will differ. The following are samples.
1. hardwood; the
2. microbes. Those microbes
3. ✓
4. Because attempts to extinguish such fires have often failed, some
5. night. By morning
6. After the ringleaders abandoned the cub they had attacked, we stayed
7. people, and so I
8. mournfulness; it seemed
9. lagoon; except
10. water. Even with plugs

■ **Exercise 5** (p. 39)   **Compound Sentences**

Answers will vary.

■ **Exercise 6** (p. 40)   **Dividing quotations**

1. "I am . . . sing," Artemus Ward commented. "So are . . . me."
2. "I . . . prejudice," W.C. Fields once said. "I . . . equally."
3. "I know . . . backbone," says Ann Landers. "This is . . . project."
4. "There . . . life," according to Harrison Salisbury. "To . . . learned."
5. "Money . . . thing," John Kenneth Galbraith commented. "It . . . anxiety."

■ **Exercise 7** (pp. 40–41) **Revising comma splices and fused sentences**

Answers will vary. The following are samples.
1. says, "You're
3. Johnny. Besides
4. home. In Oklahoma

6. William, who
8. right, for that happy marriage
9. Illinois. There
10. attack; however, Nellie's arteries
11. sweetheart. Then
12. want it to. Age is

■ Exercise 8 (p. 41)　　　Proofreading sentences for correctness

Revisions may vary; the following are samples.

1. We sold our property; then we bought . . .
2. The cabin was originally built to house four people. A family often lives in it now, not to mention all the dogs and cats.
3. Val signed up for the university chorus; however, he really doesn't sing very well.
4. The Kiwanis Club sponsors a flea market every year; it is not, however, an easy way to make money.
5. ✓
6. Most of my professors require that students be on time for class because students who come in late disturb the other students.
7. ✓
8. . . . botulism, an acute form of food poisoning.
9. It is an argument riddled with stupid assumptions.
10. I usually buy . . . paperbacks, although I never get . . . them.

4

ADJECTIVES AND ADVERBS

Students occasionally confuse adjectives and adverbs in written sentences. The traditional explanation has been that, relying on spoken language, these students select the form they have heard in conversation ("we drove slow") whether or not the form is correct. The use of the *ly* form in such a sentence, however, is no longer obligatory. Several current dictionaries accept "slow" (and other such words) as adverbs.

Another common problem, however, is related to speech: the omission of the *-d* or *-ed* of a past participle used as an adjective. Often, students can correct this problem once they are made aware of it. Those students who have difficulty determining when to use the participial form can also be referred to **7a**, page **77**.

Although multiple negation (discussed in **4e**) occurs in all dialects of English, it varies in the degree to which it is rooted in patterns that may be difficult to correct. In such instances as "She didn't eat none," a writer would need only to substitute "any" for "none," and students writing double negatives of this sort are usually quick to correct them once alerted to the problem. But instructors should also be prepared for instances in which a negated auxiliary precedes a negated subject, so that "Couldn't nobody hear" appears for the "Nobody could hear" of edited American English. Such constructions, which appear in Black English vernacular, seem like questions when no question was intended, and you may need to focus on syntax before you can help students eliminate multiple negation from their prose. When students have difficulty overcoming their use of double negatives, you can comfort them with a bit of language history: multiple negatives were acceptable in English for almost a thousand years, becoming nonstandard only in the eighteenth century.

Students might be confused about the comment on page **49** that two negatives can be an acceptable and effective means for expressing a positive. As the example on page **50** suggests, this use of the double negative can help a writer emphasize negation. Although writing instruction usually stresses the importance of being clear and direct, most people also recognize that rhetorical situations occasionally occur in which a deliberate softening of language is judicious. Like the passive voice, the double negative can be of diplomatic use when an unpleasant truth needs to be broken tactfully: "I see nothing in your application that would disqualify you from being selected."

You may want to supplement the discussion of adjectives and adverbs in the Handbook with a class focused on how to use these parts of speech most effectively. Some student writers load their prose with both adjectives and adverbs, convinced that doing so is essential to good writing. Alert your students to constructions like "ran quickly" or "cold snow," in which the adverb or adjective is redundant. Show them also how a well-chosen noun or verb can often eliminate the need for modifying a less specific term (e.g., "pebble" for "small stone" or "stagger" for "walk unsteadily").

ACTIVITIES

1. Ask students to evaluate the following paragraph from "Old Mrs. Harris" by Willa Cather, marking every adjective and adverb. Then ask them what these modifiers have revealed about the character who is being described.

> Mrs. Rosen darted quickly back into the house, lest her neighbour should hail her and stop to talk. She herself was in her kitchen housework dress, a crisp blue chambray which fitted smoothly over her tightly corseted figure, and her lustrous black hair was done in two smooth braids, wound flat at the back of her head, like a braided rug. She did not stop for a hat—her ruddy, salmon-tinted skin had little to fear from the sun. She opened the half-closed oven door and took out a symmetrically plaited coffee-cake, beautifully browned, delicately peppered over with poppy seeds, with sugary margins about the twists. On the kitchen table a tray stood ready with cups and saucers. She wrapped the cake in a napkin, snatched up a little French coffee-pot with a black wooden handle, and ran across the green lawn, through the alley-way and the sandy, unkept yard next door, and entered her neighbour's house by the kitchen.

2. Ask students to evaluate the following paragraph, underlining any adjective or adverb that contributes to meaning and crossing out any that seem superfluous.

> As soon as I make it through the gate, I quickly separate myself from the raucous crowd and immediately head toward the brightly lit midway to find my friends. I am soon assaulted by the true scents of a state fair, the sickeningly sweet smell of cheap cotton candy, and the rich, gamey odor of half-eaten corn dogs overlapping with the slightly rancid smell of stale beer. Realizing that my nearly empty stomach is growling menacingly, I reluctantly buy some french fries. They are reasonably palatable, but the abundance of warm grease quickly soaks the flimsy paper container, and I'm left wiping my greasy palms on my expensive, new jeans.

3. Ask students to determine which sentences contain past participles from which the -d or -ed has been omitted.

   a. He is a prejudice referee.
   b. He tried to prejudice the jury.
   c. New Jersey is one of the few states with legalize gambling.
   d. Will any other states legalize gambling?
   e. The coach always wanted a hand-pick team.
   f. The coach hand-picked the team.
   g. We are only interested in the finish product.
   h. We finished the game.
   i. The driver shouted a clearly pronounce command.
   j. The driver clearly pronounced the name of the street.

4. Have students consult their dictionaries for the comparative and superlative forms, if any, of the following:

Adjectives

articulate	friendly	little
base	frizzy	morose
far	graceful	ready

Adverbs

contritely	loudly	soon
early	often	very
likely	quite	well

Ask students to write sentences for three of the adjectives in comparative form, and for three of the adverbs in comparative or superlative form.

5. Ask students to write sentences using each of the following: *graceful diving, diving gracefully, hurried eating, eating hurriedly, gleeful laughing, laughing gleefully.*

Because the gerund has properties of both verb and noun, students may have some trouble deciding on correct modifiers. The following sentences can serve as illustrations:

She is known for *her rapid answers.* [adjective + adjective + noun]
She is known for *her rapid answering.* [adjective + adjective + gerund]
She is known for *her answering rapidly.* [adjective + gerund + adverb]
She is known for *her answering questions rapidly.* [adjective + gerund + object + adverb]
Answering rapidly, she defended her vote. [participle + adverb]
Answering the questions rapidly, she defended her vote. [participle + object + adverb]

In the adjective + gerund construction, the adjective tells *what* or *which* about the gerund. In the gerund + adverb construction, the adverb answers *how* or *when* about the gerund.

6. Ask students to distinguish between subject and object complements in the following sentences:

a. The traffic committee's recommendation to triple the fee for on-campus parking stickers proved unpopular.
b. You can label his argument illogical only if you can identify the errors in his assumptions.
c. The waves of laughter from the audience made the comedian happy.

d. Jim and Mary always say that their toddler is hyperactive, but the pediatrician always pronounces him healthy and normal.
e. As the warm front moved through the state, the evenings turned balmy.

7. As a class activity, have students identify the adjectives and adverbs in a paragraph from a recent essay. Then have students, working in groups of three or four, revise the paragraph by adding, deleting, or substituting adjectives or adverbs. Ask someone in each group to read the revised paragraph to the class.

ANSWERS TO EXERCISES

■ Exercise 1 (pp. 43–44) Converting adjectives into adverbs

1. behaved calmly OR calmly behaved
2. rewarded promptly OR promptly rewarded
3. remarked carelessly OR carelessly remarked
4. believed sincerely OR sincerely believed
5. visited regularly OR regularly visited
6. appealed specially OR specially appealed
7. nearly possible
8. totally incompatible
9. formerly prosperous
10. recently ill

■ Exercise 2 (p. 44)   Converting modifiers into adverbs

1. seriously
2. ✓
3. nationally
4. easily
5. regularly
6. suddenly
7. rapidly
8. exceptionally
9. ✓
10. gracefully

■ Exercise 3 (p. 45)   Using complements

Answers will vary.

■ Exercise 4 (p. 45)   Using modifiers

Answers will vary.

■ Exercise 5 (p. 48)   Finding comparatives and superlatives

1. quicker, quickest
2. more quickly, most quickly
3. thirstier, thirstiest

4. hollower, hollowest
5. more modest, most modest
6. worse, worst
7. more realistically, most realistically
8. more frightened, most frightened
9. more scared, most scared
10. more inactive, most inactive

■ Exercise 6 (p. 48)   Using appropriate modifiers

1. worst
2. most useful
3. livelier OR more lively
4. more mellow OR mellower
5. less
6. strongest
7. tiniest
8. thinner
9. better
10. more mature

■ Exercise 7 (p. 50)   Eliminating double negatives

1. They don't have any home. OR They have no home.
2. I could hardly hear OR I couldn't hear
3. We never do anything OR we do nothing
4. couldn't buy any OR could buy none
5. club didn't have any OR club scarcely had any

■ Exercise 8 (p. 50)   Correcting adjectives and adverbs

1. sells well.
2. really good.
3. our wettest month . . . have barely received
4. ✓
5. unbiased, . . . was duller than usual.
6. mechanic who estimates repairs was . . .
7. mayoral
8. Karl is much more content . . .
9. ✓
10. device of authors who write detective novels . . . seemingly innocent

5

CASE

For some students, determining the case of a noun or pronoun must be like aiming at an invisible target: what they don't see they can't hit. After all, *cat* is *cat* whether it's subject of the verb, object of the preposition, or subject of the infinitive. Indeed, students rarely have difficulty with case unless they are using a pronoun.

Throughout the history of English, pronouns have changed less than any other part of speech and thus retain their case forms more distinctively than nouns do. The case forms of pronouns, then, deserve study because they carry information about the way words function in a sentence, and that information helps to convey meaning.

Today, readers of English depend on word order and a few inflections to tell them about the relationships between words in a sentence. Writers also use the same order and inflections to convey information. Thus, any error in order (such as a misplaced modifier) or in inflection (case, number) can confuse the meaning being signaled.

Instructors should recognize that emphasis upon such points as *who* versus *whom* (**5b[1]**, **5b[2]**, and **5c**) encourages a popular stereotype of English teachers and leads otherwise articulate people at gatherings to become tongue-tied when they learn that they have been speaking to one without realizing it. ("That was my worst subject," they'll declare at parties, and then promptly discover the need to refill their plate.) Consider H.L. Mencken's comment on this issue in *The American Language*. The schoolteacher, he says,

> continues the heroic task of trying to make her young charges grasp the difference between *who* and *whom*. Here, alas, the speechways of the American people seem to be again against her. . . . [I]n ordinary discourse the great majority of Americans avoid *whom* diligently, as a word full of snares. When they employ it, it is often incorrectly, as in "Whom is your father?" and "Whom spoke to me?" Noah Webster, always the pragmatic reformer, denounced it as usually useless so long ago as 1783. Common sense, he argued, was on the side of "*Who* did he marry?" Today such a form as '*Whom* are you talking to?' would seem very affected to most Americans; they might write it, but they would never speak it.

Usage that seemed affected in 1919 may well seem even more off-putting today. Explain the distinction between *who* and *whom* to your students, but focus on more substantial issues before penalizing a writer for making the wrong choice.

ACTIVITIES

1. Ask students to write a paragraph narrating a recent event in their family or among their friends. The paragraph should include references to at least five people, all of whom are identified by name and none of whom are referred to by a pronoun. Then ask them to rewrite the paragraph using each name only once, and using a pronoun at least once for each person mentioned without making any unclear references.

2. Illustrate pronoun case by writing the following sentence on the board:

   After he finished his biology homework, Bruce wondered if anyone would like to go out for a pizza with him.

   Now substitute a proper noun:

   After Bruce finished Bruce's biology homework, Bruce wondered if anyone would like to go out for a pizza with Bruce.

   Note how pronouns are inflected, and ask students what writing would be like without pronouns.

3. Have students write a paragraph or bring to class a copy of an edited paragraph from a recent essay. The paragraph should include ten pronouns, five of which are personal pronouns; the copy should be neatly handwritten or typed. Ask them to exchange papers; then have them underline and number all pronouns in the paragraph and, on a separate sheet of paper, list in columns the pronouns, the case of each, and the reason for each case. For example,

Pronoun	Case	Reason
a. us	objective	object of preposition
b. she	subjective	subject complement

   Students could do this activity in small groups, but guard against groups in which one student who is sure of the answers completes the exercise while everyone else looks on.

4. Ask students to collect from newspapers—campus newspapers are a readily available source—three examples of pronouns correctly used and three incorrectly used. You may wish to narrow the selection to instances of a single pronoun, a single case, or a single function.

5. Distribute copies of the campus newspaper and discuss pronouns used in that issue. If there are errors in usage, ask students to correct them, giving the appropriate rule.

6. Ask students to select the one sentence from each pair that is appropriate in formal English.

a. It was I barbecuing chicken at midnight. ✓
Kim refusing to sing at the wedding rehearsal upset David and Beth.
b. Let's you and me fly to Dallas for the weekend. ✓
Could it have been them, Scott and Mike, who designed the concrete canoe?
c. Give the message to whomever answers the telephone.
Jerry wanted Elizabeth and me to weed the garden every day. ✓
d. Professor Still is a dynamic teacher which I admire.
The question has become who should be nominated to fill the vacancy.✓
e. No one could be happier than her now that the Cubs have won three games.
That cashier is the one whom she thinks the customers voted most helpful. ✓

7. Have students write sentences to illustrate the following:

a. *we* as subject complement
b. *whoever* as subject of a clause
c. *theirs* as direct object
d. *us* as object of an infinitive
e. *her* as part of a compound appositive

8. Ask students to convert possessive nouns to possessive pronouns and possessive pronouns to possessive nouns.

a. Mark's   d. the Department of labor's
b. theirs   e. ours
c. women's

ANSWERS TO EXERCISES

■ **Exercise 1** (pp. 54–55)   **Choosing correct pronouns**

1. me
2. She, I
3. she
4. they
5. her
6. him
7. him, her
8. I, her
9. he
10. him

■ **Exercise 2** (p. 56) **Combining sentences with *who* or *whom***

1. Hercule Poirot is a famous detective whom Agatha Christie finally kills off in *Curtain*.
2. We heard terrifying stories of terrorist activity from my brother who had just returned from two years active duty in the Middle East.
3. After the home run, hundreds of fans who had been halfheartedly watching a routine game were smiling and slapping each other on the back.
4. The defense attorney had shouted earlier at the district attorney, who called for the maximum sentence.

■ **Exercise 3** (pp. 56–57) **Inserting and completing**

Oral practice.

■ **Exercise 4** (p. 58) **Changing *who* to *whom***

1. Whom
2. ✓
3. whom
4. ✓
5. whom
6. whom
7. ✓
8. whom
9. [deceived] whom
10. ✓

■ **Exercise 5** (pp. 59–60) **Revising case forms**

1. As for my wife and me,
2. ✓
3. whom, my
4. John's
5. we; they
6. ✓
7. whom
8. ✓
9. ✓
10. me

6

AGREEMENT

The study of agreement might begin with a discussion of number and of the formation of plurals (section **18**). The quickest way to show students the forms of the verb is to refer to **conjugation** (pages **74–76, 556**). Although dictionaries, grammarians, and teachers refer to "plural verbs" for the sake of convenience, strictly speaking, verbs are not *plural* in the same way that nouns or pronouns are. For example, *two books* indicates two items, whereas *they swim* refers to the number of people doing the swimming rather than to two separate acts of swimming. In other words, the actual concept of plural rests in the subject in such a sentence. To convey the idea of plural action, English uses adverbs (I swam again and again), a prefix (*redo, re*think), or repetition (I swam and swam). Similarly, because the verb in English retains few inflections—notably the one that indicates a third-person singular subject—agreement poses problems chiefly in the present tense when a third-person singular subject is indicated. The declension in section **5** can be helpful in familiarizing students with the meaning of *person*.

When a sentence begins with the expletive *there*, students sometimes have difficulty determining the subject. Although *there* may, on rare occasions, serve as the subject of a clause or a sentence (as it does in the subordinate clause of this sentence and in such sentences as "There is where I live"), students are almost always safe to exclude it from consideration.

When the subject and verb are separated by an intervening element (usually a clause or prepositional phrase), students frequently identify the noun closest to the verb as the subject and make the verb singular or plural to agree with that noun: *One of the watches were broken.* OR *George is the only one of those waiters who keep the water glasses full.* Students who make this kind of error may have (1) mistakenly applied the rule that in a sentence with a compound subject the verb agrees with the closer one, (2) forgotten the subject by the time they write the verb, or (3) simply not correctly identified the subject. The first problem can be handled easily by clarifying the use of the whichever-is-closer rule. The other problems can often be resolved by having students identify and eliminate prepositional phrases as they proofread for subject-verb agreement.

Students may resist using indefinite pronouns in their writing for a number of reasons. Those who associate the use of certain pronouns with very formal writing (*few were turned away; each married a childhood sweetheart; either is acceptable*) may avoid using them by finding an alternate construction (*not very many fans, the graduates, both of the menus*) or may use them only as modifiers (*few fans, each graduate, either menu*). Second, students are often unsure about which pronouns are regularly singular and what rules govern compound subjects. Finally, students may not know how to resolve the conflict

67

between the injunction to make pronoun and antecedent agree and the increasing avoidance of the generic *he, his,* or *him* as sexist. The language of many people continues to exclude the female half of the population, however, so students should be encouraged to avoid usages that are inherently sexist. (See activities 2 and 3.) For additional information about nonsexist language see *Guidelines for Nonsexist Use of Language in NCTE Publications* (1985) and *Language, Gender, and Professional Writing: Theoretical Approaches and Guidelines for Nonsexist Usage* by Francine W. Frank and Paula A. Treichler (New York: MLA, 1989).

ACTIVITIES

1. Ask students the following riddle, which enjoyed wide currency in the 1970s but which the current generation of students has seldom heard:

   A man and his young son are in a car accident. The father is killed, and the son is rushed to a hospital where the surgeon on duty looks at him and exclaims, "That's my son!" What is the relationship between the surgeon and the injured boy?

2. Ask students to suggest nonsexist alternatives for each of the following: salesman, caveman, mailman, fireman, stewardess, and the common man.

3. Ask students to eliminate sexist language by substituting the plural for the singular in each of the following examples:

   a. Give every politician a chance to prove his honesty.
   b. A good secretary earns her pay through hard work.
   c. A college student needs to be able to write well before he/she graduates.
   d. A nurse should treat her patients as individuals.
   e. We should require every candidate for the job to submit a copy of his or her résumé.

4. Ask students to identify the function of *there* in each of the following sentences as adverb (A) or expletive (E) and to revise expletive-*there* sentences by making singular subjects plural, plural subjects singular, and changing the verb accordingly.

   a. Near the fence there are five violets and twenty-four dandelions growing. [E]
   b. Hang the picture there to cover the smudge. [A]
   c. There stand Jennifer and Linda.[A]
   d. There happens to be a perfectly logical explanation for this chaos. [E]
   e. There seems to have been a mistake; I ordered iced tea, not ice cream. [E]

5. Ask students to make a list of collective nouns that describe groups of people and use some of those nouns in sentences. Explain that once the

number is established, students should use that number consistently in the composition. Have them consult a dictionary to check current usage.

6. Have students write a paragraph comparing or contrasting two relatives, two siblings, or two friends. The paragraph should include the following elements:

   a. one expression beginning with *not to mention* or *together with*
   b. compound singular subjects both of which are preceded by *every* or *each* and joined by *and*
   c. one sentence containing expletive *there*
   d. *one* used as subject
   e. two antecedents joined by *nor*

   The elements need not follow this order, but each should be labeled appropriately.

7. Ask students to explain how context has determined the verb form in each of these sentences:

   a. All was forgiven when he replaced the broken window.
   b. Three of my neighbors jog daily, and all take different routes.
   c. Most were mailed out before the printing error was discovered.
   d. The argument is illogical, but none question its emotional appeal.
   e. None of the ice cream has melted.
   f. No apology was offered, and none was necessary.
   g. Half want to schedule the exam for next Tuesday.
   h. Do you think half is too few?
   i. Do any of the guides answer questions during the tour?
   j. Any who are enterprising will succeed.

8. Ask students to select the correct verb form and to explain their choice.

   a. Almost everybody I know (believes, believe) that football is the national sport.
   b. Marty is the only one of them who (is, are) enough of a fan to know that the national sport is really baseball.
   c. He is one of the many college professors who truly (enjoys, enjoy) the game.
   d. In the summer you can be sure that either Marty or one of his colleagues (attend, attends) every home game.
   e. Sitting on the desk in Marty's office (is, are) an autographed baseball as well as an ashtray and an dictionary.

ANSWERS TO EXERCISES

■ **Exercise 1** (p. 67)   **Reading aloud**

Oral practice.

■ **Exercise 2** (p. 67) **Choosing correct verb forms**

1. thinks
2. vary
3. was
4. provide
5. knows
6. come
7. was
8. is
9. store, jeopardize
10. is

■ **Exercise 3** (p. 70) **Choosing correct pronoun or verb forms**

1. have, their
2. needs, she
3. they
4. was; it OR were; they
5. controls, it, itself OR control, they, themselves

■ **Exercise 4** (p. 70) **Making language inclusive**

1. Doctors who treat their own children show poor judgment.
2. The nurse looks efficient in a starched, white uniform.
3. Every lawyer should be sure to tell the receptionist which parking piace to use.
4. The child's teacher gave the report to the social worker who put it on the desk so that it would be ready when the psychiatrist testified.
5. The police officer asked the woman who was robbed if the robber had pocketed her money.

■ **Exercise 5** (p. 71) **Securing agreement**

1. These computers do . . . from . . . them
2. a frustrated student . . . was . . . his or her (OR his/her OR the)
3. casserole or vegetables are ruined . . . "These ovens read
4. the words that come out of one's mouth are . . . the words that one intends . . . the words that one really thinks.
5. One of my instructors . . . was
6. kinds of labels are
7. are the mirrors . . . a person doesn't
8. people have . . . they actually look, not how they want
9. are other thoughts
10. does one ever see oneself (OR himself OR himself or herself; SOMETIMES themselves) as one (OR he OR he or she; SOMETIMES they) really is (SOMETIMES are) [See **21c**. Students may legitimately find the repetition of *one* wordy. They should also see from this exercise how awkward some of the solutions to the problem can become.]

7

VERB FORMS

Understanding the system of English verbs requires students to grasp an extensive network of relationships of tense to time, not only on a single verb but also in sequences of verbs. Some students may think that there are more verb forms than they will ever need to use and thus feel reluctant to master the differences among them. You can often motivate such students by emphasizing the function of tense, demonstrating how tense enables writers to be precise and reminding them that precision is one of the characteristics of good writing. You should recognize, however, that tense does not always establish actual time. The present tense, for example, can indicate action in the past or future as well as the present:

Sarah jogs for an hour every afternoon. [a habitual action implying past, present, and future]

Madrid is the capital of Spain. [a fact in the past, present, and future]

Paul is going to Daytona Beach during spring break. [an intended future action].

This might also be a good time to introduce students to the historical present, which is useful in writing about literature: "When Macbeth hesitates, his wife rebukes him. Lady Macbeth is one of the most memorable of all of Shakespeare's women, and many actresses dream of playing this role."

Teaching students to use the active voice may involve undoing lessons they have already learned. Some students habitually use the passive because they have been taught to avoid the first person or because they are anxious to avoid pronouns that reveal gender. Emphasize that the active voice is preferable because it is simpler and clearer. Use such examples as "A meeting has been called," or "A motion has been made" to reveal how the passive is favored in bureaucratic language, noting that these statements do not reveal who called the meeting or made the motion. Once students see how the passive enables writers or speakers to avoid assigning responsibility for action, ask them to imagine the following situation: "You have borrowed your brother's new car, skidded on an icy road, and smashed into a tree. You are not injured, but the car is ruined. When your brother asks what happened to the car, you reply, 'Your car was smashed.'" Then ask what would happen next.

Recognizing that the passive can be useful in some cases, do not insist that it be avoided at all cost. In addition to the exception noted in **29d** (pages **295–96**), the passive is unavoidable when the subject responsible for an action is unknown (for example: "She was murdered shortly after midnight").

The discussion of voice leads to the distinction between transitive (from the Latin *transitus* meaning "passing over" or "crossing") and intransitive (or

71

"not passing over") verbs, since only transitive verbs can be passive. Point out that many verbs can be either transitive or intransitive, depending upon context (for example: "She eats all day long" [intransitive, since the day is not being eaten] or "She eats chocolate." [transitive, since the chocolate is the direct object of the eating]). Once you have done so, you can reassure students by telling them that they do not need to memorize lists of transitive and intransitive verbs. What matters is the function of verbs as they appear in sentences. You might point out that just as we ride a transit system to reach a specific destination, we use transitive verbs to reach a direct object before the action conveyed by the verb can be completed (for example: "Bill raised" is not meaningful until we learn what Bill raised).

Although most students already know when to use the indicative and imperative moods (even if they cannot define what these terms mean), the subjunctive mood may be puzzling to them. Accordingly, you may wish to reserve class time for reviewing the discussion of this mood in the Handbook. One way to help students grasp the meaning of mood is to show that indicative implies certainty, imperative implies necessity, and the subjunctive implies uncertainty.

ACTIVITIES

1. Ask students to eliminate any errors in verb usage from the following paragraph:

> When I was seventeen, I meet Tommy. He my first real boyfriend. I already go out with other guys since I am fifteen, but none of them seem understand me. Within a few days, we talk about things I never talk about with anyone else before. He is captain of the football team, and I felt proud when we were seen together by kids from school. When we break up, I cried for a week, and did not want go back to school. That seem like a long time ago now.

2. Ask students to write a narrative paragraph about an event that happened in the past, using examples of both the past perfect (which shows an action that was completed before another action took place) and the past progressive (which shows a continuing action in the past).

3. Have students write one or two narrative paragraphs (nine or ten sentences) in which they do not use any form of *be* or *have*, avoiding these forms even as auxiliaries. This exercise will reveal several important points to students. First, they will become aware of how frequently they use a form of *be* (and perhaps will begin to use more varied language—see also **29d**); second, they will discover how difficult it is to establish proper tense sequences without these forms; finally, they will become much more aware of the function of tense in the language and of relationships among tenses.

4. Ask students to be prepared to discuss in class any problems that may arise when they try to convert all present tense verbs in an essay they have written to present progressive and all past tense verbs to past perfect.

5. Ask students to write a brief paragraph using *lie/lay* and *sit/set* correctly. Copies of the following paragraph might be distributed as a warm-up exercise and as a model for students to follow.

> Several things that belong upstairs were (lie/lay) on the counter. I suppose that Sarah had (sit/set) them there so that she could put them away later. I didn't do anything about them, however; I just let them (sit/set) there until she came back. I did think to ask her why she had (lie/lay) the candlestick over on its side, but decided to wait until we were (sit/set) in the other room. We (sit/set) there often in the afternoon, partly because the western exposure allows us to watch the sun (sit/set) and partly because there is a comfortable couch either of us can use if one of us wants to (lie/lay) down to rest for a while. We can even cover up with the afghan that (lie/lay) on the couch if we want to.

6. Ask students to complete these two sentences with the proper verb forms:

   a. Phil (*past tense*) the porcelain vase, but if Carolyn has (*past participle*) one, too, she won't admit it. [*bring, choose, draw, lose, steal, take*]
   b. They have (*past participle*) sweet corn. [*buy, can, eat, freeze, grow, raise*]

7. Ask students to review the difference between direct objects and subject complements. Then have students apply the following set of questions to the fifteen sentences below to determine whether a verb is transitive/intransitive, active/passive, linking/complete.

   a. Is the verb transitive or intransitive?
   b. If the verb is transitive, what is the direct object?
   c. If the verb is transitive, does the subject perform the action of the verb?
   d. If the verb is intransitive, is there a complement?
   e. If there is a complement, what kind is it?

   The order of these questions is designed to show that the first task—even if the ultimate one is to discover whether the verb is active or passive—is to decide whether the verb is transitive or intransitive since the answer *transitive* leads to questions *b* and *c* while the answer *intransitive* leads to questions *d* and *e*. Thus, the choices are limited so that an answer such as *transitive complete* is impossible.

   The following diagram clarifies the hierarchy of choices for students who insist on asking whether the verb is active or passive before they know whether it is transitive:

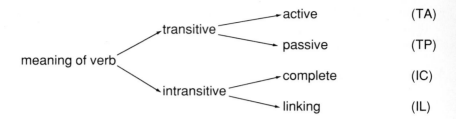

1. More hot sauce should be added to those tacos. [TP]
2. How could I have anticipated Ralph's sentence about the dead jackalope? [TA]
3. The class had been dull until yesterday. [IL]
4. I began to suspect a sense of humor upon hearing Brad identify *sea-nymph* as an exclamation. [TA]
5. Mike's days of being an outcast will cease with the end of the semester. [IC]
6. Camille went to the mountains to be alone. [IC]
7. Watching from my bedroom window, I saw her climb the tree to rescue the kitten. [TA]
8. This horse hasn't been ridden for two weeks. [TP]
9. Crystal bought a geode to add to her mineral collection. [TA]
10. Nick and Seth were applauded for their original lyrics. [TP]
11. After the moderator's long introduction, Joan began her speech on the virtues of brevity. [TA]
12. The chili con carne smelled delicious, but it was too spicy for me. [IL, IL]
13. She leaned wearily against her shopping cart. [IC]
14. Laughing uproariously at the misprint, they continued through the story. [IC]
15. Has the bill from the dentist been paid yet? [TP]

8. Some instructors may wish to give additional time to the concept of *voice*. If so, begin with a discussion of the features of a sentence containing a passive-voice verb:

   a. a verb consisting of a form of *be* and the past participle of the main verb (*were written, have been mailed*)
   b. a subject which would be the object of an active-voice verb (*The newspaper was torn. Someone tore the newspaper.*)
   c. a prepositional phrase beginning with *by* and having as its object the person or thing performing the action of the verb (This prepositional phrase is sometimes optional.)

   Then write the following sentences on the board and ask students to identify the features of the passive found in each.

a. Our meeting was canceled by the police.
b. Our meeting has been canceled by the police.
c. Our meeting was canceled.
d. Our meeting has been canceled.

When working through this activity, instructors may want to point out the five main uses of a passive-voice verb:

(1) when the subject which would be used with an active-voice verb (what Jesperson calls "the active subject") is unknown or difficult to state,
(2) when the active subject is clear from the context,
(3) when tact dictates that the active subject not be directly stated,
(4) when the passive subject is more important than the active subject, and
(5) when the passive construction aids in combining one sentence with another.

▲ **Note**: A sentence containing an indirect object as well as a direct object can also be made passive.

The judge awarded us custody.
We were awarded custody by the judge.
Custody was awarded us by the judge.

From students' compositions, select ten passive-voice sentences for a handout or transparency. Ask students to rewrite them, using the active voice.

ANSWERS TO EXERCISES

■ **Exercise 1** (pp. **80–81**)   **Using verb forms in a pattern**

1. Yes, he gave it away.
2. You have already run a mile.
3. Yes, the man drowned.
4. They have already begun that.
5. Yes, the wind blew.
6. She has already chosen it.
7. Yes, it really happened.
8. The river has already risen.
9. Yes, you did that.
10. They have already stolen it.
11. Yes, you spun your wheels.
12. They have already frozen it.
13. Yes, he clung to that belief.
14. They have already gone to the police.
15. Yes, she knew them.
16. The fire alarm has already rung.

17. Yes, the sack burst.
18. He has already eaten it.
19. Yes, you grew these.
20. Bert has already spoken out.

■ **Exercise 2** (pp. 81–82)   **Substituting correct forms of *sit* and *lie***

1. My neighbor's baby never wants to lie down. My neighbor's baby never wants to sit down.
2. Elizabeth's cat sat under the house during the storm. Elizabeth's cat lay under the house during the storm.
3. Melody sat in that position for half an hour. Melody lay in that position for half an hour.
4. Caleb often sits in the car. Caleb often lies in the car.
5. Have they lain there all along? Have they sat there all along?

■ **Exercise 3** (p. 82)   **Choosing correct verb forms**

1. laid
2. sit
3. lie (down)
4. sitting
5. setting

■ **Exercise 4 (p. 84)**   **Meanings of tense forms**

Oral exercise. Answers will vary.

■ **Exercise 5** (p. 85)   **Choosing correct verb forms**

1. ended
2. was passed
3. to move
4. to go
5. Having finished
6. Having bought
7. adjourned
8. to register
9. to meet
10. has been

■ **Exercise 6** (pp. 87–88)   **Using the subjunctive**

Oral exercise. Answers will vary.

■ **Exercise 7** (p. 88)   **Composing sentences**

Answers will vary.

■ **Exercise 8** (p. 89)　　**Correcting verb errors**

1. ✓
2. went to build
3. ✓
4. to move, obtained
5. had gone (or "companies went"), to suppose
6. ✓
7. were being hauled
8. had foreseen, to stop
9. delete "would" (". . . task and perhaps defeat")
10. ✓
11. was waiting
12. ✓

8

MANUSCRIPT FORM

Section **8** offers some general guidelines on matters of paging and format. At the beginning of almost any writing course, someone is likely to ask, "Do our papers have to be typed?" You will need to establish your own guidelines, since **8a** covers handwritten papers, as well as those that are typewritten or word-processed. Another common question is, "Do we have to have a title?" Once again, you will need to clarify what you expect. But making your expectations clear on these points should take only a minute or two, and then you can refer students to the Handbook for additional information. Given the challenge of helping students to become better writers, you may not see any reason to waste class time talking about the size of margins or whether or not to use a paperclip.

When teaching section **8**, note that **8e** addresses the importance of revision. Both professional writers and experts in composition agree that revision is essential to good writing, and you should plan to reserve class time for helping students understand what revision means and why it is important. Many students assume that revision means simply going over a first draft and making a few small changes, often in spelling or punctuation. You need to emphasize that revision is a type of writing that is part of the writing process; it means adding new material, cutting material that doesn't work, revising sentence structure, and rearranging paragraphs both to clarify and develop ideas as well as to express them more eloquently. Laboring under the unhappy belief that successful writers write effortlessly (because they know what they are doing), students are often surprised to see how experienced writers subject their work to extensive revision and are astonished to discover that the final draft of a work may have little in common with earlier drafts. Class time devoted to studying multiple drafts of an essay will almost always be time well spent. If students get discouraged by the realization that writing involves more time and work than they had anticipated, you can reassure them by pointing out that doing anything well takes time and practice, that writing would be terrifying if writers could never make changes, and that—as Donald Murray has shown in "The Maker's Eye: Revising Your Own Manuscripts"—revision can be fun:

> Making something right is immensely satisfying, for writers begin to learn what they are writing about by writing. Language leads them to meaning, and there is the joy of discovery, of understanding, of making meaning clear as the writer employs the technical skills of language.

When teaching revision, you should recognize that different writers revise in different ways. Some writers like to compose their first drafts quickly and then revise these drafts as a separate stage in the writing process. Others work best if they revise as they compose. Although writing teachers should insist upon the importance of revision, they should not insist upon any one method of revision. Instructors frequently advise students to put their writing aside for a few hours (or days if possible) and then reread it critically. This is excellent advice, for the passing of time can often help writers see a problem that had previously gone undetected or a solution to a problem that had previously seemed impossible to resolve. But students who are taught that this is the only way to revise may lose the benefit of valuable ideas that occur to them while they are still drafting or within minutes of having completed a first draft.

Because students often confuse revision with proofreading (or checking spelling, punctuation, and mechanics), it may be tempting to discount the importance of proofreading when emphasizing the importance of revision. But you should remind your students that careless errors can distract a reader's attention and undermine his or her confidence in the writer. Pointing out that books often include typographical errors despite professional proofreading, you should help students realize that a writer's eye has a tendency to see what it wants to see. Because errors are easily missed, students would be well advised to proofread their work several times, doing so aloud at least once. Reading a work aloud will not only oblige most readers to read more slowly but also serves as a safeguard against the inadvertent omission of a necessary word—or such word-processing errors as the retention of a word or phrase that should have been deleted.

ACTIVITIES

1. Show students examples of early drafts of your own that include extensive changes—the more that has been crossed out or penciled in the better. Doing so will both demonstrate what revision means and show your students that you understand the problems they may encounter when trying to say what they mean.

2. Distribute copies of different drafts of a student essay written during a previous semester. Show how the essay improved from one draft to the next and how, at some point, the author profited from receiving comments. Doing so should help students see that criticism can be productive and that it shouldn't be perceived as a personal attack.

3. Have students work in groups of three to evaluate drafts of their peers. Provide students with specific guidelines for doing so, such as the Reviser's Checklist on pages **390–92** of the Handbook or the student-generated questions on pages 34–35 of this manual. Ask them to suggest corrections or revisions, but caution them against using their time simply to look for spelling errors. Make sure to allow time for evaluators to

discuss their written comments and for the author to respond. Briefly join any group that seems paralyzed, and raise questions that can help start discussion.

4. Bring to class examples of two final drafts submitted for a grade in an earlier course, deleting the names of the authors. The two examples should offer a clear contrast between a paper that inspires confidence by a professional-looking format and another that undermines confidence by looking sloppy. Although you should emphasize that substance matters more than appearance, you can also help students to see that writers can profit from making a good impression visually but get off to a weak start by looking as if they themselves don't care about their work.

5. As an alternative to the record sheet illustrated in **8f**, ask your students to keep a journal in which they record any difficulties they encounter when writing their papers, ideas that occur for future papers, and responses to comments that you have made about their work.

ANSWERS TO EXERCISE

■ **Exercise 1** (p. 97)   **Dividing words**

Words that should not be divided:

4. NATO	8. against	14. C.P.A	17. matches
5. gripped	13. recline	16. WFAA-FM	20. patron

Words that may be divided, with hyphens marking appropriate divisions:

1. cross-ref•er•ence	7. guess-ing	12. e•ven-tu•al
2. e•co-nom•ic	9. pres-ent	15. mag•i-cal
3. fif-teenth	10. pre-sent	18. dis-solve
6. grip-ping	11. sea-coast	19. cob-webs

9

CAPITALS

Certain conventions vary from language to language, country to country: German, for example, capitalizes all nouns and words used as nouns; English capitalizes only proper nouns. Students generally overuse capital letters because they don't know the conventions. Occasionally, however, students will feel a need to give special prominence to a word, particularly if they are trying to emphasize its importance: "*Elected to Phi Beta Kappa in his junior year, Russ is a true Student.*" Although capital letters do call attention to the words they head, they tend to distract the reader and so should not be used for emphasis: "*Elected to Phi Beta Kappa in his junior year, Russ is the quintessential student.*"

In addition to cautioning students not to overcapitalize, you may want to supplement the Handbook's discussion of capitalization on two points. Advise students to add course titles to the examples of proper names in **9a**: "Political Science 101," but not "a course in Political Science"—noting such exceptions as an English or a French course because of the rule in **9a(3)**. (An example of a course title within the Handbook can be found in **9f**.) And you can clarify the note in **9c** concerning hyphenated compounds in titles by supplying examples of hyphenated compounds in which the second element is *not* a proper adjective or of equal importance with the first element (e.g., Medium-sized, not Medium-Sized) or when both elements constitute a single word (e.g., B-flat Major).

Students might also be confused about how to handle simplified secondary references to proper names that they realize should be capitalized when written in full. To clarify this point, you can provide the following example:

> The University of Michigan is expecting to make a major change in its administration this year. A spokesperson for the university refused to comment until after next week's meeting by the Board of Regents. The board last met only three days ago, and two meetings within the same month are unusual.

This example can then be supplemented by activity 2.

▲ **Note**: *The Chicago Manual of Style*, 13th ed. (Chicago: U of Chicago P, 1982), includes a detailed discussion of capitalization.

ACTIVITIES

1. Ask students to revise the capitalization in the following paragraph (adapted from "New York" by Gay Talese):

> New York is a City in which large, cliff-dwelling Hawks cling to skyscrapers and occasionally zoom to snatch a pigeon over central park, or wall street, or

81

the hudson river. Bird Watchers have seen these peregrine falcons circling lazily over the city. They have seen them perched atop the tallest buildings, even around Times square. About twelve of these hawks patrol the City, sometimes with a wingspan of thirty-five inches. They have buzzed women on the roof of the St. Regis hotel, have attacked repairmen on smokestacks, and, in august 1947, two hawks jumped women residents in the recreation yard of the Home of the New York guild for the jewish Blind.

2. Ask students to revise the capitalization in the following paragraph:

The National Football League is confronting another major drug scandal. Commissioner Pete Rozelle has promised a prompt and thorough investigation into allegations that the League has ignored repeated warnings concerning drug use among players. Reached in his New York office, the Commissioner would make no further comment at this time. The NFL confronted a similar problem two years ago, but people quickly forgot about it.

3. Ask students to supply the principles of capitalization that govern the following:

a. Jell-O; whipped cream
b. Roman Catholic church; catholic tastes
c. the Great Plains; eastern South Dakota
d. Biology 100; sophomores and juniors
e. Levis; jeans
f. Lake Mead; the Allegheny and Monongahela rivers
g. Senator Nancy Kassebaum; George Bush, president of the United States
h. Dead Sea Scrolls; worship service
i. Korean War; the infantry
j. Canis Major; aurora borealis

4. Give students a list of titles (uncapitalized) from a set of recent essays and ask them to follow **9c** as they provide proper capitalization.

5. Ask students to write down the titles of three books and three articles they have read recently (works not related to academic requirements), and three books they would like to read as soon as they have time.

6. Bring a telephone directory to class to illustrate conventions regarding names in the yellow pages.

ANSWERS TO EXERCISES

■ **Exercise 1** (p. 110) **Using words correctly**

Answers will vary.

■ **Exercise 2** (pp. **110–11**)   **Supplying capitals**

1. I; Christmas; I; Spanish; I
2. We; West; Pike's Peak, Colorado; Rocky Mountains; Glacier National Park; Mojave Desert; Mount Baker; Washington; Puget Sound
3. God's; Bible; We; Democrats; Senator Attebury
4. Robert Sherrill's; *The Saturday Night Special [and] Other Guns [with] Which Americans Won [the] West, Protected Bootleg Franchises, Slew Wildlife, Robbed Countless Banks, Shot Husbands Purposely [and by] Mistake, [and] Killed Presidents—Together [with the] Debate [over] Continuing Same*

10

ITALICS

Students who rely on italics to emphasize special meaning have yet to learn that an effective sentence emphasizes certain ideas by its diction and word arrangement and that every part contributes to both meaning and arrangement or structure. Just as the architect selects the type of exterior finish appropriate to the style of the house, so the students must choose elements of mechanics and punctuation appropriate to the meaning and the arrangement of the words.

If, however, you suggest that students try ways other than italics to emphasize ideas but do not specify those ways, students usually opt for quotation marks or (infrequently) capitalization. As a rule, these choices are equally ineffective because the problem lies with the choice of words, not with the choice of marks for emphasis (see also **16d**). Instead, students should work to master substitution (for single words) and arrangement (for relative importance of ideas). Thus, the sentence *His laugh was funny* might become *His laugh was a burst of throaty gasps* OR *With a burst of throaty gasps he laughed.*

The use of italics to identify a word used as a word sometimes confuses students because they tend to see words as individual items listed in dictionaries or vocabulary exercises or as units in a sentence; they can therefore have difficulty imagining a sentence in which a word is used as such. Examples using proper names clarify the rule: *Katherine* and *Catharine are variations of Catherine* (compare with: *Catherine addressed the envelope).* A useful rule of thumb is that if a word can be preceded by *the word*, it should be italicized (*The word philology means "love of words"; the discipline of philology is the study of language development*).

ACTIVITIES

1. Ask students to revise the following sentences, substituting more emphatic words for those that have been italicized in an attempt to give them emphasis:

   a. The wind is blowing *so hard.* [fiercely]
   b. After an avalanche buried the pass, the climbers were trapped and did not know what to *do.* [trapped and desperate]
   c. I need to see you *now.* [immediately, urgently]
   d. Smoking is *not allowed.* [forbidden]
   e. Mary Lou is one of the *nicest* people in town. [friendliest, most generous]

2. Use the following excerpt from a letter by Queen Victoria to demonstrate how excessive underlining weakens prose. She is describing a visit from Nicholas I, Czar of Russia. Note that none of Victoria's italics help us to see what the Czar actually looked like:

> A great event and a great compliment *his* visit certainly is, and the people *here* are extremely flattered by it. He is certainly a *very striking* man; still very handsome. His profile is *beautiful,* and his manners *most* dignified and graceful; extremely civil—quite alarmingly so, as he is so full of attentions and *politeness.* But the expression of the *eyes* is *formidable,* and unlike anything I ever saw before.

3. To help illustrate that different titles receive different treatment, with some set in italics and others set off by quotation marks, ask students to list the titles of their favorites: three books, three magazines, three films, three television programs, three songs. Ask students to list the titles of two textbooks they are using in other courses and the titles of two chapters from each; the titles of two journals in their major field (such as *English Journal*) and the titles of two articles from recent issues of each. Ask them to list the title of the last play or film they attended on campus and the title they would give their autobiography.

4. Have students identify which item in each of the pairs is correct:

a. *All My Children* ✓   "Consumer Reports"
b. *Chicago Tribune* ✓   Oh, Susanna
c. *U.S.S. Jackson*   Hamlet ✓
d. the *Bible*   "The Lottery" ✓
e. *Gone With the Wind* ✓   "Ghostbusters"

ANSWERS TO EXERCISE

■ **Exercise 1** (pp. 115–16)   **Underlining words that should be italicized**

1. *Newsweek*
2. *New York Times; Andria Doria*
3. *d; t; partner; pretty*
4. *Madama Butterfly; bravo* [The word is familiar enough in English not to be italicized; however, it may be italicized here because those who shouted it are, presumably, primarily Italian.]
5. *The Last Supper*
6. *Casablanca*
7. *60 Minutes*
8. *Roget's Thesaurus of Words and Phrases*
9. *The Fellowship of the Ring*
10. *NotaBene*

11

ABBREVIATIONS, ACRONYMS, AND NUMBERS

The emphasis in **11a–11e** is on spelling out words, for formal prose does not yet admit all of the convenient abbreviations students would like to use to reduce the time spent writing. Certain inappropriate abbreviations appear more frequently than others—the titles *Prof.* and *Sen.*, names of states, days, and months. Yet the writer's convenience is less important than the reader's needs. Abbreviation-laden writing channels the reader's attention away from the message and toward the symbols to be decoded, thus interfering with the process of communication.

The common Latin expressions (*e.g., i.e., et al., etc.*) deserve comment not so much because students use them in their writing but because they encounter them in their reading. Often unfamiliar with both the abbreviation and its Latin phrase, students ignore valuable information because they don't know how to interpret its relationship to the sentence they are reading. Further, they misspell such abbreviations as *etc.* (as *ect.* or *and etc.*) or *vs.* (as *vrs.*) because they have had little experience with them. *The Chicago Manual of Style*, 13th ed. (Chicago: U of Chicago P, 1982), pages 384–88, offers an extensive list of scholarly abbreviations for instructors who wish to familiarize their students with these Latin expressions.

The question of when to spell out numbers is one that students always ask. Although **11f** specifies that numbers of one or two words be written out, students often think that the numbers one through ten (or sometimes one through twenty) are spelled out while figures are used for all other numbers. Perhaps they cannot distinguish numbers in series and statistics from numbers in other usage (see "Special Usage Regarding Numbers," page **123**, number 7).

The use of *from* and *to* with dates also requires comment. Students who have developed their own abbreviations for note-taking (*in 1981–82, from 1981–82,* or *fm 81–82*) may be unaware of the distinction between *from 1981 to 1983* and *in 1981–82: from* and *to* are used together, or the hyphen is used without *from*; but *from* and the hyphen are not used together.

▲ **Note**: Additional abbreviations can be found in section **34** of the Handbook (pages **447–49**). Remind students that other abbreviations can be found in most college dictionaries.

ACTIVITIES

1. Ask students to revise the following sentences, if necessary, so that the meaning of each acronym will be clear. Tell them to put a check beside

any sentence in which the acronym is so well known that an explanation would be superfluous for an audience of their peers. (Answers may vary.)

a. The fear of AIDS has changed many persons' life-styles. (✓)
b. Meeting this month in London, OPEC will try to stabilize prices. (Organization of Petroleum Exporting Countries)
c. Only one candidate has been endorsed by NOW. (National Organization for Women)
d. Don underwent a CAT scan after he hit his head on the diving board. (Computerized Axial Tomography)
e. Twenty years ago, he was the leading member of CORE. (Congress of Racial Equality)
f. NASA is using the space shuttle as a launch pad for the preliminary exploration of Venus and Mars. (✔)
g. Many students used BASIC when they first began to learn to program computers. (Beginner's All-purpose Symbolic Instruction Code)
h. Most personal computers are now DOS-based. (Disk Operating System)
i. American and Soviet diplomats made significant achievements in their START negotiations. (STrategic Arms Reduction Talks)

2. Have students write sentences telling

a. their home address
b. the dates of employment for a recent job, preferably one at which they no longer work
c. the ideal salary for a job offered upon graduation and the ideal location of that job
d. the largest number of miles they have ever traveled in a single day
e. the number of students in their smallest class and the number of students in that class whom they know by name.

3. Ask students to write sentences about three or four statistics found in an almanac or in *The Guinness Book of Records*.

4. Ask students to review the following paragraph, making any necessary changes in either abbreviations or number:

Franklin D. Roosevelt was pres. of the U.S. longer than anyone else elected to that office. He was inaugurated in Jan., 1933 and was serving his 4th term when he died in April of nineteen forty five, shortly before the end of the 2nd w. war. On a typical working day, he might keep as many as 21 appointments and approve four pieces of legislation. Controversial but nevertheless popular, he won 523 out of five hundred and thirty one electoral votes in the election of 1936. When Roosevelt died, over ten thousand people lined Penn. Ave. to see his funeral. His home in Hyde Park, NY, is now open to the public and can be viewed w/o charge.

ANSWERS TO EXERCISES

■ **Exercise 1** (p. **121**)   **Striking out inappropriate forms**

Inappropriate forms which students should strike out are listed below.

1. a dr.
2. in Calif. and Ill.
3. on Magnolia St.
4. on Aug. 15
5. for Jr.
6. before six in the A.M.

■ **Exercise 2** (p. **123**)   **Using appropriate shortened forms**

1. on June 15 OR on June 15th
2. Dr. Ernest Threadgill OR Ernest Threadgill, MD
3. $30 million OR $30,000,000
4. Janine Keith, CPA
5. 1 P.M. OR 1 p.m. OR 1:00 P.M. OR 1:00 p.m.
6. by December 1, 1990 OR by 1 December 1990
7. at the bottom of page 15
8. 400 B.C.
9. in act 1, scene 2 OR Act I, Scene 2
10. (1990–1995) OR (1990–95)

12

THE COMMA

Because it has so many different uses, the comma poses more difficulty for students than any other type of punctuation. Recognizing that the comma signals a brief pause, many students punctuate by ear, whenever a pause seems appropriate to them. Although this practice can lead them to use the comma correctly at times, it can also lead them to send confusing or misleading signals to readers. The haphazard use of the comma can also lead to overpunctuation, discussed in section **13**. When teaching the comma, you should stress that correct punctuation is not simply an arbitrary system designed by English teachers to give them an excuse to be picky. Correct punctuation helps writers be precise, which, in turn, helps readers quickly understand the relative importance of the information conveyed to them.

You may find it useful to concentrate on the uses of the comma that signal subordinate elements (**12b** and **12d**), since students usually find punctuation more interesting (and more difficult) when they can see that it has a clear function beyond indicating a "pause." Students who have already mastered the use of the comma in a series, in a date, or in an address may still be puzzled about the need to set off introductory phrases and adverb clauses. But understanding the distinction between restrictive (or essential) and nonrestrictive (or nonessential) elements is usually the greatest challenge for students. Your own students may benefit from a class period focused exclusively on this aspect of punctuation. (See activities 3 and 4 below.)

When teaching **12b**, you can show that introductions—whether a word, phrase, or clause—are subordinate to the clause they are introducing. Doing so will enable you to relate this rule to the principle that informs **12d**. In both cases, the comma is being used to help readers distinguish the most important part of a sentence. One way to do this is to begin with introductions that are clearly transitional: "For example, Margaret Thatcher became the first woman prime minister of Great Britain." (Compare "Margaret Thatcher, for example, became the first woman prime minister of Great Britain.") You can also show how conjunctive adverbs are set off by a comma when they introduce a sentence: "However, many British women are still victims of unfair hiring practices." You might also alert students to introductory adverbs that may double as prepositions: "Above, the flag fluttered in the wind." Removing the comma in this case would suggest that something above the flag was fluttering in the wind.

You can also provide students with examples of introductory phrases and adverb clauses that are clearly nonessential to the meaning of a sentence: "In a flash, I realized that I was using the comma incorrectly." "Although we may not like to think about it, punctuation can help us write more clearly." Of course, you will also need to show that introductions often convey important information: "When beginning to exercise, you should be careful not to strain yourself." "Next to chocolate, strawberry is my favorite flavor." The point to emphasize here is that even though these introductions are conveying information that is essential to the meaning of the sentence, they are still grammatically subordinate to the main clause. At this point you would need to help your students see a distinction between **12b** and **12d**: although commas are used to set off nonessential information within sentences, they are also used to set off introductions that may be nonessential only in terms of sentence structure.

You will often need to remind students that commas precede coordinating conjunctions, several examples of which are provided in **12a**. The omission of this comma is a frequent error. But because this rule is fairly simple, and difficult to relate to the principles embodied in **12b** and **12d**, you should consider teaching it in conjunction with section **3** on the comma splice and fused sentence, reserving the study of **12b, c, d**, and **e** as a separate lesson.

When teaching **12c**, you will probably need to spend more time on coordinate adjectives than on items in a series. Two tests may help students identify coordinate adjectives. First, coordinate adjectives may be joined by *and*:

soggy, bedraggled puppy	OR	soggy and bedraggled puppy
	BUT NOT	
difficult biology exam		difficult and biology exam
crumpled typing paper		crumpled and typing paper

Second, coordinate adjectives may be reversed and still communicate the same meaning:

soggy, bedraggled puppy	OR	bedraggled, soggy puppy
	BUT NOT	
difficult biology exam		biology difficult exam
worn leather shoes		leather worn shoes
long wooden ladder		wooden long ladder

▲ **Note**: When linking main clauses with coordinating conjunctions, students should be aware of the various meanings of these connectives:

and—in addition, also, moreover, besides
but OR **yet**—nevertheless, however, still
for—because, seeing that, since
or—as an alternative, otherwise
nor—and not, or not, not either [used after a negative]
so—therefore, as a result

Advise students to consult the dictionary when they are in any doubt about the meaning of a connective. See also **3b**.

Although students seldom have much difficulty understanding that they should use the comma to separate items in a series, they may be confused about the option in **12c** that recognizes occasions when the last comma before *and* can be omitted. Students frequently ask about this point, occasionally in a weary voice that suggests they don't understand why English teachers can't agree about an apparently simple point. *Harbrace* tries to avoid being prescriptive, but there is no reason why you cannot simply advise your students to use the final comma, since doing so is not incorrect even when the extra comma is not absolutely necessary.

Although few instructors are drawn to the study of English because they want to be able to settle such weighty issues as the use of a final comma in a series, teaching from a handbook and responding to student questions can sometimes lead us to dwell upon them. Doing so can have the unfortunate result of leading students to think that good writing means putting commas in all the right places. When teaching the comma, try to identify this instruction with the writing process. As Mina Shaughnessy has shown in *Errors and Expectations*, punctuation "should not be isolated . . . from the dynamics of composition, for the process whereby writers *mark* sentences is related to the process whereby they *make* them" (28). Instruction focused on the making of sentences can help students see how the comma gives writers the opportunity to write complex and imaginative sentences. Show students that punctuation is simply one of a writer's tools, and—while tools need to be used correctly—writers need to concentrate on what they are using those tools to make.

ACTIVITIES

1. Use sentence-combining exercises to help students see how the comma expands a writer's range of syntactic options. For example:

Steve got up late.
He hurried into his clothes.
He ran down the stairs.
He climbed into his car.
He realized he had the day off from work.

[Steve got up late, hurried into his clothes, ran down the stairs, and climbed into his car before realizing that he had the day off from work.]

2. Ask students to add commas where they are needed in the following paragraph adapted from "The Barrio" by Robert Ramirez:

The train its metal wheels squealing as they spin along the silvery tracks rolls slower now. Through the gaps between the cars blinks a streetlamp and this pulsing light on a barrio streetcorner beats slower like a weary heartbeat until the train shudders to a halt the light goes out and the barrio is deep asleep.

3. Ask students to insert commas between main clauses separated by a coordinating conjunction:

a. We raked the leaves into ten small piles but Jerry argued that three large piles would look better.
b. I fertilized the garden and watered it thoroughly every week.
c. Did you buy carpet for the kitchen floor or did you decide to wait until parquet flooring is on sale before you remodel the kitchen?
d. They saved their money for a two-week vacation in New York but finally decided to rent a houseboat instead.
e. Marlene did not want to wax her car nor did she want to pay someone else to do it.

4. Have students write sentences following the pattern *Adverb clause, main clause.* Then have students rewrite the sentences using the pattern *Main clause, adverb clause.* Suggest as subordinators *as soon as, because, until, wherever,* and *provided;* or have students select from those listed on page **22.**

5. To help students distinguish restrictive from nonrestrictive clauses, have them answer each of the following questions twice in complete sentences—the first with a restrictive clause, the second with a nonrestrictive clause.

a. Who has helped you the most?

   1. An instructor who explains rules clearly helps me become a better writer.
   2. Professor Grimes, who always returns papers promptly, advised me to use subordination more often.

b. Who listens to your problems?
c. What job would you like to have upon graduation?
d. Which person do you most often compete with?
e. Who is one person you admire?

6. Ask students to explain the uses of the comma in one paragraph taken from one of their textbooks or a favorite magazine.

ANSWERS TO EXERCISES

Since punctuation is often a matter of individual preference, much of the key to exercises in sections **12–17** should be considered as merely suggestive—indicative of one instructor's preferences.

■ **Exercise 1** (pp. **128–29**)   **Linking sentences with coordinating conjunctions**

1. conduct, so another [OR and so OR and]

2. faces, and they also
3. department, or they may
4. road, for we wanted
5. Orleans, but they

■ **Exercise 2** (p. **129**)   **Inserting commas before connectives**

1. questionnaires, and they had
2. fill, for Bob
3. later, but I
4. movie, and the
5. party, but Gary

■ **Exercise 3** (pp. **131–32**)   **Punctuating adverb clauses and introductory phrases**

1. else, forget
2. know, these
3. time, I OR time I
4. noon, the OR noon the
5. downhill, the

6. ✓
7. sledgehammer, these
8. ✓
9. over, the
10. can, help

■ **Exercise 4** (p. **133**)   **Using commas and composing sentences**

Answers will vary.

■ **Exercise 5** (p. **136**)   **Using commas with nonrestrictive elements**

1. Mary Smith, who
2. ✓
3. Berry, sitting . . . window,
4. Lilacs, which have a beautiful fragrance, are
5. hometown, a little
6. ✓
7. *The Rivals*, a Mrs.
8. ✓
9. Falls, which . . . 1871, was
10. Duke, Jr., and

■ **Exercise 6** (pp. **137–38**)   **Using commas with appositives, contrasted elements, and names, dates, and addresses**

1. bugs, not
2. Avenue, San Diego, CA
3. Seattle, Washington,
4. Forks, Kansas,; April 24, not
5. January 19, 1989

■ **Exercise 7** (p. 140)   **Inserting needed commas**

1. When I was six, we moved closer to civilization,
2. It was a middle-class neighborhood, not a blackboard jungle; there was no war, no hunger, no racial strife.
3. My guess is that as the family breaks down, friendships
4. But alas, I do not rule the world and that, I am afraid, is the story of my life— always a godmother, never a God.
5. If all else fails, try
6. spring, a brilliant . . . September 22, 1979, in
7. Incidentally, supporting . . . expensive, some
8. drunkenness, nor
9. forty, and . . . them, horse and woman,
10. write, had . . . feeling, had . . . roam, but

■ **Exercise 8** (p. 140)   **Class discussion of commas**

In sentence 3 commas could be inserted as follows:

you, you   [**12b**]
realized, and   [**12a**]
it, the whole   [**12b**]
lashed up, squirming [**12d**]

In the closing sentence, rule **12d(3)** *can explain the parenthetical or appended elements.*

13

SUPERFLUOUS COMMAS

Once students have studied the rules in section **12**, the result—usually for the next essay or two—is commas, commas everywhere. Even students who had no problems with the comma before tend to overcomma their prose until they can comfortably and correctly apply the rules that their style most often calls upon. By reemphasizing the comma's relationship to structure and readability, however, you can stem this flow.

Short introductory phrases and slightly parenthetical phrases (**13c**) become the objects of students' desire to separate elements. Introductory prepositional phrases are especially likely to be set off by commas if they contain more than three words ("In modern research laboratories"). To be realistic, such phrases are increasingly set off by commas, and often it is the writer who decides whether the comma is desirable. Frequently, students insert commas before the coordinating conjunction linking the elements of a compound subject or compound verb and even before the conjunction linking coordinate adjectives—either because they confuse these structures with coordinate main clauses or because they have simply formed the habit of using a comma before any coordinating conjunction.

Also, students try to improve readability by using a comma between the subject and verb in the belief that the comma helps the reader see the most important separation in the sentence. What they do not realize is that while English sentences are binary, the separation of subject and verb by a comma works against the completion of meaning, for once readers come upon the subject or the verb, they then search out the word(s) that complete the central thought.

In addition to helping students avoid the inclusion of superfluous commas, you should also help them to see that too many commas can make a sentence difficult to read—even if each comma is correctly placed:

> When Jean, humming and smiling mysteriously, entered the crowded, hushed waiting room, she saw two sullen children, a distraught parent, and a harried receptionist, who was retrieving scattered toys.

In this sentence the number of ideas obscures the major divisions of adverb clause and main clause. The commas do not cause the problem; they are an indication of it.

To help students see the problem, ask them for revisions to improve the readability of the sentence. Allow them to see that some rearrangements change the meaning. Although creating two sentences is one option, assure them that as long as the two major divisions are clearly marked, all of the ideas can remain in one sentence:

95

Jean, humming and smiling mysteriously, entered the crowded, hushed waiting room; there she saw two sullen children, a distraught parent, and a harried receptionist, who was retrieving scattered toys.

ACTIVITIES

1. Ask students who make the errors discussed in section **13** to review section **12** and complete a justification chart for each comma they have used in a short writing sample. Ask them to make particular note of any comma they cannot justify, encouraging them to drop these commas if they can. Invite students to consult with you when they cannot explain why they have used a comma that nevertheless seems right to them.

2. Have students correct the misused commas in the following sentences:

   a. Jim is going to Arizona next month, and looks forward to seeing the Grand Canyon.
   b. He has been planning this trip for almost a year, so, he should know what it will cost.
   c. Jim has never traveled, on his own before, but he is not expecting any problems.
   d. Hiking, and camping are his favorite activities, and, he enjoys doing these alone.
   e. Anyone, who likes the outdoors, would enjoy the chance to see desert wildlife.

3. Ask students to rewrite the following sentence so that fewer commas will be necessary:

   After two weeks, David went for a second interview, feeling very nervous, but, when he saw that he was greeted warmly by the company president, vice president, and treasurer, he realized he might be offered the job.

ANSWERS TO EXERCISES

■ **Exercise 1** (p. 143)   **Explaining the use of commas**

1. **13c**
2. **13a**
3. **13c**
4. **13b**
5. **13d**
6. **13c**
7. **13b**; **13c**
8. **13b**

■ Exercise 2 (pp. 143–44)   Changing sentences

1. evaluations and also recommended
2. knowledge and presents
3. Portland and may
4. People who make requests instead of giving orders usually get cooperation.
5. Students who are willing to listen can learn much from Professor Young.

■ Exercise 3 (p. 144)   Circling superfluous commas

1. minds⊙
2. Punctuation⊙rest⊙
3. lies , units⊙and⊙
4. such as⊙volume⊙
5. world⊙periods⊙
6. sharps⊙
7. correct
8. bend⊙

14

THE SEMICOLON

The correct use of the semicolon is relatively rare in work submitted by students at the beginning of a writing course. Some students confuse the semicolon with the colon (which is discussed in section **17**). Others recognize that they don't understand how to use the semicolon correctly and decide to avoid using it at all. But the semicolon is essential in eliminating such problems as the comma splice and fused sentence (discussed in section **3**) as well as the sentence that groans under the weight of too many commas (as noted on page 95 of this manual). Once students understand the nature of a main clause (or independent clause, as it is often called), then they should be able to use the semicolon easily.

As noted at the beginning of **14**, the primary use of the semicolon is to separate closely related main clauses that are not linked by a coordinating conjunction. This rule is best taught by tying it to the problems discussed in section **3**, since punctuation becomes more meaningful when students can see it within a context in which they would actually need to use it. When teaching how the semicolon functions in this case, you can help your students by suggesting a simple check: since a main clause could be a complete sentence, and since the semicolon is used to separate main clauses not linked by a coordinating conjunction, then writers should be able to substitute a period (if they wanted to) for any semicolon used according to the rule established in **14a**. You might also point out that the semicolon visually incorporates the symbols that, when used separately, distinguish the comma and the period. This observation may help students understand how the semicolon is an intermediate mark between the short pause indicated by the comma and the full stop required by the period. To put it simply, the semicolon is stronger than a comma but weaker than a period.

Traditionally, the semicolon has been favored when a second main clause restates an idea expressed in the first, exemplifies that idea, or provides a contrast to it. Many sentences follow this pattern. You may find it useful to show students examples of sentences that contain main clauses that are only marginally related to each other and to use these sentences to discuss other options (such as treating these clauses in separate sentences). See activity 1.

Once students have mastered this primary use of the semicolon, you need to decide whether to discuss **14b**, which covers another way the semicolon can be of use. When attempting to use the semicolon to separate a series of items which themselves contain commas, students may replace the wrong comma with a semicolon. Because students often find **14b** more difficult to master than **14a**, you may want to devote class time to helping students analyze sample sentences such as those on page **148** of the

Handbook and in activity 2 below. If you do so, emphasize that the semicolon separates parts of equal grammatical rank and that it cannot separate parts of different rank (such as separating a clause from a phrase). However, dwelling upon **14b** may cause some students to lose what confidence they gained from mastering **14a**, which is of greater potential use to them. Accordingly, you might decide to focus exclusively on **14a** in some classes, mentioning only in passing that **14b** explains another situation in which a semicolon may be occasionally of use.

Students often respond favorably to instruction in the semicolon because they perceive it as a more sophisticated type of punctuation than the comma, which they have been hearing about since grade school. If your own students are slow to feel the appeal of the semicolon, you might share with them the following quotation from "Notes on Punctuation" by Lewis Thomas:

> It is almost always a greater pleasure to come across a semicolon than a period. The period tells you that that is that; if you didn't get all the meaning you wanted or expected, anyway you got all the writer intended to parcel out and now you have to move along. But with a semicolon there, you get a pleasant little feeling of expectancy; there is more to come; read on; it will get clearer.

ACTIVITIES

1. Ask students to evaluate the following sentences, adding a semicolon where appropriate and recommending either a comma and a coordinating conjunction or a division into separate sentences when the main clauses are not closely related.

   a. Some people eat to live others live to eat.
   b. Many Chinese feel that their standard of living has improved during the last ten years previously hard to obtain consumer items are now within their reach.
   c. San Francisco has many excellent Italian restaurants it is a five hour drive from Los Angeles.
   d. Housing in New York City is very expensive a studio apartment can rent for over a thousand dollars a month.
   e. Soap operas can be entertaining they are interrupted by too many commercials.

2. Ask students to add commas and semicolons to the following sentences:

   a. The selection committee includes Kurt Vonnegut the novelist Arthur Miller the playwright and Harrison Salisbury the journalist.
   b. The Mississippi is useful as a highway allowing goods from Minneapolis to be shipped to the Gulf of Mexico as a natural resource providing New Orleans with much of its drinking water and as a place for recreation providing many opportunities for boating and fishing.

c. At our New Year's Eve party we served popcorn pretzels and potato chips beer wine coolers and nonalcoholic punch and a hot buffet supper after midnight.

d. A typical shopping mall has large department stores such as Sears and J.C. Penney specialty shops like Benetton and Banana Republic and fast-food restaurants like Burger King and Taco Bell.

e. Writing involves invention or the discovery of ideas arrangement or planning how to organize those ideas and drafting or putting ideas down on paper.

3. Ask students to tell whether or not the units in each item are of equal grammatical rank and to what rank each unit belongs.

a. As soon as she spoke / because of her wit [clause / phrase]

b. She spoke with authority / when she delivered her speech [sentence or main clause / subordinate clause]

c. Phrasing her thoughts carefully / she measured the crowd's reaction while she spoke [phrase / sentence]

d. An articulate and calm speaker / a speaker of unsurpassed poise [phrase / phrase]

e. She spoke; they listened / she spoke while they listened [sentence / sentence]

f. Should have been listening attentively / as she replied [phrase / clause]

g. Offering the latest statistics, she refuted the argument that he gave / to have refuted it so effortlessly [sentence / phrase]

h. Since the proposal was defeated / her rational argument was accepted even by those who had been opposed at first [clause / sentence]

i. According to the latest statistics / against the proposal [phrase / phrase]

j. She knew she had won / she congratulated herself [sentence / sentence or main clause]

4. Ask students to write two sentences for each pattern, punctuating the sentences as in the pattern.

a. Subordinate clause, main clause; main clause subordinate clause.

b. Main clause; transitional phrase, main clause.

c. Main clause; main clause.

d. Participial phrase, main clause subordinate clause; main clause.

e. Main clause with items in a series; conjunctive adverb, main clause subordinate clause.

5. Have students collect five sentences containing semicolons and identify the rule for each use. Encourage students to locate sentences for both

14a and **14b**. Ask students what they conclude about the use of semicolons, such as how often they are found; whether they more often illustrate rule **14a** or **14b**; and whether they are found more often in informal or formal writing.

6. Reinforce rule **14a** and relate it to use of the period (**17a**) by dictating pairs of ideas that could be written as one compound sentence or as two simple sentences. Ask students to decide whether a comma or a semicolon is better. It may also be useful to include some ideas that are apparently unrelated and refer students to **23a**.

ANSWERS TO EXERCISES

■ **Exercise 1** (p. 147–48)   **Using semicolons between main clauses**

1. marriage; a family [. . . *marriage, nor is a family quarrel a broken home* is also correct]
2. use; for example,
3. sequels; from
4. cooking; later,
5. blew up; as a result,

■ **Exercise 2** (p. 148–49)   **Using semicolons to separate items in a series**

1. counseling; linguistics;
2. geologists; psychology;

■ **Exercise 3** (p. 150)   **Correcting misused semicolons**

1. paper, no
2. ate, I still
3. people: those who [OR *people—those who*]
4. minutes, the doors
5. ✔

■ **Exercise 4** (p. 150)   **Composing sentences**

Answers will vary.

■ **Exercise 5** (pp. 150–51)   **Punctuating with the comma and the semicolon**

1. courses, for
2. Mikoyama, a noted Japanese scientist, invented
3. beans, . . . peaches, . . . tomatoes,
4. healthy, energetic

5. fire, I
6. luggage, Dick
7. 1066, the . . . Hastings; 1215, the . . . Carta; 1917, the . . . revolution; and 1945, the
8. sloop; to tell the truth, however, they
9. hungry; Jack thought
10. never end; however, I reminded

15

THE APOSTROPHE

The most common error involving the apostrophe is the confusion between *it's* and *its* and *who's* and *whose*—contractions versus personal pronouns showing possession. Although this problem is noted in **15d**, your students may profit from additional discussion of this point. You might review section **6** on case immediately before assigning section **15**, and then remind students that the apostrophe is used to indicate the possessive of nouns but not for the possessive of pronouns: *Bill's* or *the school's* but not *his's* / *his'* or *it's* / *its'*. You can then draw their attention to **15b**, emphasizing that the apostrophe takes the place of whatever has been omitted in a contraction or number: *didn't*, not *did'nt* (a common error); class of *'91*, but not class of *91'*. You can give students some good, simple advice by suggesting that they double-check any contraction to make sure they have put the apostrophe where something has been left out. When students understand the difference between using the apostrophe to establish possession and using it to make a contraction, you can provide them with a useful test for safeguarding against confusing the common contractions *it's*, *they're*, and *who's* with their equally common homonyms: whenever they use one of these contractions, they should reread it substituting the two-word form in its place. If the two-word form makes sense, then they need only ask themselves if the informality of the contraction is appropriate for their audience and occasion for writing. If the two-word form does not make sense, then the possessive pronoun should probably be substituted.

When forming the possessive of nouns, students are often confused by nouns that end with *s*. Make sure they understand the option provided under **15a(1)** and note that **15a(2)** includes an example of a surname used as a plural to describe a family, since this is another instance that often puzzles students. They might welcome the following example to help clarify this point: Did you hear "John Lawlor's lecture? Are you going to the party at the Lawlors' house?"

Since the possessive case signals more than ownership alone, students may not recognize all the occasions that call for it. In *An Introductory English Grammar*, 4th ed. (New York: Holt, 1981), Norman C. Stageberg lists six relationships that are signaled (the examples here are similar to those Stageberg uses):

possession	Mary's camera
description or characterization	driver's license
origin	Dillard's prose
measure—time	a day's time
—value	two cents' worth

—space	at arm's length
subject of act	Steve's regret; he regrets
object of act	John's kidnappers; someone kidnapped him

But knowing when to use the possessive does not guarantee knowing how to use it. Many a student has avoided deciding 's or s' by writing the apostrophe above the s, thus suggesting that in the haste of getting down the idea the student intended the correct placement but failed (and students smile knowingly when the instructor says that this subterfuge is not unfamiliar). Students can follow a three-step process to select the correct form. First, they decide the word; second, they decide the number; third, they decide the sign of possession, as in these examples:

dean	(sing.) dean	**15a(1)** dean's
woman	(pl.) women	**15a(2)** women's
Richards (last name)	(pl.) Richardses	**15a(2)** Richardses'
sheep	(sing.) sheep	**15a(2)** sheep's
Secretary of State	(pl.) Secretaries of State	**15a(3)** Secretaries of State's

When teaching the possessive, you should also realize that the absence of the possessive (zero possessive) is a typical feature of dialect interference. Although the omission of the -s inflection occurs before gerunds in all dialects, a construction like "William pencil" (as opposed to "William's pencil") is characteristic of Black English vernacular. Instructors encountering this error should not assume that it is a sign of careless writing. Students who make this error repeatedly will almost certainly need extra exercises—including those in the workbooks that accompany the Handbook—before they master the use of the possessive in edited American English.

Finally, when teaching **15c** on the use of the apostrophe to form certain plurals, emphasize that the apostrophe is not normally used for plurals. Remind students that most plurals are formed by adding s or es, not by adding 's or s'. (She has many books, not book's.)

ACTIVITIES

1. Supplement **15b** by discussing the literary use of the apostrophe in dialogue written to reflect the sounds of American speech. Use the following excerpt from Sarah Orne Jewett's "The Hilton's Holiday" as an example:

> "I've be'n a-thinkin' all day I'd like to give the child'n some kind of a treat," said the father, wide awake now. "I hurried up my work 'cause I had it so in mind. They don't have the opportunities some do, an' I want 'em to know the world, an' not just stay here on the farm like a couple o' bushes."

Ask students if attempts at dialect impose any extra burden upon readers. Ask them to revise this passage, eliminating all contractions. As a follow-up exercise, ask them to compose a short speech in which they use contractions to convey the sound of someone they know.

2. Ask students to identify names of stores and products that use the apostrophe, and note that this type of cute spelling has become pervasive. Examples might include, Steak 'n Stein, Beans 'n Franks, and Quick 'n Easy.

3. If necessary, have students review **18d(5)** (forming the plural of nouns). Then ask them to write the singular and plural possessive forms for each of the following:

chemist	chemist's	chemists'
class	class's OR class' (depending on context)	classes'
committee	committee's	committees'
Elk City	Elk City's	Elk Citys'
fox	fox's	foxes'
beach	beach's	beaches'
staff	staff's	staffs' OR staves'
volcano	volcano's	volcano(e)s'
cactus	cactus's OR cactus'	cacti's OR cactuses'
member-at-large	member-at-large's	members-at-large's
people	people's	peoples'
other	other's	others'

Ask students for which, if any, they would use *of* instead of *'s* (such as "the votes of the two members-at-large" or "the ceremony honoring the mayors of the two Elk Citys"). Also single out *each other* and *one another* for discussion: although plural in meaning, the possessive forms are *each others'* and *one another's*. Ask the class to distinguish differences in meaning shown by *other's, others',* and *others.*

4. Have students supply the two forms that correspond to the one already supplied, rewording as necessary.

EXAMPLE   It is <u>Nancy's</u> gift; her gift; hers.

a. It is _____ car (*their*).
b. I ordered _____ dinners (*Ethan's and my*).
c. This racquet belongs to _____ (*you*).
d. The camper is _____ (*his*).
e. _____ favorite color is yellow (Frances's).

5. Have students write these sentences as they are being dictated.

I wonder whose essay was typed on graph paper. Whether it's hers or his makes no difference. This paper with its fine lines makes reading difficult. Who's going to argue that it's acceptable manuscript form?

ANSWERS TO EXERCISES

■ **Exercise 1** (p. 154)   **Using apostrophes to indicate the possessive case**

1. John L. Field III's acreage
2. Weinberg's house
3. Gregory's and Philip's voices
4. sister-in-law's hopes
5. Jefferson Davis's home
6. a dollar's worth
7. somebody else's turn
8. O. Henry's stories
9. men's coats
10. Anne and Betty's book [OR Anne's and Betty's book]

■ **Exercise 2** (pp. 155–56)   **Using apostrophes correctly**

1. students' [OR 1980's]
2. Hughes' [OR Hughes's]
3. boss's
4. ✔
5. '94, Marilyn's
6. It's, M.D.'s, isn't
7. *i*'s, *s*'s
8. There's, Tom's
9. NATO's, analyst's
10. else's

16

QUOTATION MARKS

Sections **16a**, **b**, and **e** contain information students will use as they write their research papers. For that reason, this section (along with **17i** on ellipsis points) can be logically included in the part of the course devoted to the research paper. Emphasis should be placed on accurate quotation as well as accurate punctuation since the respect given a piece of writing is at least in part a result of its author's respect for others' material.

As students look at a passage in their own work, they should ask: What is the controlling idea of this passage? How is the controlling idea related to the ideas in my paper? Does it support my ideas? What point does it support or illustrate? What are the two or three key phrases? Do the phrases merit direct quotation? If so, how can they be integrated into my own sentence? Would my use of the ideas be as effective if they were summarized or paraphrased? (See **34c** in the Handbook and page 194 of the *Instructor's Manual*.)

Students who learn how to evaluate sources in this fashion are more easily convinced that other sources should support their ideas, not replace them; writers who have something they think worth saying will not want too many or overly long quotations robbing them of that opportunity. At the same time, they do not risk losing their reader's patience (students often admit that as soon as they see a long prose quotation, they decide not to read it).

The following example shows the successive embedding indicated by the alternation of double and single quotation marks:

Original source
Few can read Mark Bradley's "Chronicles of a 'Suburban Rookie' at the Annual Block Party" without giggling, chortling, or roaring at the essayist's collection of neighborhood types.   —ELIZABETH COOKE

Sentence in a research paper
Although suburbanites are often considered dull, Elizabeth Cooke argues that most people cannot "read Mark Bradley's 'Chronicles of a "Suburban Rookie" at the Annual Block Party' without giggling, chortling, or roaring at the essayist's collection of neighborhood types"(Cooke 110).

Although students rarely need all three levels, they should know that a method exists for handling the situation when it arises.

When teaching the use of quotations marks, you should emphasize that writers have a responsibility to quote accurately. Students often misquote because of errors in transcription, but some do so because a small change in the quotation will make it fit more easily into their own work. Students need to understand that quotations must be exact, and that any alteration of a quotation must be recorded through the use of the ellipsis or brackets. (See

17g and **17i**.) You should also alert students to the danger of quoting out of context. Quotations should accurately reflect the views of the writer or speaker cited.

Another common problem is the overuse of quotation marks for slang or colloquial words. In an attempt to demonstrate their recognition that such words do not fit with the rest of their prose, students may add quotation marks rather than revise. If they are using slang with trepidation, ask them to consider their topic, audience, and occasion. If slang is appropriate within a particular context, then quotation marks are superfluous; if slang is inappropriate, authors should reconsider their word choice rather than their punctuation. Similarly, when students put clichés in quotation marks, ask them if they could replace these worn expressions with fresher language instead of using punctuation to call attention to weakness.

Students are often puzzled about where to put other marks of punctuation with quotation marks, so reserve some time for class discussion of **16e**. When discussing mechanics, you might also remind students that quotation marks *always* come in pairs. Urge them to double-check their prose to make sure that they have remembered to include the mate for any quotation mark they have used.

ACTIVITIES

1. Ask students to revise the following sentences, eliminating either quotation marks or quoted words and expressions, depending upon the context:

    a. Plato's concept of reality is "mind boggling."
    b. Before he met Juliet, Romeo was a "party animal."
    c. My roommate is a "nerd."
    d. Thousands of new government employees arrived in Washington to implement the "New Deal."
    e. After his visit from "the Ghost of Christmas Past," Scrooge began to realize that he had turned into an "old fart."

2. Using an essay that all students have access to, write a series of quotations which students are to check for accuracy. Make deliberate errors: an omitted word, an omitted quotation mark, transposed words, improper capitalization, and misspellings. Select different sentences for each error, and include two or three accurate sentences in the exercise.

3. Ask students to follow **16a(3)** as they quote one passage of poetry that appeals to them, locating the quotation within a brief discussion of its significance.

4. Ask students to identify direct and indirect quotations and to punctuate these sentences:

a. He wondered why he had agreed to baby-sit the twins.
b. Have I forgotten what they did the last time he asked himself.
c. Well he sighed at least they won't be letting the gerbil out of its cage now that the cat finally ate it.
d. He had forgotten to ask whether they had become toilet-trained since his last visit.
e. Perhaps I just don't remember how much fun children can be.

5. Ask students to write down an actual conversation. To concentrate on recording what is said, the students should not take part in the conversation. Allow them to use an overheard conversation, but encourage them to use the conversation of friends—pointing out that they would then be able to read their transcript back to the speakers for verification. Once the dialogue is on paper, the students should add appropriate punctuation marks and dialogue tags.

6. Refer students to section **34b** of the Handbook and ask them to interview one of their professors or a member of the community. Ask them to include both direct and indirect quotation in the written interviews they subsequently bring to class and exchange with other students for evaluation.

7. Refer students to section **34e** and ask them to gather five sentences on a topic of their own choice. Then have them write sentences that quote the passages they have collected, and ask them to provide documentation.

ANSWERS TO EXERCISES

■ **Exercise 1** (p. 161)   **Punctuating direct and indirect quotations**

Sentences containing indirect quotations may vary somewhat. Tense may vary in direct quotations.

1. Doris said, "I have a theory about you."
2. He said, "I have read David Baltimore's 'The Brain of a Cell.' "
3. A Weight Watcher, Eileen explained, "I can eat as much as I want—of vegetables like spinach, eggplant, and zucchini."
4. Clyde asked whether I would go to the opera with him.
5. Last night Pruett said, "I think that Amanda's favorite expression is 'Tell me about it!' "

■ **Exercise 2** (p. 163)   **Using quotation marks correctly**

1. "Cloning,"
2. "stoked" means "fantastically happy on a surfboard." (Option: italics instead of quotation marks)
3. "A Circle in the Fire."

4. "Sighting the Target."
5. "My grandmother often said, 'When poverty comes in the door, love goes out the window.' "

■ **Exercise 3** (p. **164**)   **Inserting needed quotation marks**

1. "The Star-Spangled Banner"?
2. "Get aholt," instead of "get hold,"
3. "Hey Jude"
4. "The Road Not Taken."
5. "No," Peg said, "I didn't . . . bananas yet!"
6. "I Want a Wife"?
7. "Black Orchid,"
8. "First Confession"; mine is "The Story of an Hour."
9. "Why cry over spilled milk?" my grandmother used to ask. "Be glad . . . to spill."
10. Catherine said, "Do the townspeople ever say to me 'You're a born leader'? Yes, lots of times, and when they do, I just tell them my motto is 'Lead, follow, or get the heck out of the way!' "

17

THE PERIOD AND OTHER MARKS

Students who perceive punctuation as a means for signaling pauses have good reason to do so, since punctuation was originally designed as a convenience for people reading aloud in a primarily oral culture. Introduced by a Greek librarian over two thousand years ago, the period, colon, and comma were the first punctuation marks to emerge in the West. A dot set high on the line signaled a period; a dot on the bottom of the line indicated a colon. Reflecting its now well-recognized status as half-stop, the comma appeared halfway up between the top and bottom of letters. Parentheses and brackets emerged around A.D. 1500, and dashes approximately two hundred years later. If you share this brief history of punctuation with your students, emphasize that the purpose of punctuation has changed over the last several hundred years, just as its physical appearance has also changed. Although writers still enjoy considerable freedom in its use, punctuation is now used not simply to signal a pause at a convenient moment but to designate grammatical structure.

Mastering punctuation thus requires a good understanding of sentence structure. (See section **1**.) If this prospect seems unappealing to students, help them to see that punctuation gives experienced writers opportunities unknown to novices. Faced with a number of marks to signal intonation patterns and the importance of ideas within sentences, inexperienced writers may simply ignore them, falling back upon the comma (often used incorrectly) for internal punctuation and the period for the end of every sentence. Such students need to learn how punctuation can enable them to communicate more effectively and write more imaginatively. The punctuation discussed in this section is ideal for such instruction. Both the dash and the parentheses facilitate the embedding structures that enable writers to create the varied sentence structure characteristic of good prose. And both brackets and ellipsis points are essential to the efficient use of sources. (See activity 9 that follows.) Encourage your students to experiment with these forms of punctuation, especially if they are unfamiliar with them. Tell them not to worry if they misuse one of these marks at first; they may use it correctly on their second or third attempt—but they'll never use unusual punctuation correctly until they try.

When teaching the exclamation point, remind students that punctuation cannot take the place of effective word choice. Well-chosen words can usually speak for themselves without marks like italics or exclamation points calling attention to them. Writers who overuse the exclamation point may sound hysterical or silly. (See activity 1.)

When teaching the colon, you might like to cite the distinction made by Robert M. Pierson in "Punctuation as Art": "Remember that colons . . . generally mean that what is to come will explain what has just gone by. They

111

imply identity, whereas semicolons imply 'separate but equal' status." Students are usually quick to master the use of the colon before a series or a quotation but much slower to use one to introduce a second main clause that explains or amplifies the main clause that has preceded it. Since the semicolon would be acceptable in this case, and the correct use of the semicolon may be more helpful to students, detailed instruction in the colon might be best reserved for only your most able students.

Once they have discovered the dash, some students tend to use it to avoid making decisions about commas, semicolons, and colons. When teaching the dash, emphasize that too many dashes can make writing look fragmented and haphazard. (See activity 2.)

"Punctuation of Parenthetical Matter" (**17f**) provides a useful summary of the different effects achieved by the dash, the parentheses, and the comma. This illustration may help students to grasp a key point: parenthetical information is still a part of the sentence in which it appears, and it should read smoothly whichever way it is set off. Although the Handbook observes that parentheses "usually de-emphasize the elements they enclose," de-emphasis does not mean deletion. Students who misuse the parentheses should be encouraged to read their work aloud, listening to how it sounds. Long, cumbersome parenthetical matter is often best moved to another sentence.

ACTIVITIES

1. Help students avoid the inappropriate use of the exclamation point by asking them to revise the following sentences, cutting any exclamation point that is superfluous and substituting new words if doing so can make the prose more emphatic:

    Mary Lou should feel pleased with herself! During the last six months, she has lost forty-two pounds! This was the first diet that really worked for her! When I saw her, I said, "Mary Lou! You look like a new woman!" She used to be so big (!) that I felt thin by comparison. Now I feel envious!

2. Ask students to revise the following paragraph (adapted from "Desperation Writing" by Peter Elbow) using other punctuation, if necessary, to reduce the number of dashes in it:

    I know I am not alone in my recurring twinges of panic that I won't be able to write something when I need to—I won't be able to produce coherent speech or thought. And that lingering doubt is a great hindrance to writing—it's a constant fog—or static—that clouds the mind. I never got out of its clutches till I discovered that it was possible to write something—not something great or pleasing but at least something usuable—workable—when my mind was out of commission. The trick is that you have to do all your cooking out on the table—your mind is incapable of doing any inside. It means using symbols and pieces of paper—not as a crutch—but as a wheel chair.

3. Ask students to write sentences with the following information, first using a colon and then a dash. Example: *Three famous women who never married are Elizabeth Blackwell, Maria Montessori, and Emily Dickinson.* (Book of Lists *278*)

> Marriage is not a prerequisite of success: the careers of Elizabeth Blackwell, Maria Montessori, and Emily Dickinson show that a woman is not successful in her job because she is married.

> Elizabeth Blackwell, Maria Montessori, Emily Dickinson—these are famous women who never married.

    a. The three most landed-on spaces in Monopoly are Illinois Avenue, Go, and B. & O. Railroad (*Book of Lists* 375).
    b. Three benefits of regular exercise are improved body tone, increased endurance, and increased self-respect.
    c. Three words beginning with *dh* are *dhak, dharma,* and *dhole.*
    d. Three famous American writers who married are Nathaniel Hawthorne, F. Scott Fitzgerald, and Robert Frost.
    e. Three U.S. presidents whose birthdays occur in March are Andrew Jackson, John Tyler, and Grover Cleveland.
    f. Nicknames for *Mary* are *Mamie, May, Molly,* and *Polly.*

4. Have students compose sentences to illustrate each of the following:

    a. a direct question
    b. an indirect question
    c. a double direct question
    d. a direct quotation containing an indirect question
    e. question marks between parts of a series

5. Parentheses comes from the Greek *parentithenai,* meaning "a putting in beside," and this exactly describes the act of interpolating material that is independent from the syntax of the sentence but that qualifies the ideas in it. Parenthetical information is apart from, yet related to, its referent. A writer must decide how much emphasis the parenthetical information should receive and then use the corresponding punctuation mark. Dashes emphasize most strongly, parentheses less so, and commas (because they are the most common of the three) least. Have students discuss the effect of the punctuation in each sentence:

    a. No one—not even his mother—recognized him after he had lost seventy pounds.
    b. No one (not even his mother) recognized him after he had lost seventy pounds.
    c. No one, not even his mother, recognized him after he had lost seventy pounds.

Ask them how the punctuation marks in each sentence reflect the writer's attitude toward the weight loss and other people's reaction to it.

6. Lists enumerated within a sentence are separated by commas, and the numbers are enclosed in parentheses. Lists in vertical columns use numbers followed by a period:

> In deciding whether to quote from a source, a writer considers (1) the authority of the writer, (2) the relationship of the passage to the thesis of the research paper, and (3) the function of the passage in the research paper.

> In deciding whether to quote from a source, a writer considers

> 1. the authority of the writer
> 2. the relationship of the passage to the thesis of the research paper
> 3. the function of the passage in the research paper.

Have students enumerate the courses required for their major field of study, the arguments for a career in their major field of study, the arguments against a career in that field, and five questions to ask when considering a career in that field.

7. Ask students to collect one or two examples of sentences punctuated according to **17a, 17e, 17f, 17h,** and **17i** (one or two illustrations of each).

8. Have students use the punctuation marks in this chapter as they revise one or two paragraphs from their essays. Then ask them to select what they think are three major punctuation revisions and explain what was gained by each.

9. Following the structure of exercise 5, use passages from several related articles (ideally those in an anthology of essays to which students have access) and ask students to quote according to instructions. Or use one long passage reproduced on an overhead transparency and highlight the words to be omitted. Ask for a direct quotation omitting the words you specify. (Specify at least one omission that will require the use of a bracketed interpolation as well as ellipsis points.)

ANSWERS TO EXERCISES

■ **Exercise 1** (p. 168)   **Using the period, question mark, and exclamation point**

Answers may vary.

■ **Exercise 2** (p. 170)   **Adding colons**

1. 12:30; quotation:
2. ✓

3. these:
4. periodicals:
5. ✓

■ **Exercise 3** (p. **170**)   **Using semicolons or colons between main clauses**

1. purpose: 3. certain;
2. purpose;   4. certain:

■ **Exercise 4** (pp. **174–75**)   **Punctuating parenthetical elements**

Punctuation setting off parenthetical matter may vary.

1. Gibbs—or is it his twin brother?—plays
2. Joseph, who is Gordon's brother, is
3. "I admit that I—" he began
4. everything—more
5. courses—for example, French and biology—demand
6. Silverheels (1918–1980) played
7. fool [sic] the
8. Body language—a wink or yawn, nose-rubbing or ear pulling, folded arms or crossed legs—can . . .
9. lakes—these
10. innovations—for example, the pass/fail system—did not

■ **Exercise 5** (pp. **177–78**)   **Using the ellipsis mark**

According to John Donne, "No man is an island . . . every man is a piece of the continent, a part of the main. . . . Any man's death diminishes me because I am involved in mankind."

■ **Exercise 6** (p. **178**)   **Using the ellipsis mark**

1. My father was dying . . . what would happen to us?
2. Our lives would have been different if. . . .

■ **Exercise 7** (p. **178**)   **Using end marks, commas, colons, dashes, and parentheses**

Answers may vary somewhat.

1. same: aluminum guardrails, green signs, white lettering.
2. "Is it—is it the green light then?" was all I managed to say.
3. again: What . . . theater.
4. typo: "The . . . refugees."
5. "Judy!" she exploded. "Judy, that's . . . say."
   She raised . . . daughter, but it wouldn't reach.
6. Emily (formerly Mrs. Goyette) caught . . . urgently.

7. wished to be—a professional dancer.
8. thinkers—conservatives or liberals—who . . . human.
9. put it, "Rose Bowl, Sugar Bowl, and Orange Bowl—all are gravy bowls."
10. "very" ("I am good and mad"), and . . . coffee, not the cup, is hot.

18

SPELLING AND HYPHENATION

Because spelling problems vary from student to student, no one approach to teaching spelling will help all students uniformly, but the suggestions that begin section **18** are sound advice to all writers. Whenever possible, instruction in spelling should be individualized to meet the needs of the class or, ideally, of each student.

One method is to compile a list of the three or four most frequently misspelled words in a set of essays and to present the words with appropriate spelling rules when class time allows. Working from students' writing, you are then sure to teach the words that need attending to rather than dwelling on words that cause the class little problem. Further, over the semester you might want to compile a class list; the words that recur in more than two sets of papers could be assigned for special study.

A second approach is to have students keep a list of words which they have misspelled in their writing. Rather than ask students to recopy the misspelling (which reinforces the error), have them write down the correct spelling and the rule or device which will help them remember the spelling. Such a list might look like this:

An Individual Spelling List

laid—like *said*	[analogy]
forfeit—not an *ee* sound	[rule reference]
minor—minority	[change of stress]
category—cat-e-gory	[syllabication]
recommend—re + commend	[structural analysis]
studying—y + ing	[rule reference]
together—to get her	[mnemonic device]
accept—to accept gifts	[use in context]

Spelling can be tested in a number of ways. Here are some suggestions:

1. Assign groups of twenty words a week chosen from the list of frequently misspelled words plus those on the class list; then dictate ten of them for the students to write down. This approach has the advantage of being quick, easy, and familiar; and students have said that it causes them to be more careful with all spellings as they prepare an essay.
2. Give each student several words to spell orally.

3. To test easily confused words, dictate words in context and ask students to write either the word or the phrase.
4. Ask students to write a paragraph using selected words.
5. Write a multiple-choice quiz, asking students to select the one misspelled word from a series of three to five words, or the one correctly spelled word from a series of misspelled words.

In short, spelling is a skill that students who want their ideas to be taken seriously must master, but testing spelling need not be limited to a single method.

For **18d** two cautions are in order. First, students should realize that not all words ending in *f* or *fe* change the ending to *ve* before adding *s* (*safes, proofs, beliefs, handkerchiefs*); some have two plural forms (*hoofs, hooves; scarfs, scarves*). Second, they should realize that *-es* (not *-s*) marks the plural in such words as *tomatoes* and *potatoes*; thus *tomatoe* and *potatoe* are incorrect singular forms.

Students who are poor spellers may find comfort in learning that English and American spelling has become regularized only within the last two hundred years. As the brief history of the English language included in section **19** reveals, English as we know it today has evolved over many centuries, during which it responded to many different influences. Spelling has evolved with the language, and it remained irregular during the years English was changing most rapidly. Shakespeare, for example, used *honor* and *honour* interchangeably, and scholars continue to debate whether his name should be spelled *Shakspere* or *Shakespeare*. Attempts to standarize spelling began only in the sixteenth century, and concern for correct spelling did not become widespread until the publication of Samuel Johnson's dictionary in 1755.

Students might be particularly interested in the spelling reforms advocated by Noah Webster (1758–1843), the most influential figure in the development of American spelling. In "Dissertations on the English Language" (1789), Webster advocated the simplication of spelling by the omission of all silent letters (so that *friend* would be spelled *frend*, for instance) and the substitution of characters with a definite sound for those that seem indeterminate (so *laugh* would become *laf*, and *character* would become *karacter*). In these reforms, he was much influenced by Benjamin Franklin's "A Scheme for a New Alphabet and a Reformed Mode of Spelling" (1768), although he did not accept Franklin's proposal for the introduction of six new characters into the American alphabet. In his dictionary of 1806, Webster eliminated the *u* in *our* words like *labour*, redundant consonants in words like *travelling*, and the final *k* from words like *publick*; he also transposed the *re* in such words as *theatre* and *centre*.

Many of the differences between American and British spelling can be traced to Webster's influence. But many of Webster's spellings never took root, and he eventually dropped such spellings as *aker, iland, stile,* and *wimmen* from later editions of his dictionary—to the regret, perhaps, of students who wish more words were spelled as they sound. That many of

Webster's eminently practical recommendations failed to become accepted can be cited as evidence of the extent to which spelling had become standardized by the nineteenth century. And that Webster sold over eighty million copies of his *American Spelling Book* during his lifetime can be cited as evidence of the extent to which Americans associate good spelling with education. In short, bad spellers today are living in the wrong century; writers these days need to observe the spellings now accepted as standard.

When teaching spelling or drawing attention to spelling errors, try to remind students that spelling is part of writing and not an end in itself. A good speller can be a poor writer, but a good writer can lose the confidence of his or her audience by making errors that suggest either carelessness or inadequate education.

ACTIVITIES

1. Ask students to substitute American spelling for each of the following British words: *apologise, cancelled, cheque, colour, defence, encyclopaedia, harbour, lustre, personalise,* and *shovelling.*

2. Ask students to consult a good dictionary and discover archaic spellings for three or four familiar words. For example: *olde* [old], *smale* [small], and *toune* [town].

3. Dictate the following passage to your students, warning them that it contains many homonyms but that they should be able to determine what words are meant from the context. After dictating the passage, allow students time to read what they have written and make any necessary changes. Try to present this as a puzzle rather than a test. If you suspect your class includes several poor spellers, consider giving each student a teammate. (Words likely to be misspelled are italicized.)

A *lot* of people have *already heard* so many *arguments* about *capital* punishment that they *cannot bear* to sit *through* another. But this issue *affects* us all, *whether* or not we realize *its* importance. *There* are two *separate* sides to the debate. Critics of the death penalty *recommend* that it be abolished because *they're conscious* of how much suffering it has caused *through* the years. They *cite* examples of prisoners who were denied *access* to a *fair* trial and good legal *counsel. Their conscience* may lead them to demonstrate at the *site* of an execution or before the *Capitol* in Washington, D.C. Defenders of *capital* punishment urge us not to *lose sight* of the *pain* suffered by the victims of violent crime. Making *exceptions* for cases involving self-defense, they *accept* the death penalty as appropriate for murderers, and *cite* shocking cases, like the man who *threw* a baby through a *pane* of glass *fourteen* floors above the street. Emphasizing that many murderers have *eluded* punishment and then killed again, they claim *it's* time to get *tough* on crime. During the *course* of the next few months, I will try to decide *who's* right.

4. Have students pronounce correctly each word listed in **18a**. Ask students what mispronunciations they hear in the speech of others (not, of course, in their speech or that of their classmates). Some frequent mispronunciations are

disastrous	pertain	recognize
escape	prescribe	relevant
everything	probable	quantity or quality

5. Have students choose the correct forms:

a. If you expect to (*accept, except*) their dinner invitation, I'd (*advice, advise*) you to (*choose, chose*) some loosely fitting (*clothes, cloths*).
b. They usually serve five or six (*coarses, courses*) (*altogether, all together*), and the table setting (*always, all ways*) (*complements, compliments*) the food. Not even the diet-(*conscience, conscious*) are unimpressed by the (*desert, dessert*)—raspberry torte.
c. (*Sense, Since*) you can do no better (*than, then*) to dine in the (*presence, presents*) of such (*holy, wholly*) gracious hosts, my (*council, counsel*) is to (*precede, proceed*) with your plans to attend what (*maybe, may be*) a (*lessen, lesson*) in attention to every (*miner, minor*) detail.
d. Use (*your, you're*) best (*stationary, stationery*) to (*rite, write, right*) a thank-you note; a genuine (*complement, compliment*) (*formerly, formally*) given is (*all ways, always*) welcome.

6. Ask students to use hyphenated words as adjectives in listing five qualities that describe their ideal spouse (such as *bluegrass-loving cowboy, well-groomed botanist, a wife with a one-day-at-a-time philosophy of life*). Also ask students to use five *-ly* adverb-adjective combinations to describe their ideal instructor (*basically optimistic adult, totally organized lecturer*).

ANSWERS TO EXERCISES

■ **Exercise 1** (p. 185)   **Adding suffixes**

1. likely, safely, surely
2. excitable, exciting, excitement
3. coming, noticing, hoping
4. using, useless
5. continuous, courageous
6. careful, hopeful, useful
7. arguing, argument, arguable
8. completely, completing
9. desirable, noticeable
10. managing, management

■ **Exercise 2** (p. 186)   **Forming present participles and past tense**

1. admitting, admitted
2. bragging, bragged
3. concealing, concealed
4. gripping, gripped
5. hoping, hoped
6. jogging, jogged
7. planning, planned
8. rebelling, rebelled
9. stopping, stopped
10. auditing, audited

■ **Exercise 3** (p. 187)   **Adding suffices**

1. variable, pliable
2. funnier, carrier
3. various, luxurious
4. easily, finally
5. supplied, stayed
6. studying, worrying
7. paid, laid
8. livelihood, likelihood
9. friendliness, loneliness
10. usually, coolly

■ **Exercise 4** (p. 188)   **Forming plurals**

1. beliefs
2. theories
3. churches
4. geniuses [RARE: genii for "spirits"]
5. Kelly
6. baths
7. heroes
8. stories
9. wishes
10. forties
11. radiuses OR radii
12. scarves OR scarfs
13. wives
14. speeches
15. tomatoes
16. phenomena OR phenomenons
17. halos OR haloes
18. children
19. handfuls
20. rodeos

■ **Exercise 5** (p. 189)   **Spelling with *ei* and *ie***

1. piece
2. achieve
3. receive
4. neigh
5. freight
6. apiece
7. belief
8. conceive
9. their
10. deceit
11. niece
12. shield
13. weird
14. shriek
15. priest

■ **Exercise 6** (p. 196)   **Converting and hyphenating compounds**

1. a three-car garage
2. gum-chewing girls
3. rust-covered pipes
4. two-year-old cheese
5. bird-lovers' club
6. thirty-dollar books
7. week-long conference
8. problem-solving parents
9. flood-control dams
10. eight-lane freeway

■ **Exercise 7** (p. 197)   **Converting phrases**

1. self-knowledge
2. tobacco-chewing men
3. hickory-smoked ham
4. night-light
5. L-shaped
6. all-purpose brush
7. ice-covered trees
8. L.A.-Rome flights
9. three-day weekend
10. five-year-old computer

19

GOOD USAGE AND GLOSSARY

A common misconception about dictionaries offers a good starting point for discussion of dictionary making and attitudes toward language: *a modern dictionary tells us how words should be used.* Ask students what they understand *should be used* to mean. Then, ask students to give an example of a word that they think a dictionary will say is incorrect usage. Someone will undoubtedly mention *ain't.* Have students look the word up in three standard college dictionaries. (*American Heritage, Webster's New Collegiate*, and *Webster's New World* will probably be represented among the dictionaries students should bring to class that day. However, to ensure that those dictionaries are represented, instructors may wish to bring them.) Have students read the usage note for *ain't* from each dictionary. They may be surprised to learn that whereas the *American Heritage Dictionary* labels *ain't* nonstandard (followed by a long explanatory usage note) and *Webster's New Collegiate* labels it substandard, *Webster's New World* accepts *ain't* as colloquial for *am not.* Such an activity helps to break down the students' view of a dictionary as the authority on words and to point out that many dictionaries are descriptive rather than prescriptive. (Instructors may find it useful to explain the distinction.)

This is the time to give attention to the usage terms dictionaries use. When students are aware that lexicographers do not always agree about which usage label, if any, to give a word, they are ready to confront the differences in meaning among such terms as *colloquial, regional*, and *informal.* Have students note the usage labels employed by their dictionaries. For example, the *American Heritage Dictionary* lists the following labels (pp. xlvi–xlvii):

1. *nonstandard*—for words not considered part of "standard, educated speech"
2. *informal*—for words "acceptable in conversation . . . [but] not . . . suitable in formal writing"
3. *slang*—for informal, usually short-lived, words whose aim is "to produce rhetorical effect, such as incongruity, irreverence, or exaggeration"
4. *vulgar*—for taboo words
5. *obsolete*—for words "no longer used except in quotation or intentional archaism"
6. *archaic*—for words "that once were common, but are currently rare and are readily identifiable as belonging to a style of language no longer in general use"

123

7. *rare*—for words used infrequently because their synonyms are used instead
8. *poetic*—for words common to poetry but not to prose
9. *regional*—for words used by or associated with one particular area

As an introduction to a few basic principles of language study, such assumptions as the following give beginning writers perspective on language:

1. Language is symbolic.
2. Living languages change.
3. Language has system.
4. Language has hierarchies (sound, syllable, word, sentence, paragraph).
5. Speech, not writing, is primary; writing is the graphic representation of sounds.

For a discussion of common but incorrect notions about language, see "Facts, Assumptions, and Misconceptions about Language," chapter 1 of Thomas Pyles and John Algeo's *The Origins and Development of the English Language*, 3rd ed. (San Diego: Harcourt, 1982).

ACTIVITIES

1. Bring a number of dictionaries to class so that students can see the differences among them. If you are willing to lug it along, the two-volume edition of the *OED* almost always interests students. Other good choices would include Fowler, a dictionary of slang, any small pocket dictionary, and a specialized dictionary within a particular field, such as *A Concise Dictionary of Literary Terms*. Explain the differences among these dictionaries to your students and emphasize that your selection is only a small sample of the resources available to them.
2. Help students understand the limitations of dictionaries by reading to them the following passage from S. I. Hayakawa's *Language in Thought and Action*, 4th ed. (New York: Harcourt, 1978):

> The writing of a dictionary . . . is not a task of setting up authoritative statements about the "true meanings" of words, but a task of *recording*, to the best of one's ability, what various words have *meant* to authors in the distant or immediate past. *The writer of a dictionary is a historian, not a lawgiver.* If, for example, we had been writing a dictionary in 1890, or even as late as 1919, we could have said that the word "broadcast" means "to scatter" (seed, for example), but we could not have decreed that from 1921 on, the most common meaning of the word should become "to disseminate audible messages, etc., by radio transmission." To regard the dictionary as an "authority," therefore, is to credit the dictionary-writer with gifts of prophecy which neither he nor anyone else possesses. In choosing our words when we speak or write, we can be *guided* by the historical record afforded us by the dictionary, but we cannot be

bound by it, because new situations, new experiences, new inventions, new feelings are always compelling us to give new uses to old words. Looking under a "hood," we should ordinarily have found, five hundred years ago, a monk; today we find a motorcar engine.

3. Read students an extended definition, like Joseph Epstein's "What Is Vulgar?" or Margaret Mead's "New Superstitions for Old," and ask students to write a definition of their own. (See section **32**.)

4. As a follow-up to exercise 4, discuss the different connotations of the following words: *peaceful, placid, serene, quiet, still, unruffled, tranquil, untroubled, unmoved* and *inert*. Begin by asking which words sound the most and least attractive.

5. This list is a supplement to exercise 5. Have students give the etymology of each of the following words:

a. aloof	h. turnpike	o. lieutenant
b. cereal	i. tuxedo	p. meander
c. gargle	j. tycoon	q. suede
d. grape	k. cartel	r. vinegar
e. laser	l. dollar	s. wacky
f. sideburns	m. glamour	t. zoo
g. telethon	n. gossip	

6. Have students use their dictionaries to identify the languages from which each of the following words was borrowed:

a. bungalow	e. judo	h. taboo
b. chocolate	f. mosquito	i. yam
c. flamboyant	g. succotash	j. yogurt
d. gruff		

7. Ask students to mark the root and the prefix or suffix of each word; then have students use the root and another affix to form a word:

a. underground	e. interlock	h. circumvent
b. admit	f. creative	i. vision
c. converse	g. judgment	j. propel
d. bisect		

8. Give students an opportunity to compare dictionaries while they learn about the kinds of information dictionaries contain. Have each student bring a standard college dictionary to class. Begin the class by asking for the name of each dictionary and listing different titles on the board. Then ask students to help list the kinds of information contained in an entry: spelling, syllabication, pronunciation, stress, variant spellings, variant

pronunciations, abbreviations, inflected forms, etymology, definitions (or-dered by most common meaning or by historical order), part(s) of speech, usage label, examples of the word in context, synonyms, antonyms, usage notes. Shift attention from the entry to the entire dictionary by asking if the dictionaries contain the following and if so, where:

abbreviations
foreign terms
geographical names
population figures
male and female first names
names of famous people
names and locations of U.S. colleges and universities
charts of weights and measures
illustrations
forms of address in letters to public figures
a history of English
a chart of Indo-European and non-Indo-European languages
a glossary of usage labels
a chart of pronunciation symbols [Call attention to differences in the use of symbols by asking students for the symbols of the sounds italicized here: *th*ing, *sh*arp, *j*ustify, *f*ather, *a*sk, and *ur*ge.]

9. As a class activity, have students consult their dictionaries for

   a. the preferred pronunciations of *aunt, creek, exquisite, harass*
   b. the plurals of *criterion, elk, parenthesis, voodoo*
   c. the number of meanings for *in, plastic,* and *run* (verb)
   d. the usage label, if any, for *bib and tucker, keckle, once-over, potlatch, you-all, yummy*
   e. the parts of speech for *best, but, while*

10. To help students understand that dictionaries do not always agree even about spelling and that sometimes two spellings are equally correct, have students consult three dictionaries for the correct spelling(s) of the follow-ing words:

    a. focused   b. programed   c. alright

11. Using the dialect survey in Roger W. Shuy's *Discovering American Dialects* (NCTE, 1967), have students identify their speech and discuss why it is more difficult to define their dialects than those of their grandparents' time. Ask whether they think regional varieties of English will disappear.

12. Have students collect examples of jargon or gobbledygook and, for one example, provide a translation in plain English. The two examples here illustrate the kind of language students should look for:

a. Rarely have I known, hither-to, the unalloyed pleasure of being the recipient of so concentrated a demonstration of domestic felicity as was lavished upon this unsuspecting beneficiary of your matchless hospitality. Truly, your hearth is a lodestone for the weary wayfarer, and your threshold an entrance to unimaginable delights.

—a Hallmark thank-you card

b. Walking through the Soils Building at the University of Wisconsin in Madison, I stopped in front of a display case containing unusual soil and mineral specimens. One descriptive card read:

"Structure built by an avian engineer using solid waste (plastic, paper, tin foil); organic debris from vegetation; and mineral soil. The soil was compacted into a platy, stratified deposit which is essentially a series of crusts of reduced hydraulic conductivity. The structure, a segment of a concretion, is formed on a tree branch close to the canopy. It is an epiphytic pedological feature, whose fate is to be translocated by free fall to the soil surface, where it will eventually be incorporated into the soil, except that part which decomposes first."

Displayed in the glass case was a robin's next.

—READER'S DIGEST

13. Divide students into teams and ask them to translate the following sentences into the proverbs that are hiding within them.

a. It is recommended that you not cause the small, strong two-wheeled vehicle to be in a certain advanced position of the large herbivorous quadruped. [Don't put the cart in front of the horse.]

b. The diurnal ingestion of a certain red or green product rich with malic acid generally insures the avoidance of interviews with practitioners well versed in the mysteries of human anatomy. [An apple a day keeps the doctor away.]

c. Thou shalt not rivet thine eyes upon the oral cavities of large equine presents. [Don't look a gift horse in the mouth.]

d. Regardless of the fact that you are mentally perturbed, it is showing consistency of reasoning to defer from indulging in spontaneous grief mechanisms expressing profound dissatisfaction over the spillage of liquid produced by the mammary gland of all mature mammals after they have given birth. [Don't cry over spilt milk.]

e. The state of being away brings into existence increasingly evident positive emotional perceptions. [Absence makes the heart grow fonder.]

Each of these examples was composed by a student in freshman English. As a follow-up to this activity, ask your own students to choose another familiar saying and translate it into jargon or gobbledygook. During a subsequent class, read the best aloud.

14. Ask students to compile examples of jargon used by one group (such as truckers, grocery clerks, fast-food employees, computer programmers, pilots, or sailors) and to write a paragraph using as much of that jargon as possible.

15. Have students revise the following sentences according to the usage recommended in the **Glossary of Usage**.

   a. All the farther I had yet to drive seems to be alot since I had already driven four hundred miles that day.
   b. Its an awful long ways from South Dakota to Pennsylvania, especially on these kind of roads, when you're kinda tired plus you're suppose to be there before dinner time because your folks are waiting on you.
   c. Be sure and stop in Milwaukee if you're fixing to have a fun vacation.
   d. Hopefully, it's okay to show up unannounced if the visit's just only for a couple of hours.
   e. No amount of coaxing will make me liable to accept an itinerary that's different than the one Lee and myself planned. The reason is because the perfect vacation is an allusion alright, but each and every summer the affects of all them glossy summer-vacation brochures gets us to making plans for a trip superior than last year's.

ANSWERS TO EXERCISES

No answers are given for the dictionary exercises in this section because answers will vary according to the dictionary used.

■ **Exercise 9 (p. 211)**   **Rewriting to eliminate jargon**

1. We have a good plan for success.
2. Don't open these doors.
3. We will discuss with the client ways to get more ads on the air.
4. Muzak makes people feel comfortable.
5. We discouraged thieves.

20

EXACTNESS

Students frequently have difficulty distinguishing between denotation and connotation. Rather than saying that denotation is the dictionary definition (dictionaries frequently include connotations in the definitions of words), try having students arrive at the concept empirically. For example, write the word *Thanksgiving* on the chalkboard and ask students to suggest words or phrases to define it. Some of the suggestions will be denotations: national holiday, day for giving thanks. Other suggestions will be connotations: turkeys, huge meals, family get-togethers, pumpkin pies, and so forth. Ask students to list all the denotations in one column and all the connotations in another. Any number of words can be treated in this manner until students are comfortable with the two concepts. Some useful words are those for family members and other loved ones (grandmother, boyfriend, best friend), prized possessions (automobile, house, other items of value), authority figures (coach, police officer, Dean of Men/Women/Students).

Students also are often mystified by advice to make their writing specific and concrete. After working through examples of abstract and specific language, it is helpful to caution students that excessive detail can interfere with their writing just as much as abstraction can (see **23b**). Some instructors may also wish to look ahead to the sections on the paragraph (section **32**, particularly **32a**) and the whole composition (section **33**, particularly **33a**) so students recognize that exact diction serves a rhetorical purpose. In particular, students might be asked to consider that a writer must transfer ideas from his or her mind to that of a reader and that this difficult task must be done with no immediate opportunity for the reader to ask questions about what the writer has said. And if that were not enough, consider some other possible obstacles:

1. Uncertainty about what to say or how to say it
2. Unconventional use of words, either because of errors in grammar or usage or because of an overly personalized language
3. A complex message
4. An audience hostile to prose and/or to the subject
5. Audience distractions (television, the smell of food, conversation, a fire siren)
6. The differences between writer and audience in values, background, education, and experience
7. An audience using definitions of key words different from the writer's

Conscientious writers assume two things: first, that the message and the audience must both be considered; and second, that if readers can misread or misunderstand, they will (sometimes going so far as to lose the meaning

129

entirely). The choice of exact words is one important method for increasing the likelihood of the message's being interpreted as the writer conceived it.

The use of figurative language is another method by which writers make meaning exact. Metaphors and similes clarify the nature of something unknown or unfamiliar by comparing it to something familiar. For example, in "his tightly knit prose" the metaphor compares the intricacies of two structures: the securely intertwined loops of a sweater (the familiar) and the coherence of the author's writing (unfamiliar); the structure of both results from the pattern of connections.

Students, however, frequently have difficulty handling figurative language well either because they don't know how to integrate it with their ideas or because, recognizing the value instructors place on such language, they want to please. They can usually benefit from specific advice about using metaphors, similes, and personification: Does the metaphor (simile, personification) make the idea clearer? Is it consistent with the tone and approach of the essay?

Often defined as "figurative language gone stale," clichés are sometimes useful, particularly when they can be turned to the writer's advantage—as many professional writers use them. However, students are well advised to be alert for clichés in their writing and to be sure that if they do use a cliché, they have not simply employed it as a kind of formula.

When discussing clichés with your students, you should make a distinction between clichés and other commonly used expressions such as vogue phrases (e.g., "sincerely," at the end of a letter). As Paul Pickrel has argued in "Identifying Clichés" (*College English* 47 [1985]: 252–61),

> The rule of the handbooks—"Avoid hackneyed and overfamiliar expressions. Use fresh and vigorous language"—is worthless if it does not go on . . . to tell us how to distinguish between the familiar phrase that is hackneyed and dispensible and the familiar phrase that must be used as it stands because it embodies an essential habit of language. (252)

Students might profit in particular from the distinction Pickrel makes between clichés and proverbs:

> Proverbs are spare, worn down to the bone by the repetition of generations, incapable of being shortened by paraphrase. Clichés, on the other hand, are usually wordy, ornate even unto blowsiness, and paraphrase will shorten them as much as it will improve them. It is impossible to find a more succinct way of saying what is said in proverbs like "A rolling stone gathers no moss" or "Make hay while the sun shines," but it is the easiest thing in the world to turn "wend my weary way homeward" into "go home" or "burn the midnight oil" into "study hard."
> A proverb encapsulates folk wisdom; it summarizes a large body of experience with the greatest economy of means. A cliché is simply an elegant variation on nothing very much, a try for style that fails. (256)

Like clichés, allusions can help writers achieve exactness. However, also like clichés, they should be used only with deliberation. The purpose of linking familiar phrases from literature or the Bible with the writer's idea is to make a point or connect ideas in a way no other words or references could. Such citations are valuable only if the audience recognizes them and understands how they make the writer's meaning exact. For example, the sentence "Apparently believing that his sound and fury signified something, the incensed customer continued his harangue" contains a reference to Macbeth's words, but the reader must recognize the allusion and the difference between the original speech and the words in this sentence in order to understand the irony of the man's continuing harangue. Of course, allusions used to pad ideas or to show off the writer's background should not be included.

ACTIVITIES

1. To make vivid the point that a variety of interpretations of a given word are possible, ask students to close their eyes (but to stay awake) and to listen to the next word or phrase spoken. After the instructor says the word *dog*, students should describe what they pictured when the word was said. The instructor should ask questions to help students describe the image precisely (breed, size, color, age, name, stance). Repeat the exercise using *tree* and then *tropical paradise* to illustrate the range of experiences and backgrounds that color the images of what are perceived as simple words.

2. On the board write this sentence: *Lynn walked into the room.* Give students a few seconds to think of several synonyms for *walk* and then call on every student (row by row) for a word to add to the list. Collecting forty or more words provides ample opportunity to discuss connotation. The exercise may be repeated by collecting synonyms for *said* or by asking males to list synonyms for *female* and females to list synonyms for *male*. The latter exercise leads naturally into a discussion of what the various connotations suggest about how the sexes view each other.

3. Have students identify the similes, metaphors, or personifications in the following sentences and comment on the effectiveness of each:

   a. Deep down in that pocket where his heart hid, he felt used. . . . The one sane and constant person he knew had flipped, had ripped open and was spilling blood and foolishness instead of conversation.
   —TONI MORRISON

   b. Winter brings blizzards, hot tornadic winds arise in the spring, and in summer the prairie is an anvil's edge.   —N. SCOTT MOMADAY

   c. Like any encyclopedia, a great cathedral cannot be read at a glance. If one's time is limited, it is best to concentrate on a few particularly glorious chapters. At Bourges, these are the center portal of the west facade and the windows. These should be read slowly, with the aid of good binoculars. —New York Times

d. The balconies that jut out of modern apartment houses are empty stages, staring and lifeless compared to the old fire escape and its dynamic design of zigzag stairs and the teasing charm of potential danger when the metal steps were wet with icy rain. —KATE SIMON

e. Bailey didn't look up from his reading so she wheeled around then and faced the children's mother, a young woman in slacks, whose face was as broad and innocent as a cabbage and was tied around with a green head-kerchief that had two points on the top like a rabbit's ears. —FLANNERY O'CONNOR

f. A mass of Latin words fall upon the facts like soft snow, blurring the outlines and covering up the details. —GEORGE ORWELL

4. Put several incomplete overused similes on the board, such as "smooth as . . . ," "thin as . . . ," or "hard as. . . . " Students should be quick to complete the expressions. As soon as they have done so, ask students to suggest similar expressions, writing them down on the board as they are offered. Fill the board as fully as you can within a few minutes, demonstrating how many trite expressions can easily come to mind. Then circle five of them and ask students to rewrite them (for example, "as hard as freshman English" or "as hard as my stepmother's eyes" for "as hard as a rock"). Read the best lines aloud to the class, and remind them that when figurative language is used in writing, it should relate to the context in which it appears: "As smooth as a shot of Jack Daniels" might work nicely when describing a college student attempting to pick someone up in a bar, but it would be ridiculous if used to describe a young child's skin.

5. Have students make a list of metaphors that use names of parts of the body. Such metaphors include

the *eye* of a hurricane   an *ear* of corn
the *brow* of a hill   the *foot* of a bed
the *nose* of an airplane   the *tongue* of a shoe
the *heart* of the matter   the *ribs* of a ship
bald cypress *knees*   the *hands* of a clock
the *face* of a cliff   the *elbow* of a river
a fine-*toothed* comb   a *cheeky* reply

Ask students to create similes for five of the italicized words.

ANSWERS TO EXERCISES

■ **Exercise 1** (pp. 228–29)   **Using exact words**

1. effects

2. childlike
3. flaunts
4. prevaricated
5. adopt
6. unfortunate
7. but OR; however,
8. intimated
9. seasonal
10. incredible

No answers are given for the rest of the exercises in this section because they will vary according to the dictionary used.

21

WORDINESS AND NEEDLESS REPETITION

Confronted by student prose in which nothing seems to happen, many English teachers offer variations on the advice given by George Orwell in "Politics and the English Language" (1946): "If it is possible to cut a word out, always cut it out." Writers can often profit from this advice, which reflects the position *Harbrace* takes in **21a**. But when offering this advice to students, instructors should present it as a concern more appropriate for revision than for drafting. Too much early emphasis upon the importance of being concise can lead to writer's block: students who are made to feel that *every* word must *always* count may be afraid to put anything on paper.

The key words in **21a** are *omit* and *meaning*. Reassure your students by pointing out that they cannot omit words until they have something to omit them from. Professional writers usually cut many of the words they have written when they revise their work, and then editors often suggest further cuts. Students can benefit from following a similar pattern: once students have composed a draft, they should have a clearer sense of the meaning they want to convey, and that, in turn, should help them distinguish the essential from the nonessential more easily. Moreover, while being concise takes time and trouble, pruning unnecessary words can be more fun than reaching for words to fill a blank page. With this in mind, you might help your students by suggesting that they deliberately write drafts that are at least a third longer than their assignments. They can then enjoy the luxury of crossing things out without necessarily worrying about being left with nothing to show for their work. And they may well discover that essential ideas emerged only after their drafts had exceeded the suggested word limit for the assignment.

Once beginning writers identify wordiness in their own prose, they are ready for systematic revisions. Simply cutting words often produces awkward or choppy sentences and restricts revision to one technique for intrasentence problems. However, a method that applies omitting, rearranging, and combining within and between sentences gives writers an orderly series of options:

1. A compound predicate is reduced to one predicate.

   a. They *called* her *up* and *asked* her to advise them about selecting roses for a hedge.
   b. They *asked* her advice about selecting roses for a hedge.

2. A main clause becomes a subordinate clause.

   a. They asked her advice about selecting roses for a hedge.
   b. *When they asked her advice about selecting roses for a hedge*, she recommended floribundas for a hedge that would bloom continuously.

3. A subordinate clause becomes a phrase.

   a. When they asked her *what roses to select for a hedge*, she recommended floribundas for a hedge *that would bloom continuously.*
   b. When they asked her about *selecting roses for a hedge*, she recommended floribundas for a hedge *of continuous blooms.*

4. A phrase becomes a word.

   a. When they asked her about *selecting roses for a hedge*, she recommended floribundas *for a hedge of continuous blooms.*
   b. When they asked her about *hedge roses*, she recommended *continuously blooming floribundas.*

5. Several words become one or are omitted entirely.

   a. When they asked *her* about *suggested* hedge roses, she *really strongly* recommended *a hedge of continuously everblooming* floribundas.
   b. When they asked about hedge roses, she recommended floribundas.

6. One sentence combines with another.

   a. When they asked about hedge roses, she recommended floribundas. She thought that for red roses they might like such varieties as "Europeana," "Vogue," and "Eutin."
   b. When they asked about hedge roses, she recommended three red floribundas: "Europeana," "Vogue," and "Eutin."
   c. "Europeana," "Vogue," and "Eutin" were the three varieties of red floribunda she recommended for their hedge.
   d. She recommended three red floribundas—"Europeana," "Vogue," and "Eutin"—for their hedge.

Words can smother thought, and too many words can alienate readers. Lean, muscular prose wastes no words. Nothing intervenes between ideas and diction, thus keeping ideas vigorous. Wordy prose is often flabby, revealing inadequate control over the expression of ideas. Most modern guides to style thus encourage writers to convey the most ideas in the fewest possible words. According to Strunk and White's celebrated *Elements of Style*, 3rd edition, for example: "A sentence should contain no unnecessary words, a paragraph no unnecessary sentences, for the same reason that a drawing should have no unnecessary lines and a machine no unnecessary parts" (23).

This analogy between writing and engineering springs from emphasis upon function and dates from an era that—in literature, art, architecture, and interior design—was reacting against the lavish ornamentation favored throughout the second half of the nineteenth century. The teaching of composition should now recognize that few readers want to live in a literary Bauhaus. Although the clean lines of precise and functional prose are preferable to aimless clutter, they may be cold and comfortless at times. Just as there are occasions when Victorian gingerbread is preferable to the formal elegance of a Mies van der Rohe apartment building, so there are times when the rhetorical flourishes of a Dickens can be preferable to the studied simplicity of a Hemingway. If we dwell too much upon the importance of being concise, we may teach our students to reject much of the literature that is our gift from the past. (For an interesting reassessment of what is widely considered to be good prose style, see Richard A. Lanham, *Analyzing Prose* [New York: Scribner's, 1983].)

Some students may have trouble distinguishing "wordiness" from the careful development of an idea. Remind them that writers have a responsibility to be precise as well as concise, and that writing efficiently does not necessarily mean that one can always write briefly. Help students see that the distinction between "necessary" and "unnecessary" words often involves more than one concern. A word or phrase may be "unnecessary" for the mechanical transmission of meaning, but "necessary" for some other rhetorical purpose—such as providing details, creating a mood, or emphasizing a point. This lesson is best learned through the discussion of examples that appear within the context of specific reading assignments.

ACTIVITIES

1. Show students two versions of a piece of your own writing that became tighter through revision. Discuss the changes with them and ask if they think you cut too much or too little. Then consider asking their advice about a piece that you are still working on.

2. Have students use direct, economical prose to revise these sentences:
   a. There are quite a few preparations at home to get ready for even today's modern picnic.
   b. The last and final step is the job of loading the necessities and things into the car. In this day and age the necessities often include Frisbees and volleyballs along with the food. This is done so that people will have something to do before the meal.
   c. After the windy gust, all the Styrofoam cups and paper plates on the picnic table were in an upset position. The major reason why they were was because Beth hadn't had time to fill the cups with lemonade drinks and lay the silverware on the plates.

3. Exercises do not replace having students reduce the wordiness in their own prose. To reduce the routine of the one-writer–one- essay class hour, use a variety of approaches and have students work with sentences and paragraphs (reserve the revision of entire essays for homework assignments).

a. Have students number and write out or type (double-space to allow room for revisions) sentences from one paragraph of a recent essays. Then ask students to revise each sentence two ways. Have students exchange papers and check the rewritten sentences for wordiness. Finally, have the writer use the revised and corrected sentences in a paragraph.

b. Bring to class a handout of wordy sentences from students' writing. Ask students to eliminate the wordiness and tell which of the six steps they used.

c. Have pairs of students revise each other's paragraphs to eliminate wordiness.

d. Have two students work separately to revise the same paragraph; then, as a class, discuss which revisions are more effective. If pairing students would result in more than six or seven sets of paragraphs to discuss, consider having groups of three to six students work together to produce one revised paragraph.

4. Have students decide which passage contains needless repetition and revise it. Then ask them to explain why the repetition in the other passage is effective.

a. My happiest memory of fall is my memory of shuffling through the fall leaves that had fallen and that lay in big drifts across the sidewalks.

b. He laughs all the time: he laughs when he gets hurt; he laughs when he is praised; he laughs when he is idle; he laughs when he works.

5. Help students understand the effective use of repetition (**29e**) by discussing the following paragraph from "I Want a Wife," by Judy Syfers:

> I want a wife who will take care of *my* physical needs. I want a wife who will keep my house clean. A wife who will pick up after my children, a wife who will pick up after me. I want a wife who will keep my clothes clean, ironed, mended, replaced when need be, and who will see to it that my personal things are kept in their proper place so that I can find what I need the minute I need it. I want a wife who cooks the meals, a wife who is a *good* cook. I want a wife who will plan the menus, do the necessary grocery shopping, prepare the meals, serve them pleasantly, and then do the cleaning up while I do my studying. I want a wife who will care for me when I am sick and sympathize with my pain and loss of time from school. I want a wife to go along when our family takes a vacation so that someone can continue to care for me and my children when I need a rest and change of scene.

6. Provide students with copies of the following two sentences by Martin Luther King. Read them aloud so that students can better appreciate their effect. Ask if the second sentence is "wordy" or if its unusual length can be justified by the writer's purpose:

Perhaps it is easy for those who have never felt the stinging darts of segregation to say, "Wait." But when you have seen vicious mobs lynch your mothers and fathers at will and drown your sisters and brothers at whim; when you have seen hate-filled policemen curse, kick, and even kill your black brothers and sisters; when you see the vast majority of your twenty million Negro brothers smothering in an airtight cage of poverty in the midst of an affluent society; when you suddenly find your tongue twisted and your speech stammering as you seek to explain to your six-year-old daughter why she can't go to the public amusement park that has just been advertised on television, and see tears welling up in her eyes when she is told that Funtown is closed to colored children, and see ominous clouds of inferiority beginning to form in her little mental sky, and see her beginning to distort her personality by developing an unconscious bitterness toward white people; when you have to concoct an answer for a five-year-old son who is asking, "Daddy, why do white people treat colored people so mean?"; when you take a cross-country drive and find it necessary to sleep night after night in the uncomfortable corners of your automobile because no motel will accept you; when you are humiliated day in and day out by nagging signs reading "white" and "colored"; when your first name becomes "nigger," your middle name becomes "boy" (however old you are) and your last name becomes "John," and your wife and mother are never given the respected title "Mrs."; when you are harried by day and haunted by night by the fact that you are a Negro, living constantly at tiptoe stance, never quite knowing what to expect next, and are plagued with inner fears and outer resentments; when you are forever fighting a degenerating sense of "nobodiness"—then you will understand why we find it difficult to wait.

ANSWERS TO EXERCISES

■ Exercise 1 (p. 243)   Revising to eliminate wordiness

Answers will vary somewhat.

1. The exact date is not known.
2. During the last two innings, many senseless mistakes occurred.
3. Long lines of starving refugees were helped by Red Cross volunteers.
4. Perhaps the chief cause of obesity is lack of exercise.
5. The skyscrapers form a silhouette against the evening sky.

■ Exercise 2 (p. 243)   Substituting one or two words for long phrases

1. now OR today OR nowadays
2. can sing
3. believed
4. seriously
5. before
6. appeared
7. near
8. can OR may break
9. while
10. too expensive

■ **Exercise 3** (p. 243)   **Striking out unnecessary words**

1. It seems obvious.
2. Because Larry was there, the party was lively.
3. All these oil slicks, massive or not, do damage to the environment.
4. As for biased newscasts, I realize that reporters have to do some editing, though they may not use the finest judgment when underscoring some stories and downplaying others.

■ **Exercise 4** (pp. 244–45)   **Condensing sentences**

1. These are dangerous pitfalls.
2. This is an aggressive act.
3. It was a carefully planned garden.
4. It was a passionately delivered speech.
5. Her husband's dishes are not as good as her father's.
6. The students' ideas were different from the advertiser's.
7. Inevitably, corporations produce goods to make a profit.
8. Predictably, before an election legislators reduce taxation to win the approval of voters.
9. A prolabor group wants two-month vacations.
10. One anti-"nuke" editorial stressed the need for state-controlled plants.

■ **Exercise 5** (p. 245)   **Reducing the number of words**

Answers will vary. The following are possibilities.

1. These invisible hazards cause many fatal accidents.
2. The United States was being invaded by foreign investors buying up farms.
3. Although my parents did not approve, I married Evelyn last June.
4. The fire chief recommended that wooden shingles not be used on homes.

■ **Exercise 6** (pp. 246–47)   **Eliminating wordiness and needless repetition**

1. The manager returned the application because of illegible handwriting.
2. It is difficult today to find a chemist who shows as much promise as Joseph Blake.
3. From time to time, a person needs to remember that anybody who is learning to walk has to put one foot before the other.
4. The yelling of fans in the stadium is so deafening that I stay home and watch the games on TV.
5. A distant hurricane or a seaquake can cause a tidal wave.
6. A comedy of intrigue (or of situation) relies on action rather than on characterization.
7. In my family, schoolwork came first, chores second, fun and games next, and discussions last.
8. Numerous products can be made from tobacco. Its nicotine is used in pesticides, and its sugar helps control blood pressure.

22

OMISSION OF NECESSARY WORDS

Whether omissions of necessary words result from the hurried, inaccurate recording of thoughts or the accurate recording of speech patterns, the effect is the same—a sentence that reads awkwardly and withholds a complete idea, thereby distracting the reader's attention until the omitted word is restored.

Two errors should receive special attention since they are made by students who usually proofread carefully for other omissions:

1. Prepositions omitted after verbs or other words—These omissions thwart the logical completion of the sentence, for example, *neither amused [by] nor interested in any explanation; overcome [by] and grateful for the comforting words; along [with] or in place of the salad.*

2. Elements in a comparison omitted—Comparisons are complete when the two subjects and the point of comparison are present. Thus, in the example in **22c**, *snow here* and *snow in Miami* are the subjects and *scarcity* is the point of comparison. But a sentence like *Wool is better for carpets* lacks the second subject, so that the point of comparison (*better*) is meaningless, yet such sentences occur frequently in commercial advertising as well as in students' writing.

Students may have difficulty understanding that there is a difference between the omission of necessary words and the deliberate omission of words that can be clearly understood from the context in which they might have appeared. You might supplement section **22** with a discussion of elliptical clauses and elliptical construction. An elliptical clause is a grammatically incomplete subordinate clause in which omitted words can be supplied from the context—for example, "When [I am] dieting, I often dream of food." Elliptical construction is a type of compound construction that allows a writer to avoid repeating a word or phrase that has appeared already in a sentence—for example, "You may succeed, but he won't [succeed]." Elliptical construction can help make writing concise by eliminating unnecessary repetition. But such constructions work only when the omitted words are identical (and not simply similar) to words that do appear in the sentence. See activity 3.

ACTIVITIES

1. Have students collect and rewrite examples of incomplete comparisons used in ads.

2. Distribute copies of a short student essay from which necessary words have been omitted. Break students into groups and ask them to supply the missing words. Compare the suggestions. If students agree about the words that are missing, you can comment on how easily writers leave out necessary words through carelessness—and urge careful proofreading. If students offer different words to fill the same gap, you can discuss how a missing word can alter meaning. Then urge students to read their own drafts aloud at least twice before handing them in.

3. Help students to understand elliptical construction by showing how words can be omitted from the following sentences. Begin with examples of elliptical clauses:

a. Calculus is one of the courses [that] he failed.
b. When [he was] re-elected to office, Lincoln had only a few more months to live.
c. Although [it is] high in calories, ice cream is still my favorite dessert.

Then ask students to consider the following examples of compound construction, pointing out that each contains a word or phrase that can be omitted because the same word or phrase has already appeared in the sentence:

a. John writes better than Carl [writes].
b. I have my ticket and Sue's [ticket].
c. My sister has been studying all semester; my brother [has been studying] for the last two weeks.
d. You are well trained but [you are] poorly educated.

Now ask them to revise the following sentences, each of which suffers from flawed construction because omitted words are not the same as the words that do appear in the sentence:

a. I am smart; you bright; she brilliant.
b. Cather's novels are widely admired, but her poetry seldom read except by scholars.
c. Lawyers protect their clients, but a judge the law.
d. Gandhi was planning a public protest; the British authorities his arrest.
e. The land belongs to the government, the buildings to private investors.

ANSWERS TO EXERCISES

■ **Exercise 1** (p. 250)   **Supplying needed words**

1. Sheila *that* Richard
2. kind *of* course
3. *During* the winter

4. *and* then OR dollar; then *she*
5. was *that* my / pair *of* shoes
6. ask *for* nor
7. Fires *that* [OR *which*] had
8. referred to *was* OR book *to* which
9. exception *that* [OR *which*] proves
10. variety *of* spices

■ **Exercise 2** (pp. 251–52)   **Supplying needed words**

1. They *have* [OR *had*] been trying
2. The consumers *had* better listen
3. Ed's income is less than *that* of his wife.
   OR Ed's income is less than his wife's.
4. Bruce admires Cathy more than Aline *does*.
   OR Bruce admires Cathy more than *he does* Aline.
5. Fiberglass roofs are better *than these*. [Answers will vary.]
6. as any *other* place.
7. I always have *liked*
8. One argument was as bad *as*
9. The ordinance never has *been*
10. more than the cranky young nurse *does*.
    OR more than *he does* the cranky young nurse.

■ **Exercise 3** (p. 252)   **Supplying needed words**

1. I had *in* my senior year a strange type of virus.
2. As far as Boston is *concerned*, I could see *that* the people
3. The group is opposed *to*
4. It *is* good to talk to a person *who* has a similar problem.
5. as mild as *that in* Louisiana. OR as mild as *Louisiana's*.
6. The concert we attended last night was so wonderful *that* . . .
   OR The concert we attended last night was wonderful.
7. The lawyer had to prove *that*
8. the hole *through* which the rabbit escaped.
9. If Jack gets a job *for* which
10. people, and *they were* still coming.

23

SENTENCE UNITY

Sentences that lack unity betray the writer's commitment to a central idea. While unrelated detail is probably more easily identified than excessive detail, students should understand that both undermine the effectiveness of the sentence—one by introducing extraneous material and the other by overwhelming the central idea in an attempt to provide adequate development for it. Apparently unrelated ideas are difficult for writers to identify since they understand the relationship and believe that what is obvious to them is obvious to the audience. A simple two-part question will help students avoid the problems: What is the relationship among ideas and how have I indicated it?

A mixed construction, which results from the use of parts of at least two possible statements, can be corrected by having students sort out the possibilities and choose the one they judge more effective. Here are two examples (from exercise 3):

> Because her feet are not the same size explains the difficulty she has finding shoes that fit.
> 1. Because her feet are not the same size, she has difficulty finding shoes that fit.
> 2. Having feet that are not the same size explains the difficulty she has finding shoes that fit.

> Does anyone here know why George resigned or where did he find a better job?
> 1. Does anyone here know why George resigned or where he found a better job?
> 2. Why did George resign and where did he find a better job?

Students may wish to rewrite the sentences themselves to produce other alternatives.

When the logical connections between subject and verb break down, the result is faulty predication (**23d**). Many, but not all, instances of faulty predication result from failure to recognize that the linking verb *be* serves as a kind of linguistic equal sign. Others are simply the result of confusion: in a sentence such as *Lions map the territory they claim for their own*, the predication is faulty because lions cannot map anything. Substituting the more accurate *mark* clears up the faulty predication.

When teaching **23e(2)**, you might add *contrast* and *enumeration* to the list of ways writers can define a term. Extended definitions often clarify what a word means by showing what it does *not* mean (contrast) or by listing its characteristics (enumeration). A formal definition might also explain the origins of a word. Refer students to **32d(7)** for additional discussion of definition within the Handbook.

You might end your discussion of sentence unity by reminding students that paragraphs and essays must be unified just as sentences must be unified. In addition to avoiding the mixed constructions and faulty predication that can destroy the unity of a sentence, writers should be careful to maintain unity of person, mood, voice, and tense (as shown in section **6** on agreement and section **27** on shifts) as they move from one sentence to another. And rather than simply avoiding mixed metaphors, they can help unify a piece of writing by using an extended metaphor—which means offering variations on one metaphor throughout a paragraph or essay. You should note, however, that extended metaphors can tire a reader's patience if extended too far. (See activity 4.)

ACTIVITIES

1. Ask students to discuss how the relationships between the ideas in the following sentences are not clear. Ask them to revise the sentences for unity.

   a. Although the visiting professor has different and refreshing views, I played badminton on September 20.
   b. The food in the cafeteria has been the subject of many jokes, and most college students do not look underfed.
   c. The ancient name for Paris, a city which has an annual rainfall of over 20 inches, was Lutetia.
   d. Brown hyenas are very shy animals and have an interesting social organization.

2. Ask students to discuss how to eliminate excessive detail from the following sentences:

   a. During eight o'clock classes last Thursday in room 331 of MacIntyre Hall which is where most of the history classes are held, the debate team held a practice debate to which all of the students enrolled in speech classes were invited.
   b. When I was about ten, tall for my age, and living in a house built during the colonial period, little of which remains today, I often walked several miles to play with neighbor children.
   c. As the classic old boat made of wood rather than the more modern fiberglass turned into the wind which was blowing about eight or ten miles an hour, the new sails were hoisted by the crew who were all medical students at the university but who welcomed the chance to get away from their heavy study schedules for an afternoon and perhaps an evening.

3. Have students identify mixed metaphors, mixed constructions, or faulty predication in the following sentences before having them revise the sentences. This exercise works well as a group activity.

    a. Although Sarah was burning the candle at both ends, she realized the need to keep her nose to the grindstone.

    b. Does the chairman of the board ride in a limousine or carry his briefcase to the office?

    c. The use of biomechanical research developed options to organ transplants.

4. Show students how an extended metaphor can help unify an essay by drawing their attention to the first and last paragraphs in Dennis Kelley's research paper on *Walden* (pages **453–79**). Ask if they can identify any other nautical metaphors in the essay. (Paragraph **2** includes references to "tide" and "sailing"; paragraph **4** to "dead in the water"; paragraph **7** includes a reference to being blown out of the water.) Because seasick reviewers felt that Dennis had gone overboard with this metaphor, he cut three lines from an earlier draft: "As the mild tide of interest ebbed, *Walden* ran aground" (originally included after "minor writer" in paragraph **9**); Thoreau "now became the captain of a shipload of social critics. Ideas that seemed revolutionary in the 1850s "found a receptive audience" became "Thoreau found a receptive audience . . ." (paragraph **17**); and "The sturdy ship launched by Thoreau in 1854 is still riding high" became "Walden remains popular today . . ."(paragraph **18**). Advise your own students that an extended metaphor can become a type of overwriting if carried too far.

5. As a supplement to exercise 4 on page **260**, provide students with model essays of definition (which can be found in *The Resourceful Writer*, second edition, or any mode-organized reader for freshman English). Then ask students to write an extended definition that will include an antonym, a dictionary definition, a carefully described example, a contrast with a word that might be confused with the term being defined, and information on the term's origins.

ANSWERS TO EXERCISES

■ **Exercise 1 (p. 254–55) Rewriting to relate ideas**

1. There are so many types of bores at social gatherings that I prefer quiet evenings at home.
2. A telephone lineman who works during heavy storms can prove a hero. Of course, cowards can be found in any walk of life.
3. Jones, who spends most of his time driving his Jaguar, was advised to hire a tutor in French immediately.

4. Professor Stetson, who likes to draw parallels between modern men and literary characters, pointed out that Macbeth was not the only man to succumb to ambition.
5. Yellowstone National Park offers truly unusual sights, but I was unable to visit there last summer because I couldn't get any vacation time.

■ Exercise 2 (p. 256)   Eliminating excessive detail

1. The fan that Joan bought for her brother arrived today. He frets about any temperature that exceeds seventy.
2. Flames from the gas heater licked at the chintz curtains.
3. After finishing breakfast, Sigrid called the tree surgeon.
4. At last I returned the library book that I had used for my Tuesday report.
5. A course in business methods helps undergraduates to get jobs and tests their fitness for business.

■ Exercise 3 (p. 258)   Eliminating faulty, mixed, or awkward constructions

1. Another famous story from American history is the one about Christopher Columbus.
2. One example of a rip-off would be the addition of a butcher's heavy thumb to the weight of the steak.
3. To have good manners is to avoid saying or doing something tactless.
4. Like a bat guided by radar, Maureen was always careful in business dealings.
5. Could anyone be certain why George resigned or where he found a better job?
6. For Don, money does grow on trees, and he frequently shakes the limbs.
7. She has difficulty finding shoes that fit because her feet are not the same size.
8. I felt as insignificant as a grain of sand in the desert.
9. When children need glasses, they may make mistakes in reading and writing.
10. The National Weather Service predicted subnormal temperatures in late March.

■ Exercise 4 (p. 260)   Defining terms

The answers will vary.

24

SUBORDINATION

Subordination and coordination both involve combining two or more simple sentences to create a new sentence in which the grammatical relationship between the ideas is clearly defined. When one idea is subordinated to another, it is of lesser grammatical rank. That is, it operates on the secondary level of the sentence (as do adjectives and other modifiers). However, although a subordinate clause is of lesser grammatical rank, it is not necessarily of lesser rhetorical importance. Compare:

1. Sarah, who lived in Des Moines for six years, has just received her commercial pilot's license. [The subordinate element contains information unrelated to and of lesser importance than the main clause.]
2. As soon as Sarah flew to Seattle, Beth and I drove to Portland. [The subordinate clause establishes the time relationship and is just as important as the main clause.]
3. Although your request for a five-thousand-dollar raise has been denied, you will receive two more paid holidays. [The negative information in the subordinate clause is rhetorically more important than the positive information in the main clause.]

When two simple sentences are coordinated, they are said to be of equal grammatical rank, and, ideally, they are of equal rhetorical importance. Occasionally, however, they may not be equally important rhetorically. Compare:

1. Tom sent Judy's gift to Grand Isle, and Judy sent Tom's gift to Birmingham. [The two clauses contain information of equal grammatical and rhetorical importance.]
2. Tom canceled his trip to Grand Isle, for Judy had already left for Europe. [Although both clauses are of equal grammatical importance, the first clause might well be of greater rhetorical importance than the second.]

Students often do not understand that coordination normally establishes an equal relationship between clauses. Rather, they see coordination as a convenient way to link ideas without developing them. Believing that *and* is a transition that guarantees paragraph unity, beginning writers often link everything with and, creating prose that offers no relief for the reader. A useful stylistic point to emphasize to students is that professional writers use a large percentage of complex sentences and that compound sentences are relatively rare.

For useful discussion of subordination and coordination, see chapter 3 in Mina P. Shaughnessy's *Errors and Expectations* (New York: Oxford UP,

147

1977) and chapter 4 in Joseph M. Williams's *Style: Ten Lessons in Clarity and Grace* (Glenview, IL: Scott, 1984).

ACTIVITIES

1. Give students a paragraph from a professional essay that includes examples of compound, complex, and compound-complex sentences. Ask them to rewrite the paragraph entirely in simple sentences by eliminating subordination and coordination but not eliminating any of the paragraph's content. Ask them to compare the two versions and consider how boring writing would become if writers were never able to subordinate or coordinate ideas. Then break the class into small groups, assigning each the responsibility for introducing appropriate subordination and coordination into selected student paragraphs that are dominated by short, simple sentences.

2. Ask students to write a main clause containing a subject, a verb, and a direct object. Have students exchange papers and add one subordinate clause. Repeat, again asking for a subordinate clause. Repeat, asking for one set of coordinate elements. Have students read and discuss the resulting sentences.

3. Ask students to write down three goals they want to achieve before the end of the semester. Have them rank the goals from most important to least important and then write a sentence using subordination to reflect the ranking. Ask them to follow the same procedure for three goals to be met within a year, three before they graduate, and three within five years after graduation.

4. Ask students to combine the following sentences in as many ways as possible and to identify which idea is stressed in each. Have them begin with coordination and then move to subordination.

   a. (1) I was walking through the park.
      (2) An elderly lady was walking through the park.
      (3) A thief stole the elderly lady's purse.

   b. (1) Marlene is a dentist.
      (2) Her hobby is breeding tropical fish.
      (3) Her husband is a film editor.
      (4) His hobby is baking bread.

   c. (1) Eloise and Donald were waiting for a table.
      (2) Two women dressed in evening gowns were seated at a table beside the window.
      (3) A waiter spilled tangerine sherbet on one woman.

5. Too many elements in a sentence impede the main idea. Have students suggest revisions for these sentences:

a. The family who bought the custom-designed ranch house that Avery Realty had on the market for eight months when sales were especially slow decided to ask that the previous owners return the water softener which was to remain in the house.

b. Wearing the furry hat that his grandchildren who lived in Bismarck had given him when they learned that the only one he had was a green felt one that belonged to his brother who knew how cold North Dakota winters were, Carl walked to the diner where the owner cooked breakfast and said that a hungry man could eat three eggs as easily as two, so three eggs were what a customer would always get.

6. Ask students to make the following sentences more positive by subordinating negative information presently stressed in a main clause:

a. Although your essay is well written, your topic is uninteresting.

b. The African elephant is still endangered in its natural habitat despite recent efforts to control poaching.

c. You need to lose weight if you want to live longer.

d. Because the city is building two new schools, your taxes will be higher next year.

e. After having enjoyed a wonderful meal, I was sorry that the restaurant was so expensive.

Now ask students to revise the following sentences so that negative information is emphasized:

a. Although he embezzled thousands of dollars from the company, John was always well-liked by his colleagues.

b. After a frightening heart attack, Margaret decided to eat a healthier diet.

c. Desperate to pass the course, Karen studied all week for the final exam.

d. Robots can make factories more efficient because they eliminate many jobs.

e. Although it was destroyed by bombing during the Second World War, Dresden now has a number of carefully restored buildings.

ANSWERS TO EXERCISES

The following revisions are suggestions. Many other revisions for subordination are possible.

■ **Exercise 1** (p. 264) **Using subordination to combine short sentences**

[1,2] Now that I have just read *The Idea of a University*, I am especially interested in Newman's views regarding knowledge. [3,4,5] Newman says that

knowledge is a treasure in itself, that it is its own reward, not just a means to an end. [6,7,8] Before reading this essay, I had looked upon knowledge only in terms of practical results—such as financial security. [9,10] Now I accept Newman's definition of knowledge, which is worth pursuing for its own sake.

■ **Exercise 2** (p. 265)   **Using subordination to improve sentence unity**

1. After she had selected a lancet and sterilized it, she gave the patient a local anesthetic and lanced the infected flesh.
2. I did not hear the telephone ring yesterday because I was taking a shower, but I got the message in time to go to the party.
3. Although an oncoming bus crowded a truckload of laborers off the road when the two ambulances tore by, nobody got hurt.
4. Because Jean Henri Dunant, a citizen of Switzerland, felt sorry for Austrian soldiers wounded in the Napoleonic Wars, he started an organization, which was later named the Red Cross.
5. Stressing career education, the administrators not only required back-to-basics courses but also kept students informed about job opportunities.

■ **Exercise 3** (p. 267)   **Simple, compound, and complex sentences**

Answers will vary.

1. a. The men were sentenced to six years in prison for smuggling marijuana into Spain.
   b. The men smuggled marijuana into Spain, so they were sentenced to six years in prison.
   c. The men who smuggled marijuana into Spain were sentenced to six years in prison.
2. a. After condemning the property, the council ordered the owner's eviction.
   b. The council first condemned the property; then, it ordered the owner's eviction.
   c. After the council condemned the property, it ordered the owner's eviction.
3. a. Having applied for a patent on his invention, Uncle Oliver learned of three hundred such devices already on the market.
   b. Uncle Oliver applied for a patent on his invention, but he learned of three hundred such devices already on the market.
   c. When Uncle Oliver applied for a patent on his invention, he learned of three hundred such devices already on the market.
4. a. Delaying every tourist, the border guards carefully examined passports and luggage.
   b. The border guards delayed every tourist, for they carefully examined passports and luggage.
   c. The border guards delayed every tourist while they carefully examined passports and luggage.

25

MISPLACED PARTS AND DANGLING MODIFIERS

This section can be fun to teach, since misplaced parts and dangling modifiers are often amusing. You might begin teaching misplaced parts and dangling modifiers by sharing humorous examples with your students. Such examples clearly reveal how faulty sentence structure can make a writer seem foolish. (See activities 1 and 2.) Once students have grasped that misplaced or dangling modifiers can undermine meaning, they should be better prepared to consider examples in which error is less readily apparent. (See activity 6.) Although context often enables readers to decipher badly structured sentences, an awareness of the problems discussed in section **25** can help students understand a fundamental truth about language: the meaning of the words we use is usually determined by the order in which we use them.

The split infinitive, **25a(5)**, is a good example of a "rule" that is often misunderstood. The key word is "awkward"; it implies the existence of split infinitives that are *not* awkward. In taking this position, *Harbrace* recognizes the importance of flexibility when deciding questions of syntax. Instructors who were raised to believe that an infinitive can never be split might note that the need for flexibility on this point was recognized even in the golden age of prescriptive grammar. According to Simon Kerl's *A Common-School Grammar* (1868), "It is *generally* [emphasis added] improper to place an adverb between *to* and the rest of the infinitive."

ACTIVITIES

1. Ask students to identify the misplaced parts in the following sentences and suggest a better sequence of words:
    a. Many students dislike living in dormitories that have never been away from home before.
    b. Students are often charged high rents by landlords who want to live close to campus.
    c. Sarah gave her paper to the teacher in a plastic folder.
    d. Her teacher gave an assignment for organic chemistry which is easy.
    e. Students may have trouble getting loans to attend schools needing money.

2. Ask students to correct the dangling modifiers in each of the following sentences:
    a. Lying in a pool of blood, I saw the deer.
    b. Being obscene, I think pornography should be censored.
    c. After graduating from college, a job was hard to find.

    d. Watching television, the frequent commercials were annoying.

    e. Having grown up in Wisconsin, cold weather does not bother me.

3. Ask students to discuss the differences in meaning:

    a. (1) Only Jamie said that the novel was inspiring.

        (2) Jamie only said that the novel was inspiring.

        (3) Jamie said only that the novel was inspiring.

        (4) Jamie said that only the novel was inspiring.

        (5) Jamie said that the only novel was inspiring.

        (6) Jamie said that the novel was only inspiring.

    b. (1) Almost everyone was in tears.

        (2) Everyone was almost in tears.

    c. (1) Merely sweeping the floor once a week is satisfactory.

        (2) Sweeping merely the floor once a week is satisfactory.

        (3) Sweeping the floor merely once a week is satisfactory.

        (4) Sweeping the floor once a week is merely satisfactory.

4. Ask students to revise each sentence, eliminating "squinting" modifiers:

    a. Chewing gum slowly calms his nerves.

    b. People who chew gum in public frequently make a bad impression.

    c. I remember painfully removing gum that had stuck to my shoes.

    d. Scraping often takes more patience than I have.

    e. Let's remember to have always guaranteed gum remover just in case we have this problem again.

5. Ask students to revise the following sentences, eliminating split infinitives when doing so will make the sentence easier to read. If the modifier sounds awkward in any other position, the sentence should be left unchanged.

    a. The inflation rate is expected to not increase this year.

    b. The secretary of the Treasury testified that she expected interest rates to gradually move lower.

    c. Nevertheless, the cost of housing is expected to more than double in some parts of the country. [✔]

    d. Congressional leaders have promised to before the end of the year reduce the budget deficit.

    e. Many analysts expect the government to eventually raise taxes.

6. Ask students to identify the sentence modifiers [SM] and dangling modifiers [DM] in these sentences:

    a. During the discussion of favorite authors, James Michener and Kurt Vonnegut were mentioned first. [DM]

    b. Speaking of contemporary fiction, who has read Gail Godwin's novels? [SM]

c. Kevin suggested the stories of Elizabeth Bowen saying that Caroline Gordon's stories were also some of his favorites. [DM]

d. Considering the number of books published each year, I would like to read two or three a week. [SM]

e. Feeling fortunate to read two or three a month, the number of good books grows faster than I can keep up with. [DM]

ANSWERS TO EXERCISES

■ Exercise 1 (p. 270)   Placing single-word modifiers correctly

1. killed *only* one person
2. cost *nearly* a hundred dollars
3. Mercedes until he could *almost* see
4. daydreams *even* when you
5. show *hardly* any interest

■ Exercise 2 (p. 270)   Bringing related parts together

1. evening news in every part of the country carried
2. steaks with hickory sauce on them for his children
3. spaghetti on paper plates to hungry customers
4. clear on Monday why plagiarism is wrong

■ Exercise 3 (p. 271)   Eliminating squinting modifiers or needless separation of related parts

1. Because he was sleepy, Bill failed to lock the back door.
2. Melissa said she had gone last week. OR Last week Melissa said she had gone.
3. The game warden warned the hunter not to carry a loaded rifle in the car.
4. Arlene promised to pick up some milk when she went to the store. OR When she was going to the store, Arlene promised to pick up some milk.
5. The puppy advertised in last night's paper is eight weeks old and is a registered Labrador retriever.

■ Exercise 4 (p. 273)   Eliminating dangling modifiers

1. While I was waiting for my friends to say goodbye, the moon rose above the horizon.
2. We ended the meeting by standing and repeating the pledge.
3. Once mixed thoroughly, the ingredients must be frozen within an hour. OR Once you have mixed the ingredients thoroughly, you must freeze them within an hour.
4. Prepare to make an incision in the abdomen as soon as the patient is completely anesthetized.
5. After we had walked for six blocks, it began to rain, and we ran the rest of the way.

6. ✓
7. Having deteriorated in the last year, the streets were bumpy.
8. Just as we were ready to pitch camp, the windstorm hit.
9. ✓
10. Because their house had burned to the ground, the Welches had to build a new one.

26

PARALLELISM

A special kind of coordination, parallelism strengthens writing in several ways. Because it relies on repetition of grammatical structures, it is a particularly effective way to present complementary or contrasting ideas. When several complementary ideas are to be expressed, their similarity is heightened and coherence is improved if they are expressed in constructions that correspond to each other. (Some parallel constructions occur so frequently that they may not be recognized as such—compound subjects and objects, coordinate adjectives. Others call attention to themselves through the deliberate repetition of lengthy structures or the use of signal words such as *not only* and *but also*.) Arranging parallel items in climactic order emphasizes the items themselves as well as their degrees of importance. Finally, parallelism is perhaps the most common means of achieving balance and rhythmic flow in prose.

Of course, neglecting other techniques for achieving emphasis or coherence in favor of parallelism can lead to monotony, and parallelism is inappropriate when imposed on elements that are not parallel in thought. Reassure students by pointing out that you do not expect them to use parallelism whenever they write. But once they have been helped to see that parallelism can help make writing memorable, students should be encouraged to experiment with its use. Because students often have difficulty writing introductions and conclusions, you might advise them that the sense of ordered emphasis provided by parallelism can be especially useful when introducing a thesis or drawing a number of points together with a strong sense of closure. As suggested by activity 5, parallelism can also help unify a paragraph—a point you might return to when teaching section **32**.

ACTIVITIES

1. Illustrate how some quotations are often famous because parallelism has made them memorable. Possibilities abound—from Julius Caesar ("I came, I saw, I conquered") to John F. Kennedy ("Ask not what your country can do for you; ask what you can do for your country"). Here are a few from Winston Churchill:

   I have nothing to offer, but blood, toil, sweat, and tears.

   Never before in the history of human conflict was so much owed by so many to so few.

   We shall not flag or fail. We shall fight in France, we shall fight on the seas and oceans, we shall fight with growing confidence and growing strength in the air, we shall defend our island, whatever the cost may be, we shall fight on the beaches, we shall fight on the landing grounds, we shall fight in the fields and in the streets, we shall fight in the hills; we shall never surrender.

Ask students to find new examples, using a dictionary of quotations if necessary. Then ask them to choose one example and use it as a model for a sentence of their own that will be identical in structure but different in content.

2. Ask students to correct the faulty parallelism in the following sentences:
   a. I bought apples, oranges, a peach, and plums. [plums and a peach, or peaches and plums]
   b. He admired the Koreans for their intelligence and the way they could do things with their hands. [intelligence and dexterity]
   c. To eat the food in the school cafeteria, you have to be crazy, starving, or have nowhere else to go. [crazy, starving, or desperate]
   d. He was wearing an expensive jacket that was made of leather. [expensive leather]
   e. She likes traveling, to read, making a garden, and her younger brother. [traveling, reading, and gardening. She also likes her younger brother.]

3. Ask students to write down a series of parallel sentences beginning with *I know that.* Although students begin with the obvious (*I know that today is Tuesday. I know that tomorrow is Wednesday*), as a rule they move on to more reflective thoughts. In any event, they are practicing parallel forms in addition to characterizing themselves by the pieces of information they choose to include. Such constructions as *To _____ is to _____ or I remember when _____* may also be used.

4. Ask students to write one sentence containing coordinate nouns, verbs, infinitive phrases, participial phrases, and dependent clauses (*Wearing cowboy gear and swaggering through the crowd to advertise the rodeo and to promote Laramie Days, the father and son laughed and whooped as they greeted visitors and even while they sold tickets*). Have students label each coordinate pair or revise the sentence if any element is missing.

5. Ask students to identify the parallel elements (set here in boldface) in the following paragraph.

   In any event, it is **futile to investigate** the referee's role and **seek to determine** whether he should have intervened to stop the fight sooner. That is not where **the primary responsibility lies**. **The primary responsibility lies** with the people who pay to see a man hurt. The referee who stops a fight too soon from the crowd's viewpoint can expect to be booed. **The crowd wants the knockout; it wants to see a man stretched out on the canvas.** This is the supreme moment in boxing. It is nonsense to talk about prize fighting as a test of boxing skills. No crowd was ever brought to its feet **screaming and cheering** at the sight of two men **dodging and weaving** out of each other's jabs. The time the crowd comes alive is **when a man is hit hard over the heart or the head, when his mouthpiece flies out, when blood squirts out of his nose or eyes, when he wobbles under the attack** and his pursuer continues to smash at him with pole-ax impact. —NORMAN COUSINS, *Who Killed Benny Paret?*

6. Ask students to write a six-sentence paragraph using at least one set of parallel elements in every sentence. Then have students revise the paragraph, saving only the most effective parallel constructions.

7. Ask students to identify the parallel elements in the following sentence by Ernest Hemingway and ask them why they think Hemingway wrote such a long sentence. Then ask them if they think such a long sentence could be written without parallelism.

> If the spectators know the matador is capable of executing a complete consecutive series of passes with the muleta in which there will be valor, art, understanding, and, above all, beauty and great emotion, they will put up with mediocre work, cowardly work, disastrous work because they have the hope sooner or later of seeing the complete faena that takes a man out of himself and makes him feel immortal while it is proceeding, that gives him an ecstasy, that is, while momentary, as profound as any religious ecstasy; moving all the people in the ring together and increasing in emotional intensity as it proceeds, carrying the bullfighter with it, he playing on the crowd through the bull and being moved as it responds in a growing ecstasy of ordered, formal, passionate, increasing disregard for death that leaves you, when it is over, and the death administered to the animal that has made it possible, as empty, as changed, and as sad as any major emotion will leave you.

ANSWERS TO EXERCISES

■ Exercise 1 (pp. 276–77)   Underlining parallel structures

1. bees, birds, or bats.
2. bought by the yard and worn by the foot.
3. To say that some truths are simple . . . to say they are unimportant.
4. Reading through *The Origin* . . . eating Cracker Jacks and finding an IOU note.
5. mountains taller than Everest, valleys deeper than the Dead Sea rift, and highlands bigger than Australia.
6. who do not need flowers, who cannot be surprised by joy
7. Booms attract an oversupply; busts generate an undersupply.
8. Think before you speak. Read before you think.
9. They must accept the criticism of others and be suspicious of it; they must accept the praise of others and be even more suspicious of it.
10. had once tried, had once reveled, had let

■ **Exercise 2** (p. 277)　　**Inserting words needed for parallel structure**

1. and *of* Mt. Rushmore
2. and *to* sail
3. and *that* I could not
4. than *by* talking
5. hour or *for a* day OR hour or *a* day

■ **Exercise 3** (p. 278)　　**Using parallel structures for parallel ideas**

1. ✓
2. to play the piano and *to listen* to the Boston Pops
3. *productive people* and lazy people OR the ones who do most of the work and *the ones who hardly work at all*
4. was thoughtful *and quiet* when OR *in a thoughtful and* quiet mood
5. whether the trip would be delayed or *whether I would be ready to start on Friday*

■ **Exercise 4** (p. 279)　　**Writing sentences of parallel structure**

Answers will vary.

27

SHIFTS

Coherent prose—writing that is consistent, orderly, and logical—usually includes shifts made necessary by the content: the mood of verb changes from the indicative to subjunctive as the writer distinguishes a fact from a condition contrary to fact; direct discourse alternates with indirect discourse to indicate shifts from speech to thought. Such shifts are needed because they help develop the writer's message. A deliberate shift in tone or style can also provide humor or emphasize a key point. (See activity **4**.)

Some shifts, however, produce inconsistencies that destroy coherence by sending out conflicting information about the relationship of ideas. In the first pair of sentences in **27a**, for example, the shift of tense from *argued* to *discusses* conflicts with words showing that the activities are simultaneous (*during, while*). In the second example, the shift from subjunctive to indicative not only signals an illogical condition but also weakens the parallel structure. Such shifts as these obscure meaning and interfere with coherence, and they are among the shifts most likely to be made by students.

Shifts in person and number are also common in student prose, either because the writers have forgotten what pronouns they are using or because a particular passage inspires them to address readers directly in the second person. Students are often quick to correct this error once it is pointed out to them (and to look for it when reviewing the work of their peers), but instructors should comment on shifts with some caution. People often make mistakes when they are afraid to make mistakes, and emphasizing minor errors can sometimes lead students to make errors of another sort. For example, the fear of using sexist language, or uncertainty about agreement when using such words as "everybody," can lead to shifts in person and number—as can the earnest wish to avoid repeating the same word, or the determination to avoid using the first person *I* because some teacher declared that good writers never do so. When responding to student prose, recognize that while unnecessary shifts can be annoying, they seldom interfere with communication. *And when teaching* **27**, point to the regularity with which "needless" appears throughout this section—reminding students that writers, like drivers, often need to shift before they can get where they want to go.

ACTIVITIES

1. Ask students to identify the needless shifts in the following sentences:

   a. If I was poor and you were rich, would we still be friends?

b. David has been nominated to fill the vacancy, and almost everyone agrees he would be a conscientious chairman.
c. One should practice daily if you want to be a concert violinist.
d. Those who have done our best should never be apologetic.

2. Have students write a paragraph alternating the direct discourse of two speakers and the indirect discourse of a third person.

3. Ask students to correct any needless shifts and to justify any needed ones in the following paragraph.

> The Silver Dome Roller Rink is the Friday night hangout for teenagers in my hometown. As one made his way through the door, he is greeted with flashing lights, loud music, and a sea of kids skating round a rickety wooden floor. To the right was the counter where you rent your skates if you don't have a pair of your own. On the left is the refreshment area, where guys with cigarettes hanging out of their mouths tried to look tough whenever the girls are looking. It may sound boring now, but when I was in junior high school, I could think of no place I would rather be.

4. Use the following passages to illustrate how a deliberate shift in diction, style, or tone can be rhetorically effective. Then ask students to be alert for similar shifts in their reading.

> We must be a little wary when Brander Matthews tells us that Cooper's books "reveal an extraordinary fulness of invention." As a rule, I am quite willing to accept Brander Matthews's literary judgments and applaud his lucid and graceful phrasing of them; but that particular statement needs to be taken with a few tons of salt. Bless your heart, Cooper hadn't any more invention than a horse; and I don't mean a high-class horse, either; I mean a clothes-horse.
> —MARK TWAIN, *Fenimore Cooper's Literary Offenses*

> That pathology is grounded upon the doctrine that all human ills are caused by the pressure of misplaced vertebrae upon the nerves which come out of the spinal cord—in other words, that every disease is the result of a pinch. This, plainly enough, is buncombe. The chiropractic therapeutic rests upon the doctrine that the way to get rid of such pinches is to climb upon a table and submit to heroic pummeling by a retired piano-mover. This, obviously, is buncombe doubly damned.
> —H. L. MENCKEN, *Chiropractic*

> If you look at the composition of most ACLU affiliates and chapters, the overwhelming majority of members are lawyers, academics, enlightened businessmen, and a very few union officials. Blue-collar workers are seldom represented. The rights that have appealed most to workers are economic rights, and they don't see the ACLU and other civil liberties organizations as being particularly concerned with take-home pay and benefits. But when a worker can lose his job if he won't piss into a bottle, the Fourth Amendment, at least, becomes much less abstract, and that's why a coalition between the usual civil-liberties activists and workers is not only plausible but potentially effective.
> —NAT HENTOFF, *Presumption of Guilt*

ANSWERS TO EXERCISES

■ **Exercise 1** (pp. 281–82)   **Correcting needless shifts**

1. came
2. that city hall be the polling place
3. dragged it down again
4. Every witness questioned was taken to police headquarters.
5. live on your skin OR that one should bathe OR live on our skin and that we should bathe

■ **Exercise 2** (p. 283)   **Correcting needless shifts**

1. grabbed, snatched
2. it reduces stress and strengthens the body
3. ✓
4. whether we knew when he OR asked had Sam arrived
5. All cooks have their
6. there was somebody
7. he will make
8. It will be useful.
9. fortress; inside, the
10. and whether I wanted to go to the hospital

■ **Exercise 3** (p. 284)   **Eliminating needless shifts**

Answers will vary. The following are possibilities.

[1]He is a shrewd businessman, or so it has always seemed to me. [2]He has innocent-looking eyes in a baby face, and he speaks softly when he talks. [3]When questioned about who recommended he make a recent stock purchase, he answers, "I work hard and do a lot of research." [4]He does not mention one name; moreover, his reluctance to discuss business transactions is evident. [5]Take these comments for what they are worth; they may help you in your dealings with this sharp operator.

28

REFERENCE OF PRONOUNS

Faulty pronoun references are a common error in student writing, and you may want to address this issue early in your course by linking it to the discussion of case in section **5** and agreement in section **6** rather than deferring it until you turn to strategies for writing effective sentences.

The clarity of pronoun-antecedent references depends not only on agreement in person and number but also on the proximity of a specific, expressed antecedent for the pronoun. Thus, broad reference or intervening words may create ambiguity or obscurity that interferes with the reader's understanding of ideas. Although experienced writers may occasionally use broad reference, it rarely increases clarity and precision, so students would profit more by concentrating on the constructions that do. To ensure clarity, inexperienced writers may be advised to make each of their pronouns refer to a specific word.

Every writer, experienced or inexperienced, must recognize the different meanings of *it* in order to avoid confusing the reader. To change meanings when repeating a word within a sentence violates the reader's one-word–one-meaning expectation. Thus, these various meanings of *it* should not be placed near each other:

1. *it* as pronoun (*I read the book as soon as I bought it.*)
2. *it* as an expletive (*It is not surprising that he won a scholarship. It is impossible for them to sing on key.*)
3. *it* as an indefinite in expression of time or weather (*It is raining. It is noon.*)
4. *it* as an indefinite in the *it* + noun + *who* or *that* construction (*It is Larry who suggested a scholarship to honor Professor Williams.*)
5. *it* as a word (*One of the original forms of it was hit.*)

When teaching section **28**, recognize that context can often make vague or ambiguous pronoun references reasonably clear—especially to the writer who has provided the context. But remind your students that they should always consider the needs of their audience. Writers usually know what they are writing about, but readers often know only what writers tell them. A pronoun reference may seem clear to a writer well aware of what he or she is writing about, but unclear to readers who are further away from the material. Emphasize that clarity is essential to effective communication. Writers who expect their readers to "figure things out," may find their work going unread. Clear pronoun references are thus not only a courtesy to readers, they also help ensure the successful transmission of ideas.

ACTIVITIES

1. Ask students to revise each sentence in three ways: by repeating the antecedent, by using a synonym, and by recasting the sentence.

   a. When four-year-old Cory and two-year-old Brad play together, he always knocks down the blocks.

   b. Our daughter prefers looking through her microscope to cleaning her room. This takes up at least two hours every Saturday morning.

   c. As Greg and his uncle shook hands, he thanked him for the helmet and jersey.

2. Ask students to eliminate the broad reference in each of the following:

   a. They accepted our challenge to play softball once a week. This means we'll have to practice seriously if we expect to win.

   b. Her research paper was written, her finals had been canceled, and her aunt had sent her one hundred dollars. That was not the case for her roommate.

3. Have students revise each sentence to eliminate ambiguous, remote, or obscure references.

   a. If you say it, then it's true that he practices the piano ten hours a day.

   b. It's seven-thirty and it's still raining, but it will pass soon.

   c. Buy them a damask tablecloth or sew them some calico napkins and place mats. It won't matter because they are both nice.

   d. It's a fact that it hasn't been the same since Mary left.

   e. Because Chris had been promoted, it meant he was able to buy a new car. It was what he wanted.

4. Ask students to look for examples of broad pronoun reference in the school newspaper, locating one example that is clear and one that is unclear. Make sure they can explain why the references are clear or unclear. Then remind them to edit their own use of pronouns with this concern in mind.

ANSWERS TO EXERCISES

■ **Exercise 1** (p. 287)   **Eliminating ambiguous, remote, or obscure references to pronouns**

1. Kate's dislike for Christine did not end until Christine invited her to play tennis with her cousins from England. OR Kate's dislike for Christine did not end until she invited Christine to play tennis with her cousins from England. [Note: "her cousins" belongs to the woman who does the inviting;

if the cousins were also invited players, the sentence would read "until Christine invited her and her cousins" or "until she invited Christine and her cousins."]

2. function keys that are not clearly identified often cause confusion.
3. In his book, Morris does not say what to do.
4. peaceful. It is well-stocked with fish. Near the shore
5. As Mrs. Young was walking down the hill, she spoke to Betty. OR As Betty was walking down the hill, Mrs. Young spoke to her.

■ **Exercise 2** (pp. **289–90**)　　**Correcting faulty reference of pronouns**

1. ice melted all over the inside
2. but Chinese food is their favorite food
3. assistants can manage these machines easily and quickly
4. The essay says that
5. ✓
6. My decision not to attend the family reunion was very disappointing to my grandparents.
7. Anne told Theresa, "I have to go to Chicago next week."
8. might cover the roads and make them useless
9. Extra fees that seemed unreasonably high surprised many freshmen.
10. Ellen plays only Country and Western tapes in her car.

29

EMPHASIS

As noted in section **26**, parallelism can be an effective tool for achieving emphasis, and you might remind your students of this when teaching section **29** (and consider teaching these two sections consecutively). Help your students to see that emphasis is best achieved through a variety of techniques. In addition to using parallel construction, writers can choose a number of other ways to achieve proper emphasis for their ideas. They may deliberately structure a sentence so the key words appear either at the beginning or the end—the most important positions in a sentence—or they may use a periodic sentence, reserving the main idea for the end of the sentence and leading up to it with less important details. Similarly, writers arrange ideas in an order of climax to emphasize what they consider to be most important. These three techniques are similar in that they rely on placement to create the emphasis. But writers also achieve emphasis through diction—by choosing active verbs that are forceful and vigorous or by selecting important words for repetition. Finally, writers construct sentences of varied lengths to signal to readers that certain ideas are important.

Once students have decided which ideas are most important and why, they are ready to try out these techniques—one at a time or in combination—until they find the most effective one for each idea. Experimenting with the options, students eventually come to rely on three or four with which they feel most comfortable; they should be encouraged to use other techniques occasionally, too. Finally, students should look at each sentence in the context of the whole paragraph; revision is called for if any technique is overused or misapplied, obscuring important points through emphasis on those of less significance.

ACTIVITIES

1. As a supplement to exercise 1, ask students to revise the following sentences so they each end with a word worth emphasizing:

   a. She was an excellent student, if her grades can be relied on.
   b. She took all the courses an accountant needs to have.
   c. She is the best qualified candidate that we have interviewed so far.
   d. However, her references are weak, in my opinion.
   e. Let's look for someone with more experience before we hire her.

2. Have students analyze one body paragraph from a recent essay by answering these questions.

a. How many sentences does the paragraph contain?
b. How many words does each sentence contain? What is the average number of words per sentence?
c. In which sentences are important words at the beginning or end?
d. Which sentences are loose?
e. Which sentences use the order of climax?
f. Which sentences use active voice?
g. What are the one or two most important words? How often is each word repeated?
h. Not counting dangling modifiers, how many times are words emphasized by being out of usual order? Which sentences are inverted? How many of the inverted sentences are questions?
i. Which sentences are balanced?

After students answer these questions, ask them to list conclusions drawn from the analysis. Have them write a paragraph describing their methods of emphasis and suggesting one way to improve their arrangement of ideas.

3. Have students select four sentences from a paragraph in an essay that did not satisfy them. Ask students to rewrite the sentences using each of the eight techniques in section **29** for each of the sentences and to devise some simple tabular arrangement that will allow them to compare the resulting sentences. Students will see that not all methods suit every sentence.

   For each of the original sentences, have students select the revision they find most effective. Ask the students which methods they are most comfortable with. Have them put their favorite revised sentences into a paragraph and make any changes necessary for ease of reading.

4. Have students use a paragraph which they enjoyed writing or which they think is particularly effective. Ask them to rewrite the paragraph using any three of the eight emphasis techniques. Once they finish, ask them to label each use. Then have them rewrite the paragraph using three of the remaining five methods. Ask them which paragraph they prefer. The goal here is not to achieve flawless arrangements but to explore the possible combinations; the discovery of combinations that do not work well together can be just as valuable as the discovery of those that do.

5. Have groups of students write a paragraph consisting of one topic sentence, one or two sentences of support, one or two sentences of examples, and a concluding sentence. All sentences should be in subject-verb-object order, in active voice, in loose rather than periodic structure, and of approximately equal length. Ask groups of students to exchange and rewrite paragraphs.

6. Use the following example to illustrate the bureaucratic anonymity conveyed by the repeated use of passive voice:

Applications for student loans must be received by August 15th. All applications must be submitted in triplicate, and late applications will not be processed. A committee has been formed to screen these applications. The financial need of every applicant will be assessed, and their credit history will be reviewed. Three references are required. All applicants will receive notification once a decision has been made. Questions can be addressed to this office between 9:00 and 17:00 on Mondays, Tuesdays, and Thursdays, provided that they are directed to the appropriate loan officer. Your business is valued by Amalgamated Savings, the bank dedicated to personal banking services.

7. As a supplement to **29e**, read to students the short opening chapter of Dickens's *Hard Times*:

The One Thing Needful

"Now, what I want is Facts. Teaching these boys and girls nothing but Facts. Facts alone are wanted in life. Plant nothing else, and root out everything else. You can only form the minds of reasoning animals upon Facts: nothing else will ever be of any service to them. This is the principle on which I bring up my own children, and this is the principle on which I bring up these children. Stick to Facts, sir!"

The scene was a plain, bare, monotonous vault of a school-room, and the speaker's square forefinger emphasized his observations by underscoring every sentence with a line on the schoolmaster's sleeve. The emphasis was helped by the speaker's square wall of a forehead, which had his eyebrows for its base, while his eyes found commodious cellarage in two dark caves, overshadowed by the wall. The emphasis was helped by the speaker's mouth, which was wide, thin, and hard set. The emphasis was helped by the speaker's voice, which was inflexible, dry, and dictatorial. The emphasis was helped by the speaker's hair, which bristled on the skirts of his bald head, a plantation of firs to keep the wind from its shining surface, all covered with knobs, like the crust of a plum pie, as if the head had scarcely warehouse-room for the hard facts stored inside. The speaker's obstinate carriage, square coat, square legs, square shoulders—nay, his very neckcloth, trained to take him by the throat with an unaccommodating grasp, like a stubborn fact, as it was—all helped the emphasis.

"In this life, we want nothing but Facts, sir; nothing but Facts!"

The speaker, and the schoolmaster, and the third grown person present, all backed a little, and swept with their eyes the inclined plane of little vessels then and there arranged in order, ready to have imperial gallons of facts poured into them until they were full to the brim.

8. Use the following example to supplement **29h**:

Most control recommendations merely perpetuate the myth that with proper care a handgun can be as safe a tool as any other. Nothing can be further from the truth. A handgun is not a blender.

—JOSH SUGARMANN, *The NRA Is Right*

ANSWERS TO EXERCISES

■ **Exercise 1** (p. 292)   **Revising for emphasis**

Answers will vary. The following are possibilities.
1. Rock music affects the brain's alpha waves.
2. The shot came from Tim's direction.
3. Colorado Springs used to have a program to train young figure skaters for national competition.
4. Never before had it entered my mind to challenge the decisions Marla made or to offer ideas of my own.

■ **Exercise 2** (p. 293)   **Converting loose sentences into periodic, periodic into loose**

Answers may vary somewhat. The following are possibilities.

1. Despite everything, Italy remains cheerful.
2. Old habits and reflexes persist, even where people want better relations.
3. The Milky Way Galaxy, one of billions of other galaxies strewn through the vastness of space, is entirely unremarkable.
4. Nervously backing away from the arguments she should have had with my father, turning aside from the talks she should have had with me, she was then (as always, as she had been all her life) sweet and apologetic.
5. "I just oppose it if I don't know anything about something, or if I don't understand it," Mays told me, almost with pride.

■ **Exercise 3** (pp. 294–95)   **Arranging ideas in order of climax**

Answers may vary somewhat. The following are possibilities.

1. industry, efficiency, and wisdom
2. sun-drenched orchards, golden-flecked birds, and diamond-eyed children
3. his pet dog was tired of the leash, his taxes were going up, and his health was failing
4. The commission is faced with a deficit. Something must be done at once. Unless we act now, the city will be bankrupt in five years.
5. autographed books for teenagers, wrote letters to senior citizens, attended a community festival, and promised prosperity to all.

■ **Exercise 4** (p. 296)   **Substituting verbs for emphasis**

1. Frogs eat flies and mosquitoes.
2. My brother manipulates other people.
3. Every Saturday, cartoons teach children violence.
4. Bad pizza tastes like cardboard.
5. The professor usually requires that students write a ten-page paper each term.

■ **Exercise 5** (p. 297)   **Using repetition instead of synonyms**

1. Sometimes we cheat . . . ; sometimes we cheat . . .
2. . . . he gripes about the weather, gripes about heavy traffic, gripes about high prices, and gripes about his meals.

■ **Exercise 6** (p. 298)   **Writing emphatic sentences to show contrast**

Answers will vary.

■ **Exercise 7** (pp. 298–99)   **Writing short and long emphatic sentences**

Answers will vary.

■ **Exercise 8** (p. 299)   **Preparing for a discussion of emphasis**

Answers will vary.

■ **Exercise 9** (p. 299)   **Revising for emphasis**

Answers will vary. The following are possibilities.

1. Even if it might help us find a cure for cancer, I think creating viruses with DNA should stop.
2. Jokes referring to minorities or to religion offend many people.
3. All around us were fields of wild flowers.
4. Fools talk about each other; wise people talk about ideas.
5. When the fleeing robber tripped over the patrolman's foot, the gun fired.
6. At the close of a hot day, the storm broke in all its fury.
7. Milburn caught a fast pass and gained thirty yards before the referee blew the whistle.
8. Two years ago, late in the fall, in a shop on Tremont Street, I asked her to marry me.
9. Although their art was crude, some of the people showed a great deal of originality.
10. By the simple device of choosing the least likely suspect whose alibi is airtight, I can identify the guilty person in every Agatha Christie novel.

30

VARIETY

To understand the importance of variety, students need to be reminded about the importance of audience. Student prose often lacks variety simply because inexperienced writers have never been encouraged to consider this aspect of composition. Experienced writers vary their sentence lengths and types because they realize that variety helps to hold the attention of their readers; writers who do not consider their relation to readers may think variety nothing more than yet another abstract concern dreamed up by English teachers to justify bad grades.

When teaching section **30**, you should thus begin with a discussion of audience, reminding students that audiences change from one writing occasion to another, but asking them to consider what kind of writing holds their own attention and what kind puts them to sleep. Some students will focus on content, reporting that they like to read about sports or gossip, but others will raise issues such as "too many long sentences." You might recognize that writers sometimes have topics that are so interesting that their work will be read no matter how unimaginatively it is written. But you should then point out that writers do not always have that luxury, and that good writers know how to rescue a potentially dull subject. You might remind them, at this point, that some audiences are more sympathetic than others: a parent or a friend may want to read any letter they write simply because they wrote it; and English teachers will read to the end of almost any essay because that is part of their job. But you can then motivate students to consider introducing more variety into their prose by emphasizing how much writing goes unread and how badly writers feel when they discover that their letters, memos, and reports have been put aside because they did not hold someone's attention.

Unfortunately, there is another reason why student prose often lacks variety: students are often afraid to experiment with their writing because they are worried about making mistakes. A short, simple sentence offers less risk than a long compound-complex sentence. Coordination is less demanding than subordination. And keeping subjects and verbs invariably next to each other reduces the likelihood of making an error in agreement. The more teachers emphasize the perils of minor errors, the less likely they are to inspire students to take chances. If we want students to write engagingly about what is important to them—as opposed to writing correctly about what seems like a safe topic for a teacher—then section **30** is well worth teaching. But it is unrealistic to expect variety from students who have been taught that being correct is more important than being interesting.

Since most students begin their sentences with the subject and give little thought to the length of their sentences, sentence beginnings and varying sentence lengths are the first topics to discuss. In addition to the suggestions in **30b** for varying sentence beginnings, you might use these patterns:

1. an infinitive or infinitive phrase (*To cut the logs into firewood, he used a chain saw.*)
2. an introductory series (*The porcelain vase, the hand-painted platter, and the domed butter dish—these the movers packed in a special carton.*)
3. a noun clause as either subject or direct object (*That they kept their promise pleases me.*)

When discussing sentence lengths, try to avoid arbitrary rules, such as two longs, a short, a medium, and a long. Length should vary according to the kinds of information presented. Because it involves qualifications of and relationships among ideas, adequate development—explanations, illustrations, and other supporting material—tends to require sentences that are longer than topic sentences or transitions. But not all supporting sentences are long—an abrupt change in length may be used for emphasis. And not all topic sentences are short—they may include a transition in addition to the several ideas directing the paragraph. Variation for its own sake is ineffective; the goal is variation that attends to the needs of both the ideas and the audience.

Once they have been asked to consider the lengths of their sentences, many students will use coordination as the easiest way to avoid a series of short choppy sentences. You may need to return to section **24** for a review of subordination and to remind students that sections **26** and **29** also contain advice that can help them both structure longer sentences and determine what sentences are best left short. Although most students will readily understand the advantages of varied sentence lengths, you may need to review section **1** before you can expect successful experiments with sentence structure.

ACTIVITIES

1. Ask students to rewrite the following paragraph, introducing more variety into sentence length and type:

   The locker room is quiet before the game. The players are thinking about their goals. Their faces show tension. The tension increases as the game gets closer. The players are afraid of making a mistake. They don't want to let their teammates down. The atmosphere after a game depends upon who wins. There is great enthusiasm in the locker room after a win. But the players remain silent after a loss. Winners like to celebrate. Losers want to cry.

2. Have students write a paragraph of five or six sentences, each sentence beginning with the subject and consisting of twelve to fifteen words. Ask students to rewrite the paragraph, varying both sentence lengths and

beginnings. Then have students exchange papers and revise the original paragraph. Ask them to discuss the merits of each revised paragraph. (If class size prevents a whole-group discussion of all the paragraphs, divide students into groups of three and proceed as above.)

3. Have students analyze one paragraph from the first essay of the semester and one from the most recent essay by answering these questions for each:

   a. How many words does each sentence contain? What is the longest sentence? Why? (complexity of ideas, wordiness, and so on) What is the shortest sentence? Why? Where does it occur? (beginning, middle, end)
   b. Which sentences are declarative? interrogative? imperative? exclamatory?
   c. Which sentences begin with the subject? a sentence connective? an adverb? an adverb clause? a prepositional phrase? a participial phrase? an infinitive? an infinitive phrase? an appositive? an absolute? a series? a noun clause?
   d. Which sentences are simple? compound? complex? compound-complex?
   e. In which sentences do words intervene between the subject and verb?

   Asking students *which* sentences, instead of merely how many, requires them to look closely at patterns and to discover whether the variety, if any, is confined to one section of the paragraph or is evenly distributed throughout. Have students describe their findings by writing a one-paragraph summary for each paragraph analyzed.

4. Have students choose three ways of varying sentence structure and include them in the revision of one paragraph from a recent essay. Then have students revise the original paragraph again by using three different methods.

5. Ask students to supplement exercises 3 and 7 by choosing, from their reading, a paragraph with good sentence variety. Assign each student a teammate with whom he or she can exchange paragraphs, explaining to each other the context in which the paragraph originally appeared and how it illustrates variety.

6. Ask students to underline or highlight the first three or four words in every sentence in early drafts of upcoming writing assignments. Ask them to watch for repetitious sentence openings—not only the use of the same words, but also the repeated use of the same patterns.

ANSWERS TO EXERCISES

■ **Exercise 1** (p. 302)   **Studying the structure and variety of sentences**

Answers will vary.

■ **Exercise 2** (p. 302)   **Combining sentences to relate ideas**

Answers may vary. The following are possibilities.

1. A supernova appeared in 1986, the first time in four hundred years that one was visible to the naked eye.
2. Instead of buying a new car, Suellen bought a 22-foot sailboat that she could sail by herself.
3. With thirty seconds of play left, Cooper stole the ball from Jackson, dribbled down the court, and at the sound of the buzzer shot at the basket, but the ball bounced off the backboard and onto the floor.
4. In a thrill-packed game yesterday, my favorite ball club, the Minnesota Twins, defeated the Cleveland Indians when the right fielder drove in another one of his winning runs.
5. In his *Kinship with All Life*, J. Allen Boone describes his ability to communicate with animals, such as conversing mentally with a dog, ordering ants to leave his home—which they do—and even taming an ordinary housefly.

■ **Exercise 3** (pp. 304–05)   **Preparing to discuss sentence beginnings**

Answers will vary.

■ **Exercise 4** (p. 305)   **Varying the beginnings of sentences**

Answers will vary. The following are possibilities.

1. a. Studded with razor-sharp pinnacles, a limestone plateau stretched ahead of them.
   b. Stretching ahead of them, a limestone plateau was studded with razor-sharp pinnacles.
2. a. *Dr. Who*, the British science fiction saga, may be the longest-running television series anywhere.
   b. The British science fiction saga *Dr. Who* may be the longest-running television series anywhere.
3. a. Asking questions about how many tasks the machines could perform, potential franchise buyers crowded around the booth that displayed small household robots.
   b. Crowding around the booth that displayed small household robots, the potential franchise buyers asked questions about how many tasks the machines could perform.

4. a. Using the simplest scientific tools while she was hiding from the Nazis in a farmhouse, Rita Levi-Montalcini initiated study into the development of the central nervous system.

   b. While she was hiding from the Nazis in a farmhouse, Rita Levi-Montalcini initiated study into the development of the central nervous system, using the simplest tools.

5. a. Sampling the location, destination, and passenger load of each car, a new, smart elevator reroutes individual elevators to eliminate long waits in the hall and stops by elevators too full to admit additional riders.

   b. Rerouting individual elevators to eliminate long waits in the hall and stopping by elevators already too full to admit additional riders, a new, smart elevator samples the location, destination, and passenger load of each car.

■ **Exercise 5** (p. 307)   **Revising loose, stringy compound sentences**

Answers will vary. The following are possibilities.

1. Although it is easy to keep clean, the small house is too cramped.
2. Growing tired of the long, cold winters, our friends the Comptons moved to Arizona, but there they had to endure long, hot summers.
3. Plastic can be sliced in thin sheets to form computer disks, molded in cases for keyboards and monitors, and removed from one's wallet to purchase equipment one cannot afford.
4. Although he did not mention the amount spent for maintenance, Keith kept asking the library board about the budget and about increasing the amount spent on books and salaries.

■ **Exercise 6** (p. 308)   **Varying subject-verb sequence**

Answers will vary. The following are possibilities.

1. Marcella, like her sister, is an excellent diver.
2. San Francisco, although south of Portland, Oregon, is colder in the summer.
3. The manager, sympathizing with the employees, supported their decision to ask for shorter hours.
4. Ron, hurrying to get home before the storm broke, flooded the engine of his car.
5. Doyle Washington, a popular football star years ago, is now manager of a health club.

■ **Exercise 7** (pp. 308–09)   **Preparing to discuss sentence variety**

Answers will vary.

31

LOGICAL THINKING

Because students frequently feel intimidated by the study of logic, a low-keyed, matter-of-fact approach does much to allay their fears. Instructors might begin by helping students see how they already use different forms of reasoning when making daily decisions. (See activities 1 and 2.) Drawing upon simple examples, you should help students become familiar with the principles of logical reasoning before expecting them to examine the logic of their own writing or to compose carefully reasoned arguments.

As suggested by the organization of section **31**, induction is often easier to teach than deduction. But instruction in both inductive and deductive reasoning is essential if students are to grasp the important lesson that valid conclusions can be arrived at by different means. Many instructors prefer to teach induction and deduction as entirely separate lessons, turning to deduction only after students have mastered induction. This strategy is often effective because it encourages students to learn one thing at a time, with what is usually the easier lesson coming first, thus building the confidence of students confronting potentially threatening material. Instructors should note, however, that writers often combine both induction and deduction within a single essay; students should not be made to think that writing must be as rigidly structured as a syllogism in a textbook.

Because of its flexibility, the Toulmin method is sometimes taught as an all-purpose alternative to induction and deduction. But there are at least two advantages to teaching Toulmin after introducing students to the fundamentals of deduction: a term like *warrant* can be easily grasped by someone already familiar with *premise*, and the flexibility of Toulmin's method is best appreciated by students who already have some experience in attempting to compose syllogisms that are both *valid* and *true*. (A syllogism may be valid but untrue when a logical conclusion is derived from a false premise. See activity 4.) Toulmin may be most useful when offered simply as one of a number of approaches from which students can eventually select the method of reasoning that works best for a particular writing occasion.

By introducing students to Toulmin (a new feature in the eleventh edition), section **31** expands the number of choices available to students when they argue, rather than insisting on the superiority of any one method. For further reading on the Toulmin method, see Stephen Toulmin, *The Uses of Argument* (Cambridge: Cambridge UP, 1958–64); Charles W. Kneupper, "Teaching Argument: An Introduction to the Toulmin Model" (*College Composition and Communication* 20 [1979]: 187–91); James F. Stratman, "Teaching Written Argument: The Significance of Toulmin's Layout for Sentence-Combining" (*College English* 44 [1982]: 718–33); Gail Stygall, "Toulmin and the Ethics of Argument Fields: Teaching Writing and Argument" (*Journal of Teaching*

Writing 6 [1987]: 93–107); and Annette T. Rottenberg, *Elements of Argument*, 2nd ed. (Boston: Bedford, 1988).

Teaching logical thinking requires some discussion of fallacious reasoning, and students often enjoy discovering logical fallacies. (See activity 5.) You might supplement the list of fallacies (from *fallacia*, Latin for "deceit") in **31c** with two more, in which important aspects of the issue at hand are ignored while feelings are exploited: *ad populum* (or "to the crowd") arguments appeal to widely held concerns that, once invoked, obscure reasonable discussion (for example, "This novel is an insult to Islam!"); *ad misericordian* (or "to pity") arguments appeal to the heart rather than to the head (for example, "I deserve to pass this course because my best friend was just killed in a car accident"). Care should be taken, however, not to place so much emphasis upon the identification of fallacies that students new to the study of logic will become paralyzed by the fear that almost anything they say is likely to be wrong.

For additional reading in logic and argument, see Jeanne Fahnestock and Marie Secor, "Teaching Argument: A Theory of Types" (*College Composition and Communication* 34 [1983]: 20–30); David S. Kaufer and Christine M. Neuwirth, "Integrating Formal Logic and the New Rhetoric: A Four-Stage Heuristic" (*College English* 45 [1983]: 380–89); and Marie J. Secor, "Recent Research in Argumentation Theory" (*The Technical Writing Teacher* 14 [1987]: 337–54).

ACTIVITIES

1. Introduce students to induction through the following exercise. Ask all students to stand and then imagine that they are tired at the end of a long and busy day. They want to go home, but they also need to talk with you about an assignment due the next day and cannot call you about it. They have come to your office, and you are not there. They must then decide if you are likely to return soon enough to justify waiting. Urging students to sit down when they think they have sufficient information to justify waiting, give them one piece of evidence at a time. (For example: The door is unlocked. The door is open. The light is on. There is a cup of coffee on your desk. Steam is coming from the coffee, etc.) Some students will sit down earlier than others, and a few may insist on standing unless they "see" you coming down the hallway. But most students will sit when they hear about the steaming coffee—thus providing a useful demonstration of how an inductive leap should be based on enough evidence so that it seems reasonable to others.

2. Ask students to cite sufficient evidence to justify one of the following decisions:

   a. dropping a class

    b. accusing a roommate of stealing
    c. signing a long-term lease
    d. getting married
    e. driving out of their way to shop in a particular grocery store

3. Although students often know what conclusion they want to reach and have specific evidence to lead to that conclusion, they frequently have difficulty recognizing unstated assumptions that underlie their arguments. Composing a good premise is, for most students, the greatest stumbling block in learning to reason deductively. Help students understand deduction by composing syllogisms on the board, providing only the conclusion and minor premise. Then ask them to determine the unstated major premise in each of these enthymemes:

[Major Premise:	Students who major in chemistry are able to get good jobs after college.]
Minor Premise:	I am a chemistry major.
Conclusion:	I will get a good job when I graduate.

[Major Premise:	A fair exam can be completed in the time allowed for it.]
Minor Premise:	No one in the class could finish more than half of Mr. Bloom's exam.
Conclusion:	Mr. Bloom's exam was unfair.

[Major Premise:	Government has a responsibility to help protect public health and safety.]
Minor Premise:	Smoking cigarettes in public buildings can injure the health of nonsmokers and cause a fire hazard.
Conclusion:	Smoking should be banned in city hall.

4. Help students understand that a faulty premise will ruin an argument by giving them additional examples of syllogisms that are valid but untrue. For example:

Major Premise:	All athletes are stupid.
Minor Premise:	Bill is an athlete.
Conclusion:	Bill is stupid.

Major Premise:	Southerners are racist.
Minor Premise:	Mary Lee is a Southerner.
Conclusion:	Mary Lee is racist.

Major Premise:	Women make bad administrators.
Minor Premise:	Katherine Adams is the new dean.
Conclusion:	Dean Adams will be a bad administrator.

Point out that these examples all reflect prejudice; other enthymemes may also rest upon unexamined assumptions that can be easily questioned by anyone who does not share the same bias. Then ask students to compose two syllogisms, one that is valid and untrue (as in these examples) and one that is both valid and true.

5. Ask students to identify logical fallacies they discover in advertisements, newspaper editorials, and letters to the editor.

6. Have students contrast the assumptions and evidence in arguments given by opposing sides in some local issue.

7. Have students discuss the use of induction and deduction in the following passage:

> Proponents of economic specialization would of course attack the idea that import replacing is economically constructive. Specialization, they would argue, represents the division of labor on a regional or an international scale; division of labor is efficient; and, therefore, specialized economies form and persist because the arrangement is efficient. Adam Smith, for one, believed this.
>
> The argument has two major flaws. In the first place, the reasoning is circular. It assumes that a result—in this case, efficiency—is its own cause. One might as well say that rain is beneficial to plants and that that is why it rains. The second flaw in the argument is that specialized economies are not efficient in any case. That is why they are commonly poor or else subsidized. To be sure, their specialties are sometimes (not always) efficiently produced. But that is not the same as saying these economies are efficient. An economy that contains few different niches for people's differing skills, interests, and imaginations is not efficient. An economy that is unresourceful and unadaptable is not efficient. An economy that can fill few of the needs of its own people and producers is not efficient.
>
> —JANE JACOBS

8. Have students analyze the following passage according to the Toulmin method of reasoning, identifying the warrant, data, and claim.

> Until, and even into, the last century, strong, capable women were needed to pioneer our new land; with their husbands, they ran the farms and plantations and Western homesteads. These women were respected and self-respecting members of a society whose pioneering purpose centered in the home. Strength and independence, responsibility and self-confidence, self-discipline and courage, freedom and equality were part of the American character for both men and women, in all the first generations. The women who came by steerage from Ireland, Italy, Russia, and Poland worked beside their husbands in the sweatshops and the laundries, learned the new language, and saved to send their sons and daughters to college. Women were never quite as "feminine," or held in as much contempt, in America as they were in Europe. American women seemed to European travelers, long before our time, less passive, childlike, and feminine than their own wives in France or Germany or England. By an accident of history, American women shared in the work of society longer, and grew with the men. Grade- and high-school education for boys and girls alike was almost

always the rule; and in the West, where women shared the pioneering work the longest, even the universities were coeducational from the beginning.
—BETTY FRIEDAN, "The Feminine Mystique"

9. Give students copies of the following letter, reprinted from the January 8, 1988, issue of the *Journal of the American Medical Association* (page 272). Ask students to determine what evidence led the physician to make his or her decision and what unstated assumptions underlie that decision. Then ask them to write a short essay for or against what this physician did.

It's Over, Debbie

The call came in the middle of the night. As a gynecology resident rotating through a large, private hospital, I had come to detest telephone calls, because invariably I would be up for several hours and would not feel good the next day. However, duty called, so I answered the phone. A nurse informed me that a patient was having difficulty getting rest, could I please see her. She was on 3 North. That was the gynecologic-oncology unit, not my usual duty station. As I trudged along, bumping sleepily against walls and corners and not believing I was up again, I tried to imagine what I might find at the end of my walk. Maybe an elderly woman with an anxiety reaction, or perhaps something particularly horrible.

I grabbed the chart from the nurses station on my way to the patient's room, and the nurse gave me some hurried details: a 20-year-old girl named Debbie was dying of ovarian cancer. She was having unrelenting vomiting apparently as the result of an alcohol drip administered for sedation. Hmmm, I thought. Very sad. As I approached the room I could hear loud labored breathing. I entered and saw an emaciated, dark-haired woman who appeared much older than 20. She was receiving nasal oxygen, had an IV, and was sitting in bed suffering from what was obviously severe air hunger. The chart noted her weight at 80 pounds. A second woman, also dark-haired but of middle age, stood at her right, holding her hand. Both looked up as I entered. The room seemed filled with the patient's desperate effort to survive. Her eyes were hollow, and she had suprasternal and intercostal retractions with her rapid inspirations. She had not eaten or slept in two days. She had not responded to chemotherapy and was being given supportive care only. It was a gallows scene, a cruel mockery of her youth and unfulfilled potential. Her only words to me were, "Let's get this over with."

I retreated with my thoughts to the nurses station. The patient was tired and needed rest. I could not give her health, but I could give her rest. I asked the nurse to draw 20 mg of morphine sulfate into a syringe. Enough, I thought, to do the job. I took the syringe into the room and told the two women I was going to give Debbie something that would let her rest and to say good-bye. Debbie looked at the syringe, then laid her head on the pillow with her eyes open, watching what was left of the world. I injected the morphine intravenously and watched to see if my calculations on its effects would be correct. Within seconds her breathing slowed to a normal rate, her eyes closed, and her features softened as she seemed restful at last. The older woman stroked the hair of the now-sleeping patient. I waited for the inevitable next effect of depressing the respiratory drive. With clocklike certainty, within four minutes the breathing rate slowed even more, then became irregular, then ceased. The dark-haired woman stood erect, and seemed relieved.

It's over, Debbie.

Name Withheld by Request

ANSWERS TO EXERCISES

■ Exercise 1 (p. 317) Analyzing arguments

1. Coal is not a simple substitute for oil or natural gas to produce electricity.
2. The unstated major premise is that anything that is a bulky commodity and has its share of disadvantages is not a good substitute for oil or natural gas. The minor premise is that coal is a bulky commodity and has more than its share of disadvantages as a fuel. The conclusion then follows.
3. The selection might also be considered an inductive argument with the conclusion that coal is not a simple substitute for oil or natural gas, supported by evidence in the form of a number of examples enumerated in the second paragraph. The examples are not supported by proof and might well be questioned by the careful reader.
4. Answers will vary since any of the supporting examples might be questioned.

■ Exercise 2 (pp. 317–18) Supplying the missing premise

1. Nice persons smile all the time.
2. Good writers are easy to understand.
3. A circle around the moon means that it will rain tomorrow.
4. Whatever the Constitution says is true.
5. Magnificent tennis players are probably good swimmers.

■ Exercise 3 (p. 321) Identifying the fallacies

Answers may vary.

1. *Oversimplification:* Crimes are caused by many things, not merely drug trafficking. *False cause:* Drug trafficking is not the cause of most crimes.
2. *Hasty generalization:* The unstated premise is that women vote only for candidates who are good-looking. *False cause:* His good looks will not necessarily cause women to vote for him.
3. *Hasty generalization:* The unstated premise is that all journalists must be good spellers.
4. *Hasty generalization:* The unstated premise is that people who walk self-confidently don't get mugged. It might be argued that this statement is true with the qualifier "probably."
5. *Oversimplification:* There are many other reasons why jails are full. *False cause:* The fact that there are people who don't have money for necessities is not necessarily the cause of jails being full.

6. *Hasty generalization:* The unstated premise is that all women are not good at math.
7. *Non sequitur:* Being sick may have had nothing to do with Mary's missing class. *False cause:* Sickness did not cause Mary to miss class.
8. *Non sequitur:* It does not follow that you should vote for Bill because he is the most popular boy in the class.
9. *Hasty generalization:* The unstated premise is that baseball players are authorities on the right blade to use for the smoothest shave.
10. *Either . . . or fallacy:* There are politicians who are interested in other things as well as ones who are interested in both their own and other people's welfare.
11. *Non sequitur:* It does not follow that a person who frowns all the time is sick.
12. *Bandwagon:* Just because all of your friends have bought cars does not necessarily make it a good idea for you.

32

THE PARAGRAPH

The primary purpose for using paragraphs is to make writing readily understandable to the reader. In modern writing, each new paragraph alerts the reader to expect a change—a new idea, a new approach to an idea, or further information about an idea. Occasionally, a new paragraph begins simply to break up a long expanse of prose. The length of a paragraph varies according to whether it appears in newspapers or magazines (short paragraphs) or in more formal kinds of writing such as essays and encyclopedia articles (longer paragraphs).

Approached from another perspective, the need to make paragraphs unified, coherent, and well developed helps the writer explore and shape ideas. In fact, lapses in unity and coherence often reflect lapses in thinking. The patterns of arrangement discussed in section **32** aid in displaying ideas clearly. Derived from Aristotle's topics of invention, these methods of paragraph development often serve to generate ideas—the purpose for which Aristotle intended them.

Because students have difficulty understanding coherence, it is useful to begin by discussing various kinds of relationships—coordinate (*and*), obversative (*but*), alternative (*or*), causative (*because, for*), conclusive (*so*), inclusive (*colon*). The discussion might move to the ways of developing coherence described in **32b**—repetition of key words and ideas, repetition of pronouns, parallel structures, and use of transitional expressions. Finally, instructors may wish to discuss coherence as the set of relationships made explicit by the ordering and arrangement of sentences within a paragraph—that is, the relationships that go beyond the sentence.

Although they may grasp the principles of unity and coherence, students often write a series of short, choppy paragraphs, each of which has a clear focus, but none of which are adequately developed. Appraising paragraphs that have nothing apparently wrong with them, even good writers can fail to see what is not on the page—those missing details that, once included, help distinguish the good from the exceptionally good. Class time devoted to development is usually well invested. Without making students feel that a long paragraph is necessarily a good paragraph, emphasize that careful development is central to writing well.

When teaching development, you might point to the difference between paragraphs in a newspaper and paragraphs in a book, showing students that newspaper paragraphs are short because of conventions usually limited to journalism: the need to have justified margins in multiple columns and boxes, the need to appeal to a general audience that includes many unsophisticated readers, and the possibility that the story may be scanned but not read completely. As writers of paragraphs and essays in college, students should expect a more attentive audience—an audience eager for details and capable of reading a series of closely related sentences without getting dizzy or bored. Make sure, however, that students understand that developing the main idea of a paragraph is not the same as simply restating the idea in other words—a common flaw in the work of students who are pushing themselves to fill a fixed quota of words but unable to think of anything new to add to a suspiciously thin paragraph. The strategies discussed in **32c** and **32d** can help students learn to develop their paragraphs, but some students may best benefit from a conference in which you ask questions raised (but unanswered) by their work. Students often know more than they realize and omit necessary details because they have forgotten that they are writing for an audience for whom the missing details are by no means obvious.

For further reading, see Richard Braddock, "The Frequency and Placement of Topic Sentences in Expository Prose" (*Research in the Teaching of English* 8 [1974]: 287–302); Frank J. D'Angelo, "The Topic Sentence Revisited" (*College Composition and Communication* 37 [1986]: 431–41); and Rick Eden and Ruth Mitchell, "Paragraphing for the Reader" (*College Composition and Communication* 37 [1986]: 416–30).

ACTIVITIES

1. Compose paragraphs that can serve as models for students preparing to write similar paragraphs. Help students evaluate these paragraphs in small groups. The following five models were created by Vivian I. Davis (see pages 14–19 of this manual) to show her students different levels of development and coherence before they composed paragraphs of their own on the same assignment: "Describe a person whose personal appearance gives people false impressions of his or her personality."

Paragraph 1

My friend, Dana, is petite. She is only 4′6″ and weighs about 80 pounds. Dana wears size four shoes and can buy most of her clothes on sale in the children's department. Her big bright green eyes, her happy surprised smile, her flat chest and too soft voice make Dana seem like a girl of 10 or 12. Though she is 15 years old, an honors student, and an excellent debater, my friend can still get into the movies at half fare. In a crowd of loud, giggly, bubble gum chewing preteens, Dana, without her high heel pumps and with her hair tied in two big puffs with bright colored ribbons, passes for a shy, run-of-the-mill little girl. In reality, Dana is aggressive because she feels she will be overlooked. She has an active social life and makes it her business to get to know everybody.

Paragraph 2

Most everybody thinks the coach is the funniest man alive when they first meet him. Our football coach is hardly 5′8″. Lots of women are taller than that! Most freshman football players are looking over the coach's head. When he comes out on the field I always hear people in the stands giggling and making unkind remarks about Coach. He looks like his name, Alphonso Waddington, as he takes to the field with his head tucked down and his arms flapping like duck wings against his pudgy sides. The coach is pigeon-toed and bowlegged. No one can tell if he's walking or running; if he's serious or playing some kind of trick to confuse the opposition. Coach Waddington has developed a way of talking that sounds like a dog barking. I'm sure it's his way of compensating for not getting the respect he is due not only for being one of the finest coaches in the league, but for his courage, compassion and his no-nonsense ways with his teams.

Paragraph 3

Someone I know now looks real smart in appearance but his grades don't show it. You might think he would have all A's, but he lucky to get a pass with all C grade. Some people like this guy I mention make you think they really, really smart by they don't never recite in class or talk alot to no other peers.

Paragraph 4

Actors always give people a wrong impression of their personalities. Because they always look like some character, not their real selves. They could be young but wearing make-up of a old person or even limping or with grey hair or a hearing-aid or barely walking on a walker. When you see them you would never guess they are around thirty year old and maybe real sharp both mentally and physically. That goes to show you can't trust your own eyes if it's an actor.

Paragraph 5

Peppers is a friend of mine, but his grandmother is one whose appearance gave me the wrong impression of herself. Everybody knew she was raising Sonny Peppers and his two older sisters, but nobody ever asked why. Since Sonny was my age I used to go over Pepper's house a lot—about once a week I would think. His grandmother was always at home. Either working in the kitchen which could be seen from the living room. Or sometimes she was upstairs. I would just kind of knock and open the door all at the same time. Mrs. Peppers, in the same fashion as all the other families living in our little town, never had her door locked. As soon as I got inside the door, she always yelled "Well, well, who's here?" I'd just say, "Melvin," thinking nothing of it. Then I'd ask her if Sonny was at home. If he was there, she called him. If not, she said, "not now. Come back later on." All this time I thought she could see me. I thought she could see everthing. She was always looking right at you. Believe it or not, I've been over there when her tv set was on. But Mrs. Peppers who didn't look anything like a grandma, not old or senile or anything, was bind!

2. Ask students to think for five minutes about a recent experience and to jot on a piece of paper as many of the ideas and details that come to mind as possible. These jottings will probably be phrases or even single words; students should make no attempt at this point to structure sentences or to organize the material in any way. After the five minutes are up, ask students to create unified groups from the jottings and to structure as many sentences as necessary to include all of the points in each group. When that activity is completed, have students write a paragraph based on the

sentences; ask them to use the coherence techniques in **32c** to make the relationships among the sentences clear.

A variation on this activity is useful to teach the value of various methods of development. Begin the activity in the same way, but have the students jot any concrete, sensory details that come to mind—how someone or something looked, sounds they heard, smells they remember, tastes, textures. Then ask them to create unified groups of details and write one paragraph about each group. Any method of development (or combination of methods) that works for the material can be used as a principle for grouping—classification, comparison-contrast, narration, and so on.

3. Have the class suggest sentences following the patterns listed below. Then have each student write a paragraph developing that sentence.

   a. A sentence stating what someone might have learned from an experience or how someone feels about an experience.
   b. A sentence stating a fact or opinion.
   c. A sentence stating a subject that has several parts.

   (This activity is adapted from Erika Lindemann, *A Rhetoric for Writing Teachers* [New York: Oxford UP, 1982].)

4. Ask students to evaluate the unity of one of their paragraphs by justifying the function of every sentence in the paragraph.

5. Have students analyze one of their essays to discover which categories of transitions are most frequently used and which, if any, are not used or are used infrequently. Have students share their analyses with the class. Ask students to compare their use of coherence strategies with those of other students and, if possible, with those of a professional writer.

6. Bring to class copies of two or three student paragraphs. In each, label the ways coherence is gained (by pronouns, key words, transitions, or parallel structure). Then ask students to analyze a paragraph they have written recently and revise it to improve unity.

7. Distribute copies of a professionally written paragraph from which you have removed as many of the aids to coherence as you conveniently can. (You may have to rewrite the paragraph slightly to remove parallel structures and repetition of key words or ideas.) Discuss with the class how the paragraph could be given coherence. If time permits, have the students attempt a revision of the paragraph before showing them the original paragraph (an overhead projector is useful for this, or you can distribute copies or read the paragraph to the students).

8. Distribute a sheet which contains at the top the first sentence of a paragraph and at the bottom the last sentence. Have students write a minimum of three sentences (and probably no more than five) to complete the paragraph. (This activity is adapted from Erika Lindemann, *A Rhetoric for Writing Teachers* [New York: Oxford UP, 1982].)
9. In random order, type and number sentences from a student- or professionally written paragraph. Ask students to determine what the proper order should be and explain why. Then read the original paragraph.
10. Have students collect paragraphs to illustrate the common arrangements of ideas discussed in **32b(1)**. Ask them to identify the topic sentence or controlling idea of each paragraph.
11. Select one topic sentence from each student's essay. Ask students what question(s) implied in the topic sentence must be answered in the development of the paragraph.
12. To emphasize the use of criteria in classifying objects into parallel, nonoverlapping categories, bring to class an apparently random assortment of silverware (knives, forks, teaspoons, sugar spoons, serving spoons, pickle forks, steak knives, stainless, silverplate, plastic, and so on). Ask students to group items according to function, material, pattern, finish.

ANSWERS TO EXERCISES

■ **Exercise 1** (p. 325)   **Developing a paragraph**

Answers will vary.

■ **Exercise 2** (p. 325)   **Revising a paragraph**

Answers will vary.

■ **Exercise 3** (p. 328)   **Identifying topic sentences**

Paragraph 9: Ambivalence as a defining sensibility is something new.
Paragraph 10: (Implied) The small living room was cluttered and untidy.
Paragraph 11: Certainly the [U.S.] political problems, difficult and delicate though they may be, are not insoluble.

■ **Exercise 4** (pp. 328–29)   **Writing paragraphs with topic sentences in varying locations**

Answers will vary.

■ **Exercise 5** (pp. 333–35)   **Identifying paragraph patterns**

It should be pointed out that many of these paragraphs combine the methods described in the text.

Paragraph 21: Chronological and topic-restriction-illustration
Paragraph 22: Topic-restriction-illustration
Paragraph 23: Specific to general
Paragraph 24: Chronological
Paragraph 25: Spatial description
Paragraph 26: Question-answer

■ **Exercise 6** (p. **335**)   **Writing three paragraphs**

Answers will vary.

■ **Exercise 7** (p. **335**)   **Finding three examples in student's own writing.**

Answers will vary.

■ **Exercise 8** (pp. **338–39**)   **Indicating linking devices**

The student should have marked the paragraphs as follows: Pronouns are circled, repeated words and phrases are underlined, conjunctions are bracketed, transitional phrases are double underlined, and parallel structures are enclosed in parentheses.

Paragraph 30

¶ (Electronic music) is a new departure from orthodox, or generally accepted, music [in that] (it is) electrically originated or modified sound. (This sound is) the output of electric pianos, organs, synthesizers, saxophones, guitars, flutes, violins, trumpets, and many other instruments. (It is) the product of composers (who) use tape recorders and tape manipulation to distort, for better or worse, conventional sounds. Also (it is) the sounds we hear in concerts and on records that use amplification to boost or alter the volume of instruments.

—MERRILL C. LEHRER, "The Electronic Music Revolution"

Paragraph 31

¶ There are obvious advantages for the writers of allegorical tales like country music's to have a conventionalized geography to reinforce the message. [But] why does country music use *this* image of America? Why is country music (so pleased with) the South and (so upset with) the North? The answer to this question lies (not in) the actual geography of the United States, (but in) how country music's audience perceives the geography of the United States. (It is) not a question of what America is (but of what America means) to these people. As a result, the question (has to do with) far more than just a style of singing; (it) (has to do with) the attitudes of the millions of Americans who listen to country music—

attitudes (about regional differences) in American society, (about the role of the media) as part of the American power structure, and (about the value of progress) in general.

—BEN MARSH, "A Rose-Colored Map"

■ **Exercise 9 (p. 339)** **Revising sentences and adding linking devices**

Answers will vary.

■ **Exercise 10 (pp. 343–44)** **Developing sentences with details and/or examples**

Answers will vary.

■ **Exercise 11 (p. 344)** **Rewriting their own paragraphs**

Answers will vary.

■ **Exercise 12 (pp. 353–55)** **Identifying topic sentences, transitions, and methods of development**

Transitions: Pronouns are circled, repeated words and phrases are underlined, conjunctions are bracketed, transitional phrases are double underlined, and parallel structures are enclosed in parentheses.

Most of these paragraphs use a combination of methods of development.

Paragraph 55

Topic sentence:	Yet along with this feeling . . . national community.
Methods of development:	Cause and effect, narration

¶ [Yet] along with this feeling had come a deep sense of belonging to a national community. The Westerner who (developed a farm) (opened a shop) or (set up in business as a trader) could hope to prosper only as (his) own community prospered—[and] (his) community ran (from the Atlantic to the Pacific) and (from Canada down to Mexico) If the land was settled, with (towns) and (highways) and (accessible markets) (he) could better (himself) (He) saw (his) fate in terms of the nation's own destiny. [As] its horizons expanded, [so] did (his) (He) had, in other words, an acute dollars-and-cents stake in the continued growth and development of (his) country.

—BRUCE CATTON, "Grant and Lee"

Paragraph 56

Topic sentence:	It is not an unpleasant place to be, . . . but to like a place like that you have to want a moat. (Or

implied: In spite of its natural beauty, one would
have to like isolation to like Alcatraz Island.)

Methods of development: Description, contrast

¶ Alcatraz Island is covered with (flowers) now: (orange and yellow nasturtiums,) (geraniums,)
(sweet grass,) (blue iris,) (black-eyed Susans,) (Candytuft) springs up through the cracked
concrete in the exercise yard. (Ice plant) carpets the rusting catwalks. "WARNING! KEEP
OFF! U.S. PROPERTY," the sign still reads, (big) and (yellow) and (visible) for perhaps a
quarter of a mile, [but] since March 21, 1963, the day (they) took the last thirty or so men
off the island and sent (them) to prisons less expensive to maintain, (the warning has been
only *pro forma*) (the gun turrets empty) (the cell blocks abandoned) (it) is not an unpleasant
place to be, out (there) on Alcatraz with only (the flowers) and (the wind) and (a bell buoy)
moaning and (the tide) surging through the Golden Gate, [but] to like a place like (that) (you)
have to want a moat.

—JOAN DIDION, "Rock of Ages"

Paragraph 57

Topic sentence: (Implied) The explorations of NASA and Columbus have many similarities, especially the responses they received to requests for funding.

Methods of development: Comparison, narration

¶ Both NASA and Columbus made (not one) but a series) of voyages. NASA landed men on
six (different parts) of the moon. Columbus made four voyages to (different parts) of what
(he) remained convinced was the east coast of Asia. As a result both NASA and Columbus
had to keep coming back to the Government with (their) hands out, pleading for
refinancing. In each case the reply of the Government became, after a few years: "(This)
is all very impressive, [but] what earthly good is (it) to anyone back home?"

—TOM WOLFE, "Columbus and the Moon"

Paragraph 58

Topic sentence: Sound has shaped the bodies of many beasts.
Methods of development: Cause and effect, description developed by
examples

¶ Sound has shaped the bodies of many beasts. Noise tapped away at (the bullfrog) (until) (his)
ears became bigger than (his) eyes. Now (he) hears so well that at the slightest sound of
danger (he) quickly plops to safety under a sunken leaf. (The rabbit) has long ears to hear
the quiet "whoosh" of the owl's wings, [while] (the grasshopper's) ears are on the base of

his abdomen, the lowest point of his body, where he can detect the tread of a crow's foot or the stealthy approach of a shrew.

> —JEAN GEORGE, "That Astounding Creator—Nature"

Paragraph 59

Topic sentence: All I know about grammar is its infinite power.
Methods of development: Definition, comparison

9 Just as I meant "shimmer" literally, I mean "grammar" literally. Grammar is a piano I play by ear, since I seem to have been out of school the year the rules were mentioned. All I know about grammar is its infinite power. To shift the structure of a sentence alters the meaning of that sentence, as definitely and inflexibly as the position of a camera alters the meaning of the object photographed. Many people know about camera angles now, but not so many know about sentences. The arrangement of the words matters, and the arrangement you want can be found in the picture in your mind. The picture dictates the arrangement. The picture dictates whether this will be a sentence with or without clauses, a sentence that ends hard or a dying-fall sentence, long or short, active or passive. The picture tells you how to arrange the words and the arrangement of the words tells you, or tells me, what's going on in the picture. *Nota bene* [Note well].

> —JOAN DIDION, "Why I Write"

■ **Exercise 12 (p. 355)** **Writing paragraphs using various methods of development**

Answers will vary.

33

THE WHOLE COMPOSITION

Effective teachers convince their students that they are interested in what students have to say and not simply waiting for the chance to correct mistakes. Emphasizing the whole composition can help students feel that their ideas matter at least as much as the skill with which they express them, and this perception can encourage reluctant writers. Many writing teachers thus begin their courses with section **33**, believing that writing is best taught through assignments that are long enough to encourage the development of thought. According to this strategy, grammar, mechanics, punctuation, diction, style, and paragraphing can be addressed as the need arises within the context of the students' writing.

Whether you decide to assign essays at the outset of your course or to begin with shorter units better suited to the needs of a particular class, you should note that this section introduces students to a number of key terms essential to the teaching of writing. You can help students understand *purpose* by asking them to consider why they write on any specific *occasion*. You might ask: "Are you writing to please yourself? To entertain someone? To teach something? Or to persuade someone about something?" Students who dislike writing may say their purpose is "to finish the assignment," but most students are quick to learn that writing benefits from having a clearly defined purpose. You may need to explain that having a clear purpose does not mean that a writer can have only one goal in a single piece of writing. You may also need to clarify the distinction between *thesis* (**33d**) and purpose, since students occasionally confuse the two: the thesis is the main idea (or *what* a writer wants to communicate); the purpose is the reason for writing (or *why* a writer has chosen a particular topic and thesis). To convey this distinction in jargon-free language, you can ask two simple questions: "What's the point?" and "Why is it worth making?"

Some students find *audience* more difficult to understand, often because they are not accustomed to thinking of writing as a form of communication. For many students, writing for an audience means writing for a teacher—and an individual instructor with specific expectations is certainly the audience for much college writing. But writing teachers should help students learn to write for larger audiences, since much of the writing they will do after college will be read by more than one person. Since a "general audience" may be the most difficult type of audience to visualize, you can help students by suggesting that they write for a "general audience" they can actually see: the other students in the class. Asking students to envision their audience as the entire class (rather than just the instructor) can be especially effective when combined with peer editing.

Students should not be deprived, however, of the chance to write for specialized audiences if they wish to do so. You might encourage students to define their audience and to experiment with writing for different audiences through the simple device of asking them to specify their audience (e.g., the class, high school students getting ready to go to college, working mothers, etc.) along with the other information (such as name and date) that you require on each submission. For further reading on audience see Lisa Ede, "Audience: An Introduction to Research" (*College Composition and Communication* 35 [1984]: 155–71); Peter Elbow, "Closing My Eyes as I Speak: An Argument for Ignoring Audience" (*College English* 49 [1987]: 50–69); and Duane H. Roen and R. J. Willey, "The Effects of Audience Awareness on Drafting and Revising" (*Research in the Teaching of English* 22 [1988]: 75–88).

Focusing upon audience can often help students find an appropriate subject. For example, when students see themselves writing for the entire class, they will usually recognize that some topics will interest their readers more easily than others. But writers can just as easily begin with a subject and then ask themselves what audience would be the most receptive to an essay on this topic. The point to emphasize is that, wherever a writer begins, the subject should ultimately be appropriate for the audience.

Choosing a good subject can be difficult, and students frequently report that they don't know what to write about. You can reassure them by pointing out that professional writers are often unsure about what they want to write about—and that choosing a topic is usually time-consuming. Emphasize the importance of prewriting, and remind students that they will put themselves at an enormous disadvantage if they postpone choosing a topic until they actually sit down to write. Encourage students to think about writing during the various blocks of time that occur even on a busy day (e.g., while walking across campus, waiting in a line at the bank, mowing a lawn). Of course, you can also help students decide what they want to write about by giving good assignments—assignments that are broad enough to give students room to make choices, but specific enough to focus these choices in a particular direction. For example, instead of asking students to write a 500-word essay describing a person, place, or thing, you might ask them to write about a place that they either miss or are happy to avoid, including enough detail so their audience can understand why they feel as they do about this place.

Although presented as if they were a sequence of steps, the rules in section **33** are interdependent. They represent parts of a process upon which there are many variations. Encourage your students to move freely among these parts and to examine their own composing habits in light of the steps presented in the Handbook. Doing so means avoiding assignments that would force all students to follow the same linear process. For example, some students like to make a formal outline before they write (and some may need to start doing so), but other students write well with only an informal plan in mind, and others like to consider organization only after they have composed a first draft. Insisting that all students compose a formal outline before they start to write may benefit some students but alienate others. Recognize the need for flexibility, and try to help students to discover the process that works best for them.

Although revision is often treated as a separate stage in the writing process, some writers (such as those who compose their drafts on word processors) make significant revisions while composing their first draft. The discussion in **33g** recognizes that revision occurs throughout the writing process. It emphasizes both large-scale revision (clarifying, restructuring, deleting, or adding ideas as meanings emerge) and small-scale revision (editing sentences; correcting errors in spelling, mechanics, punctuation, and grammar). Students often resist revising, perhaps because revising papers that have already been graded seems futile. When they do revise, they rarely concern themselves with more than "a thesaurus philosophy of writing" (Nancy Sommers, "Revision Strategies of Student Writers and Experienced Writers" *College Composition and Communication* 31 [Dec. 1980]: 381), tinkering with words rather than with ideas. Students can be encouraged to develop the revision approach that experienced writers use; in particular, they need to consider their purpose and the reader's expectations, and to work toward making the relationships among their ideas clear. As Sommers notes, "experienced writers explained that they get closer to the meaning by not limiting themselves too early to lexical concerns" (386). Since section **33** encourages students to revise for clarity of ideas (one hallmark of an experienced writer) rather than revising individual words by simply substituting, omitting, or adding words, the student paper is presented in two forms. The first shows the paper undergoing revision, and the second shows the product.

Many of Ruth Vanderhoek's revisions are stylistic, eliminating wordy passages, improving diction, and the like. Notice particularly the revision of the introduction, which eliminates *drunk drivers* in response to the instructor's comment and reduces the number of *drivers* in the paragraph. (Unfortunately, the revised opening fails to include any new details that would help make the essay get off to a livelier start.) Other changes involve larger issues such as development and focus. The addition of new material to paragraph 6 adds some much-needed detail to illustrate the absent-minded driver, and changing "aggressive in their driving" to "irresponsible or stubborn" helps link this paragraph to those that precede it. Note that new sentences were added to the ends of paragraphs 3, 5, and 6—contributing to the essay's unity—and that the conclusion is now more emphatic.

As the instructor noted, the revision is a big improvement, but it is by no means a perfect essay. It was chosen for the Handbook because it embodies the sort of changes that can be reasonably expected from one draft to another, rather than representing a dramatic transformation unlikely to occur from one draft to another. As the instructor remarked, the major problem with the revision is that the categories continue to overlap. Both stubborn and absent-minded drivers are certainly "irresponsible," if that term has any meaning. Ask your students to consider alternative ways to classify bad drivers. (See activity 6.)

Writing answers to essay examinations (**33h**) is a kind of "'writing by formula.' Writing-by-formula is also necessary in college . . . [for] when writing under pressure, students who command a repertoire of formulas for organizing answers to essay exams save time" (Erika Lindemann, *A Rhetoric for Writing Teachers*, New York: Oxford UP, 1982, 158). When discussing the essay test, a good strategy is to review methods of paragraph development by analyzing essay examination questions from various fields (such as psychology, biology, child development, nursing, physics, literature, music, engineering). Explain that, regardless of students' knowledge of the subject, they can structure an answer. The students' first task is to identify the type(s) of development implied by the questions. Then they can employ formulas for organizing the answers.

ACTIVITIES

1. Tell students about any difficulties you have had in your own writing, focusing if possible on any problems you had in high school or college. Ask them to share any bad experiences they have had when writing essays. Ask also if writing makes anyone nervous, identifying and discussing the causes of anxiety about writing.

2. Ask students how they think professional writers differ from them in work habits, interests, and background.

3. Ask students whether there is any truth in the following statements:
   a. Good writing is spontaneous and natural.
   b. The essay is a form of writing that is not much used any more.
   c. Essays are usually equated with dull information.
   d. Students' essays should be written to please the instructor.
   e. As long as the ideas are clear, grammar and spelling are relatively unimportant.

4. Ask students to keep a journal in which they write for at least ten minutes a day. Explain that writing regularly for one's own benefit in this way can help generate topics for writing that they will share with others. Urge them to avoid writing about the weather and what they eat, focusing instead on their reactions to classes, conversations, books, films, and events.

5. Help students understand audience by asking them to teach or explain a process they are familiar with to an audience of children and then to an audience of college students.

6. Help students understand criticism by asking them to explain the instructor's comment on the revised student essay in the Handbook (page **396**). Break them into groups with different responsibilities that could lead to further improvement in the essay. For example, they could list five new details that describe stubborn drivers.

7. Ask students to analyze several short articles to determine whether the purpose of each is expressive, informative, or persuasive. Have them explain what clues they used to determine the purpose. If an article has more than one purpose, have students explain which purpose is dominant and why. Since students will probably refer to audience when explaining purpose, the interdependence of the steps in the process can readily be emphasized.

8. Ask students to select a subject employing the suggestions in **33b**. Then have them explore the subject using the strategies in **33c**: listing, questioning, applying perspectives, surveying development strategies. This activity also works well as a class discussion.

9. Have students compare articles on the same or similar topics written for a specialized and for a general audience. They might, for example, select an article from a professional journal in their field and then look for a comparable topic in a popular magazine. If they are unfamiliar with appropriate journals, have them ask their instructors.

10. After students have written an essay, ask them to list in chronological order and in as much detail as possible all of the steps that they went through as they wrote. Use their lists to clarify the concept of writing as a process: Which part of the process is the most difficult? Which is the easiest? Which are students most likely to rush through?

11. Have students collect examples of different strategies for opening paragraphs (quotation, rhetorical question, anecdote, example, statistics, or a combination of these) and then rewrite one of the opening paragraphs using a different strategy or combination of strategies.

12. Type up the first sentence from each student's introduction. Discuss the effectiveness of the sentences in gaining an audience's attention.

13. After students have completed an essay, ask them to write a sentence outline of it as a way to check the sequence and importance of ideas.

14. Have students begin revising by using peer-editing techniques. Peer editing can be done by simply having students exchange papers and, using the Reviser's Checklist (pages **390–92**), write comments upon their

classmates' work, or it can be done by dividing the class into small groups and having students give an oral critique (this approach works best if students bring several copies of their draft to class).

Peer editing is useful because it enables students to see that others have problems similar to their own, and because students are usually better critics of others' writing than of their own. Peer editing gives them practice in seeing which questions to ask and what to look for. However, it should not be attempted without preparing the class and providing well-defined guidelines.

a. Make sure students know exactly what they are looking for. Early editing sessions are perhaps best limited to working with a single paragraph—perhaps the introduction. Later sessions can focus on the structure and style of the entire draft.

b. Stress that the criticism should be constructive, beginning with strengths and taking the student writer's stated intent into consideration. Weaknesses should be pointed out, but the student critic should try to explain why a given point is a weakness and how to fix it.

c. Outline a procedure for editing. For instance, tell students to read quickly through a draft and jot a brief note about what they expect to find in each paragraph. Then have them read the paper more carefully, considering (1) thesis, (2) unity, (3) coherence, (4) arrangement, (5) conclusion, if any. Then have students write a comment noting what they found to be the main strong points and the main weak points in the paper.

Whatever guidelines you use, remember that students can seldom evaluate prose as quickly as an experienced instructor can. Without adequate direction, time, and encouragement, your students may give only a superficial response to each other's work. For useful discussion of collaborative learning, including a list of student-generated guidelines for editing, see pages 33–35 of this manual.

ANSWERS TO EXERCISES

The answers will vary in each of the exercises 1–9.

■ **Exercise 10** (p. 404)   **Analyzing the composition**

Outline: "The 'Miracle' of Technofix"
  I. Introduction: Technofix
    A. Definition
    B. Example (quotation)
  II. Detailed example: Development of synfuels as technofix response to energy crisis
    A. Government funding of research, giving oil companies tremendous profits

   B. Lack of research on environmental impact of synfuel use
       1. Environmental damage, pollution
       2. Hazardous-waste disposal
       3. Occupational dangers
III. Detailed example: Green Revolution as technofix solution for world hunger
   A. Most energy- and chemical-intensive methods of agriculture too expensive for poor countries
   B. Entire countries at risk of crop decimation from a single breed of plant disease or pest
IV. Detailed example: Wonder drugs as technofix answer to disease
   A. Inadequate testing for long-range effects
   B. Overprescribed and overused
   C. Ineffective results and unintended side effects
 V. Conclusion: Erroneous belief in technofix as progress

Thesis: Somehow this nation has been caught . . . modern high technology.
Purpose: To warn readers against the belief that high technology can provide a panacea for the world's problems.
Audience: General

34

THE RESEARCH PAPER

Students often dread the research paper, seeing it as altogether different, and much more difficult, than any other writing assignment. Instead of recognizing that the same process operates in both—defining, shaping, collecting, and revising—they concentrate on collecting information. Students may divorce writing a research paper from writing essays for several reasons:

1. A research paper is usually longer and more formal than an essay.
2. It is often given more class time and more time for writing than any other essay.
3. It requires conventional research format (formal outline, citations, lists of works cited).
4. It may be weighted more heavily in the final grade than any other essay.

With this perception, students tend to fall into one of two traps: they may procrastinate, avoiding a troubling assignment until they cannot hope to do well; or, convinced that a research paper is measured by the length of its bibliography, they may plunge into extensive and prolonged research, reserving relatively little time for writing and almost none for revising. Losing sight of the composing process, students often submit papers that consist primarily of undigested blocks of source material. You can help students balance their attention to steps in the process by reviewing each of the rules in section **33** in terms of the research paper, by helping students focus their subjects, and by allowing time for revision after a conference on an early draft. Thus, by commenting on the entire process and by including time for revision, you can help students avoid the temptation either to procrastinate or to overemphasize a single aspect in a multistage process.

To help students overcome anxiety about doing a formal research paper, you might assign a series of short papers—each of which involves working with sources—as an alternative to one long paper due at the end of the semester. Assigning a series of short papers not only reduces the anxiety of students who fear that their final grade will be determined by a single assignment, but it also gives students more than one chance to learn how to work with sources effectively. Experience gained in research, paraphrase, summary, and quotation can be carried over from one assignment to another, enabling students to master and subsequently demonstrate skills that may elude them on their first attempt. Students who are assigned more than one short research paper can also be asked to use both MLA and APA style documentation. An additional advantage to this approach is that it spares instructors from the burden of reading sets of long papers during the last hurried days of the semester.

But since students are often asked to write long research papers in college, they might benefit from the experience of writing one under your direction. If you choose to assign a long paper rather than a series of short ones, establish a clearly defined schedule that allows adequate time for each step in the research process, including at least one student-instructor conference while the work is in progress. As part of the research paper unit, conferences allow you to offer specific suggestions during the writing process, and these conferences benefit both you and the student by focusing on writing. The students prepare for the conference by writing whatever is required, making a list of questions to ask, and arriving on time. You prepare by signing up students for conference times and by making a checklist of items to comment on. (Since a day of fifteen-minute conferences is exhausting, you should also schedule a break or two.) The students come away encouraged by individual attention; you are reassured that students are writing their own papers. Make sure, however, that students understand in advance what is expected of them during these conferences as well as the consequences of missing a conference.

Throughout the research paper process, emphasize that students must eventually do more than report information. They must take charge of the information they gather and write in their own voice with a clearly defined purpose. As noted on page **405** of the Handbook, the purpose of a research paper may be primarily informative or persuasive. In addition to illustrating MLA and APA style documentation, the two model papers in **34** can be used to illustrate this distinction. Dennis Kelley's survey of criticism on *Walden* is primarily informative; Sharon Johnson's essay on test anxiety is primarily persuasive. Emphasize that a good research paper must have a thesis, whatever its purpose may be, and note that the purposes for doing research overlap. Both papers present information to support a thesis, thus attempting to persuade readers that the thesis is valid. The difference between the two can be grasped by asking "What are we to do with the information provided by these papers? Is the information provided simply to help us understand something or is it designed to inspire action?" Kelley's paper is informative because it does not recommend any action; Johnson's is persuasive because it urges treatment for test anxiety.

You can use both papers to help students learn to incorporate summaries and paraphrases into their own text. It is useful to emphasize that direct quotation should be used sparingly, since too many quotations (especially long quotations) obscure the writer's own voice. Remind students that they are writers, not simply compilers. To help students avoid papers that assume a scrapbook quality—those all-too-common papers in which odds and ends from other writers have been pasted together by someone whose own voice is seldom heard—try to devote several classes to teaching students how to integrate information into their own prose. Class work on paraphrase, summary, and the identification of key lines in long quotations may be more valuable than discussing questions of format that can be resolved by referring to the Handbook. (See activities 3 and 4.) Practice in using these skills can help students both to write better and to avoid inadvertent plagiarism through inadequate paraphrase.

A candid discussion of plagiarism and its penalty informs the student and protects the instructor. In explaining the various kinds, be sure to stress the writer's responsibility for quoting accurately, paraphrasing carefully, and acknowledging honestly all of the sources cited. Students understand that copying sentences verbatim without proper documentation and passing another student's paper off as their own are examples of plagiarism. However, they usually do not know that misrepresenting the facts of publication, paraphrasing without a citation, or duplicating the order of another writer's examples are also examples of plagiarism. Tell the students to bring the original source as well as their use of it to you if they have any doubts about their use of materials. Thus, they can have troublesome summaries or paraphrases evaluated before they write the final draft of their paper.

Much plagiarism springs from misunderstanding and lack of experience. You can reduce the likelihood of encountering it by making your expectations clear and by providing students with practice in attribution and documentation—especially in cases that do not involve direct quotation, such as the use of another writer's idea or data. You should also be prepared to help students who overdocument their papers. Afraid of being charged with plagiarism, some students will provide a half-dozen parenthetical citations to the same source on a single page. When this is the case, help students synthesize these citations through reorganization and paraphrase. (See activity 6.)

Students often prefer to choose their own topics for research, and doing so can inspire research that is more meaningful to them than work on an assigned topic. When given this option, they may choose topics that involve research in other disciplines. Some writing teachers welcome the chance to read material in disciplines other than their own, but care should be taken when evaluating such papers. Reading a paper on test anxiety, for example, an English teacher can ask a number of questions that do not require study in this particular aspect of psychological research: Does the paper have a clear thesis? Is it supported with adequate data? How recent is the research? Does it involve a variety of sources? Does the writer rely too heavily upon a single source? Does the paper reveal signs of selective research (by suggesting that all the evidence points in one direction), or does it indicate that different studies have achieved different results (a probability in most fields)? Are there any unsupported claims in the paper or undocumented data that are not common knowledge? Is the documentation correct? Questions of this sort can help you evaluate papers in disciplines other than your own, but encouraging students to choose their own topics does not mean that you have to read papers in fields you prefer to avoid. (See activity 8.)

If you assign works of literature as subjects for a research paper, here are a few cautions:

1. Do not assume that students possess the skills to read literature critically. They need help to understand a literary work so their inexperience in interpreting literature does not unfairly hamper their ability to write a good essay. (See **35a**.)
2. Show them how list making, the journalist's questions, and the three kinds of writing (**33c**) can be applied to literary terms in order to produce a topic.
3. Place on library reserve copies of the subject's most important articles and books so students have equal access to them.
4. Select at least three or four works—all, preferably, by different authors—to relieve the strain on the library's resources and to appeal to a variety of interests and reading abilities.
5. To avoid students' relying on *Masterplots* or *Readers' Guide* for their information, you may want to distribute a list of bibliographic resources (with call numbers if possible) for students' use.

For further reading on the research paper, see Richard L. Larson, "The Research Paper in the Writing Course: A Non-Form of Writing" (*College English* 44 [1982]: 811–16); and James Strickland, "The Research Sequence: What to Do Before the Term Paper" (*College Composition and Communication* 37 [1986]: 233–36).

ACTIVITIES

1. Ask students to write a short argument (of 500–750 words) on a topic on which information is available in current newspapers and magazines. Emphasize that you are interested in learning their own opinions in their own words, but ask them to include both a useful fact they learned through reading and a short, direct quotation that conveys a published opinion on this topic. Ask students to cite only one or two sources and to specify them in the paper (e.g., "According to a column by George Will in the April 10th issue of *Newsweek,* . . . "). This exercise can help students gain confidence in working with sources before attempting a research paper; it also helps them see that the need to work with sources is not limited to long, formal papers.

2. To give students practice in research and make the model essay on *Walden* more meaningful to them, ask students to discover five facts about Thoreau, other than his dates of birth and death (1817–1862). Refer students to the reference works listed on pages **415–17** of the Handbook. To encourage the students to consult more than one source, you can define "fact" as a specific piece of information verified by two independent and reliable sources.

3. Ask students to paraphrase several short passages that you have chosen, either in a reader to which all students have access or on a handout.

Without revealing the names of the authors, choose three examples for discussion during the following class: a paraphrase that is too close to the original, one that distorts the meaning of the original passage, and one that successfully conveys the meaning of the passage in other words and structure. Repeat this exercise, eventually asking students to paraphrase aloud or on the board.

4. Ask students to summarize the following passage, quoting, if they wish, one key phrase of no more than ten words:

> Punitive notions of disease have a long history, and such notions are particularly active with cancer. There is the "fight" or "crusade" against cancer; cancer is the "killer" disease; people who have cancer are "cancer victims." Ostensibly, the illness is the culprit. But it is also the cancer patient who is made culpable. Widely believed psychological theories of disease assign to the luckless ill the ultimate responsibility both for falling ill and for getting well. And conventions of treating cancer as no mere disease but a demonic enemy make cancer not just a lethal disease but a shameful one.
>
> Leprosy in its heyday aroused a similarly disproportionate sense of horror. In the Middle Ages, the leper was a social text in which corruption was made visible; an exemplum, an emblem of decay. Nothing is more punitive than to give a disease a meaning—that meaning being invariably a moralistic one. Any important disease whose causality is murky, and for which treatment is ineffectual, tends to be awash in significance. First, the subjects of deepest dread (corruption, decay, pollution, anomie, weakness) are identified with the disease. The disease itself becomes a metaphor. Then, in the name of the disease (that is, using it as a metaphor), that horror is imposed on other things. The disease becomes adjectival. Something is said to be disease-like, meaning that it is disgusting or ugly. In French, a moldering stone façade is still *lépreuse.*
>
> Epidemic diseases were a common figure for social disorder. From pestilence (bubonic plague) came "pestilent," whose figurative meaning, according to the *Oxford English Dictionary,* is "injurious to religion, morals, or public peace—1513"; and "pestilential," meaning "morally baneful or pernicious—1531." Feelings about evil are projected onto a disease. And the disease (so enriched with meanings) is projected onto the world.
>
> —SUSAN SONTAG, *Illness as Metaphor*

5. Discuss the model abstract on page **491**, and then ask students to write an abstract for Dennis Kelley's research paper on *Walden.*

6. Write a paragraph that includes at least a half-dozen separate references to the same source, preferably the same page of an essay that your students have access to. Make sure each reference ends with parenthetical documentation citing the author and page. Then ask students to revise the paragraph, consolidating the references so only one parenthetical citation is necessary but all attributions remain clear.

7. Collect several examples of sources seamlessly integrated into a writer's text. (You could use samples from your own or your colleague's writing, from well-written journal articles, and from publications such as *Smithsonian* or *National Geographic.*) Using an overhead projector to display

the writings, discuss the techniques used. Then pass out sample informative paragraphs and ask students to write three or four sentences for each in which they integrate paraphrase and summary with their own ideas. Next, have students write a couple of sentences using attributive statements. Finally, have them write a couple of sentences in which they use brief direct quotations from the sources.

8. Ask students to write a 250-word proposal, defining the topic they want to research and explaining what they hope to accomplish. Treat this as an exercise in argument, explaining that you will approve only those topics for which there is a clear rationale and which can be adequately researched on your campus in the time allowed.

9. Bring to class photocopies of title pages and copyright pages for several books (or show them on an overhead projector). Select material carefully to avoid at first such complications as subtitles and copyright pages with both printing dates and copyright dates. But since students are likely to encounter those complications in their own research, provide potentially confusing examples after students have mastered those that are simple and straightforward. Discuss how to identify the city of publication when more than one city is listed. Ask students which information belongs in a bibliographic entry and in what order. Then have them write the entry.

10. Arrange for students to tour the university library. If there is an opportunity to consult with the staff members who conduct the tours, explain what subjects students have selected and ask that appropriate reference tools be pointed out. Encourage students to ask about library facilities and reference tools appropriate to their own research.

11. Ask students to bring to class their working bibliographies, at least six blank 3 x 5-inch cards, and a rubber band or large paper clip. Students should have an opportunity to compare and correct bibliographic forms. To hand in the cards, students arrange them in proper bibliographical order. This exercise has the advantage of testing students' ability to use the forms with sources that they will eventually include in the list of works cited.

12. Ask students to interview another instructor about his or her research.

13. As an alternative to a research paper, assign an annotated bibliography.

14. Use the discussion of APA style to comment upon how certain writing conventions vary from one discipline to another. Ask students to share experiences they have had with research in other disciplines.

15.

If you think the use of the first person is inappropriate for writing in the social sciences, ask students to write a new introduction and conclusion to Sharon Johnson's research paper on test anxiety.

16. Generate interest in the paper on test anxiety by asking students to discuss their own feelings when they prepare to take a test. If the class shows interest in this topic, you can ask them to respond to the following short test, assuring them that the results are for their own information, that they will have no bearing on their final grade, and that you are not attempting a psychological diagnosis.

Test Anxiety Scale (TAS) Items

(T) 1. While taking an important exam I find myself thinking of how much brighter the other students are than I am.
(T) 2. If I were to take an intelligence test, I would worry a great deal before taking it.
(F) 3. If I knew I was going to take an intelligence test, I would feel confident and relaxed, beforehand.
(T) 4. While taking an important examination I perspire a great deal.
(T) 5. During course examinations I find myself thinking of things unrelated to the actual course material.
(T) 6. I get to feel very panicky when I have to take a surprise exam.
(T) 7. During tests I find myself thinking of the consequences of failing.
(T) 8. After important tests I am frequently so tense that my stomach gets upset.
(T) 9. I freeze up on things like intelligence tests and final exams.
(T) 10. Getting a good grade on one test doesn't seem to increase my confidence on the second.
(T) 11. I sometimes feel my heart beating very fast during important tests.
(T) 12. After taking a test I always feel I could have done better than I actually did.
(T) 13. I usually get depressed after taking a test.
(T) 14. I have an uneasy, upset feeling before taking a final examination.
(F) 15. When taking a test my emotional feelings do not interfere with my performance.
(T) 16. During a course examination I frequently get so nervous that I forget facts I really know.
(T) 17. I seem to defeat myself while working on important tests.
(T) 18. The harder I work at taking a test or studying for one, the more confused I get.
(T) 19. As soon as an exam is over I try to stop worrying about it, but I just can't.
(T) 20. During exams I sometimes wonder if I'll ever get through college.
(T) 21. I would rather write a paper than take an examination for my grade in a course.
(T) 22. I wish examinations did not bother me so much.
(T) 23. I think I could do much better on tests if I could take them alone and not feel pressured by a time limit.
(T) 24. Thinking about the grade I may get in a course interferes with my studying and my performance on tests.
(T) 25. If examinations could be done away with I think I would actually learn more.
(F) 26. On exams I take the attitude, "If I don't know it now there's no point worrying about it."
(F) 27. I really don't see why some people get so upset about tests.
(T) 28. Thoughts of doing poorly interfere with my performance on tests.
(F) 29. I don't study any harder for final exams than for the rest of my course work.
(T) 30. Even when I'm well prepared for a test, I feel very anxious about it.
(T) 31. I don't enjoy eating before an important test.
(T) 32. Before an important examination I find my hands or arms trembling.
(F) 33. I seldom feel the need for "cramming" before an exam.
(T) 34. The University ought to recognize that some students are more nervous than others about tests and that this affects their performance.
(T) 35. It seems to me that examination periods ought not to be made the tense situations which they are.
(T) 36. I start feeling very uneasy just before getting a test paper back.
(T) 37. I dread courses where the professor has the habit of giving "pop" quizzes.

Note: The Test Anxiety Scale may be used by researchers without obtaining permission of author or publisher. The answer of a test-anxious student to each statement is indicated in parentheses.

ANSWERS TO EXERCISES

■ **Exercise 1** (p. 407) **Choosing a subject**

Students are unlikely to obtain a range of reliable sources on flying saucers. A general audience is almost certain to be interested in pandas, and programs to breed them in zoos would be appropriate for an eight-page paper. Answers will vary for the other subjects, but here are some possibilities.

censorship:	censorship of books in school libraries; the conflict over Salman Rushdie's *Satanic Verses*
drug abuse in wresting:	drug abuse in major-league football; steroid abuse among college athletes
Shakespeare and women:	women in *As You Like It;* the characterization of Portia
Leonardo da Vinci:	da Vinci and aviation; efforts to rescue *The Last Supper*
the Japanese economy:	the Japanese car industry; learning from Japanese management techniques
U.S. Immigration Policy:	the amnesty program for illegal aliens; granting asylum to political refugees

■ **Exercise 2** (p. 420) **Focusing the subject**

Answers will vary.

■ **Exercise 3** (p. 420) **Preparing a working bibliography**

Answers will vary.

■ **Exercise 4** (p. 430) **Paraphrasing and summarizing**

Answers will vary.

■ **Exercise 5** (p. 451) **Evaluating the MLA paper**

The paper's thesis is first introduced at the beginning of paragraph 2. (It is restated in the conclusion.) The organization is straightforwardly chronological, covering criticism from 1854 to 1985. An alternative method of organization for a critical survey would have been to write an essay of classification (e.g., "Most criticism of *Walden* falls into one of three categories . . . "). Kelley's greatest risk in organizing the paper chronologically was that the essay might easily have grown too large; a secondary risk is that chronological organization might suggest lack of synthesis and control over the material. Kelley successfully avoided these risks by integrating his source material into well-written sentences of his own and by advancing a clear thesis which gives focus to the history of *Walden* criticism and demonstrates that the author is doing more than simply reporting the views of others. Instructors who object to Kelley's thesis or question the value of critical surveys can still use this paper for teaching MLA documentation, since Kelley cites a variety of sources correctly.

■ **Exercise 6** (p. 504)   **Outlining the APA paper**

Outline

Thesis: Test anxiety is a recognized psychological syndrome that can be treated effectively.

Introduction: Personal experience with test anxiety

    I. The size of the problem
       A. The approximate number of students affected
       B. Sex differences among victims
       C. Cultural differences among victims
   II. Definition of test anxiety
       A. Distinction from simple nervousness
       B. Symptoms of test anxiety
          1. Domination by negative feelings
          2. Loss of concentration
 III. Disappointing research results
       A. Problems in measuring test anxiety
          1. Exaggerated reports
          2. Biased tests
       B. Lack of academic improvement through treatment
 IV. Evidence of successful treatment
       A. Recent research based on large samples
       B. Effective methods of treatment
          1. Responding to both worry and emotionality
          2. What teachers and parents can do

Conclusion: Reintroduce personal experience and recommend other victims get professional help

■ **Exercise 7** (p. 504)   **Changing documentation styles**

(Yardley, 1985, p. 24)
("Review," 1854, pp. 5, 7)
(Graebner, Fite, & White, 1975, p. 447)
(Krutch, 1948, p. 103)
(Howe, 1933)

35

WRITING FOR SPECIAL PURPOSES

Instructors who believe in the importance of helping students learn to write for a variety of disciplines can use this section to teach two types of writing for special purposes that generate many questions from students—namely, writing about literature and business writing. (A third, writing in the social sciences, can be taught through discussion of the essay on test anxiety in section **34**.) When teaching section **35**, you should make sure students understand that, although writing for special purposes often involves conventions that may be limited to a single discipline, good writing in any discipline is characterized by the lessons conveyed in previous sections of the Handbook. Whether writing an essay about Shakespeare or a memo about a change in office procedure, students should remember their responsibility to write clearly and grammatically, keeping their purpose, audience, and occasion in mind as they organize and develop their thoughts.

Because the teaching of writing was once considered to be less important than the teaching of literature, many English departments have become polarized between teachers of writing and teachers of literature, as if the two had nothing to do with each other. Instructors with degrees in rhetoric or composition may be tempted to assert the importance of their field by excluding literature from writing courses, just as other instructors have assumed that helping students to write better had absolutely nothing to do with the study of great literature. Instructors who find themselves caught between these two camps may hesitate to incorporate literature into the writing course for fear that doing so will be perceived as an attempt to avoid their responsibility to teach writing. But teachers teach best when they care about what they are teaching, and instructors who love literature can successfully integrate its study into the teaching of composition as long as they proceed with the needs of their students clearly in mind. Writing cannot be divorced from reading, and the reading of literature can generate numerous topics for writing. Students may also welcome the opportunity to write about literature as an alternative to writing on topics drawn from their own experience, since the subject for their writing is provided by the text they have before them, reducing the difficulty many have with invention.

The development strategies discussed in section **32**, and more briefly in section **33**, can all be adapted for writing about literature in **35a**. For example, you might ask students to describe a setting or compare and contrast two characters. Essays of classification might also focus on character. ("How would you classify the people of Gopher Prairie? Do they fall into any recognizable groups?") Essays of definition might be derived from analysis of a key term in a literary text (e.g., "What does Milton mean by 'honour' in this poem?"). And writing essays of cause and effect can help students understand the outcome of a work of literature (e.g., "Why does Blanche DuBois end up in a mental hospital?").

Of course, there are many other possibilities for assignments in writing about literature. As the Handbook points out, students can write essays of analysis that determine how the various parts of a work combine together, essays of interpretation that establish the theme or meaning of a work, and essays of evaluation that appraise the merit of a work. Class discussion is usually essential before students feel confident undertaking assignments like these, but all three can generate good essays when students understand both the work they are writing about and your expectations regarding their papers. Whatever essays you assign, try to encourage students to think for themselves, and do not make them feel that the success of their writing depends upon revealing the "correct" meaning of a text. With this in mind, make sure your students understand that literature can inspire many valid interpretations, and that good critics often help us to see a text in a new way. Their thesis should be of their own choosing—and if original, so much the better, as long as it is adequately supported.

Students often benefit from being cautioned about ways in which writing about literature can be disappointing:

1. Unless a summary has been assigned (as a means, perhaps, of appraising reading comprehension), summarizing a work is usually pointless since the writer is simply repeating information already known to the audience. (This point is worth emphasizing, since students often get bogged down in summary when writing about literature.)
2. Writers are usually wise to avoid insisting that their interpretation precludes any other; the discovery of a particular theme, for example, does not necessarily mean that it is the only theme in the work.
3. Essays should be grounded in the text, and students should be careful not to end up writing more about themselves than the work under consideration (e.g., "While reading this story, I was reminded of my own trip to Florida last year.").
4. Evaluation should not be confused with bias. Help students to see that there is a difference between complaining "This is a bad story because it is long, and I hate long stories" and arguing "The problem with this story is that the author explains too much, coming right out and telling us in detail what a more skillful writer would suggest indirectly."

As the organization of section **35** suggests, fiction often provides the best vehicle for the initial study of literature. "Wants," by Grace Paley (pages **511–13**) should help you appraise the ability with which your students can read fiction and help you determine subsequent assignments. Because this story is so short, it was possible to include it in the Handbook as a focus for the explanations of setting, plot, characters, point of view, tone, and symbolism that follow the Paley piece.

35

Students who associate fiction primarily with plot may be confused by the apparent lack of action in "Wants." When teaching it, you might note that the narrator is unreliable. Like many of Wharton's works, *The Children* is about changing social mores, but it does not cover twenty-seven years; the narrator is confusing her reading with her own experience. (Two lines in the story establish that the narrator's first marriage had lasted twenty-seven years.) Focusing upon the narrator's passivity, you might point to how she is sitting when the story begins and sits down again once she has returned her books. Students should easily recognize that a woman who holds on to library books for eighteen years may have trouble getting things done, but they are less likely to understand the allusion to *The House of Mirth,* a novel in which a beautiful and charming protagonist loses her position in society and eventually her life in part because she is unable to make decisions at key moments of her life. In this regard, it is significant that the narrator loses interest in *The House of Mirth*; this is a sign of change, like the sycamores noted in the Handbook. (If students charge you with reading too much significance into the Wharton allusions, you can respond by observing that the author makes a point not only of mentioning the titles but also of informing us that they "are more apropos now than ever.") Finally, you might also draw attention to Paley's use of figurative language (the remark which "like a plumber's snake, could work its way through the ear down the throat, halfway to my heart" and getting "under the rock" of a man's reasons). Depending upon your students' response to Paley, you can either turn to a few stories with a strong narrative element or move on to other stories devoted, like "Wants," to the revelation of character or mood.

Short reading assignments in poetry can also be easily incorporated into the teaching of writing. Although many students fear that poetry is too difficult for them, these fears can be dissipated through carefully chosen texts. Good poetry is difficult in the sense that it is, like all good literature, complex and also in that it is highly condensed. When students try to read a poem as quickly as they read a paragraph, they can easily get discouraged. Help them to see that poetry is best read slowly and reflectively, but do not make them feel that they must necessarily dwell upon every word, detecting a symbol behind every article and an image in every preposition. Since the explication of poetry becomes easier when writers have access to appropriate critical language, you should help students understand such terms as imagery, meter, and alliteration, but this language should not be emphasized so much that students are left feeling they would be foolish to attempt writing about poetry in their own words.

When teaching plays, you might give students the chance to read key scenes aloud, assigning different roles briefly to different students. This simple device often helps make a play come alive in the classroom. Before asking students to write about the drama, you might share with them the following definitions (from Shaw's *Concise Dictionary of Literary Terms*):

comedy A ludicrous, farcical, or amusing event or series of events designed to provide enjoyment and produce smiles or laughter. More specifically, *comedy* (from Greek words meaning "merrymaking" and "singing") refers to any literary selection written in a light, familiar, bantering, or satirical style. Even more specifically, the term applies to a play of light and amusing character that has a happy ending.

The pattern of dramatic comedy is the reverse of tragedy. Comedy begins in difficulty (or rapidly involves its characters in amusingly difficult situations) and invariably ends happily; tragedy may, and often does, begin in happy circumstances and always ends in disaster. Not all comedies are humorous and lighthearted, although the great majority are. Occasionally, a comedy can be serious in tone and intent as, for example, Dante's *Divine Comedy,* but even this is a comedy of a special sort because its action begins in Hell and ends in Heaven. Comedy differs from burlesque and farce in that it has a more closely knit plot, more sensible and intelligent dialogue, and more plausible characterization. In general, a comedy secures its effects by stressing some oddity or incongruity of character, speech, or action. When these effects are crude, the comedy is termed "low"; when they are subtle and thoughtful, the comedy is called "high." Other types of comedy are numerous; three may be mentioned: (1) comedy of *humors,* involving characters whose actions are controlled by some whim or humor; (2) comedy of *manners,* involving the conventions and manners of artificial, sophisticated society; (3) comedy of *intrigue* or *situation,* depending upon plot more than characterization (such as Shakespeare's *The Comedy of Errors*).

tragedy A calamity, disaster, or fatal event. In literature, *tragedy* refers to any composition with a somber theme carried to a disastrous conclusion. From a Greek term meaning "goat song," tragedy involves death just as the sacrifice of goats, totems of primitive peoples, did in ancient rituals.

Specifically, *tragedy* is applied to a dramatic work, in prose or verse, that traces the career of a noble person whose character is flawed by some defect (jealousy, excessive ambition, pride, etc.) and whose actions cause him to break some moral precept or divine law, with ensuing downfall and destruction.

In the eighteenth century, writers of tragedy began to consider men and women of the middle classes as protagonists. In today's theater, tragedy is often concerned with proletarian themes; in such plays, the cause of downfall is the evils of society rather than flaws in character or the intervention of fate. . . .

Theater of the Absurd An avant-garde style of playwriting and presentation in which conventions of structure, plot, and characterization are ignored or distorted. In this contemporary form of drama, an irrational quality of nature is stressed, and man's isolation and aloneness are made central elements of conflict. In Theater of the Absurd (*absurd* means "senseless," "illogical," "contrary to common sense"), characters may appear in different forms and identities and may change sex, age, and personality; the presentation may have no fixed or determinable setting; the sequence of time is fluid and indefinite. . . .

Even though **35b** is devoted to business letters and résumés, memos, and reports, it also provides an opportunity to review all of the elements of clear, effective writing. Business writing must accomplish its purpose in relatively few words (usually one typed page or less). Thus, every word must contribute to the message without confusing or offending the reader.

Four of the elements to review include the following:

1. *Formulating and developing a thesis.* Because "time is money," a business person wants to know immediately why the letter was written and what action, if any, the writer expects. The opening paragraph contains the thesis, which is developed by careful explanation and relevant details in the body paragraphs. The concluding paragraph should state who does what next.

2. *Analyzing an audience.* Here the writer should consider how the addressee will react. Will he or she be pleased by the request (an order for camping gear), irritated (a demand that certain repairs be made to an apartment before the rent is paid), or both (a rush shipment of bayberry candles the week before Christmas)? If the response is likely to be at least in part negative, the writer should organize the letter so that the reader is not overpowered by the negative elements. The tone should be neither insulting nor patronizing.

3. *Diction.* Clear, exact words convey precise images (a *Zenith 19-inch portable color television, model number 194467792,* instead of *my new color television*). As much as possible, avoid such phrases as *time frame* or *analyzation of invoiced goods as per your aforementioned authorization* which are not only imprecise and therefore inefficient, but also boring.

4. *Mechanics and spelling.* Readers of business prose expect standard spelling and mechanics; anything less creates a negative impression. It goes without saying that the addressee's and company's names must be spelled correctly. In letters of application and résumés especially, accuracy is imperative; more résumés are eliminated for reasons of sloppiness and misspelling than for any other.

Students who are applying for jobs should be advised to prepare their résumés before writing letters of application. Writing a résumé should not be a hurried affair. For each of the four major sections students should answer several questions as they collect and organize material:

Personal data
1. How should I give my name (no nicknames)?
2. Is it necessary to include both my school address and my home address? If so, what format should I use?

Suggested Format:

Diane Bellows

Until May 20, 1989
1830 Lexington Avenue
Louisville, KY 40227
(502) 698-3137

After May 20, 1989
2158 Claussen Trail
West Lafayette, IN 47906
(317) 712-8798

Educational background
1. What is the formal name of the school(s) I have attended? (for example, Massachusetts Institute of Technology, not M.I.T.)
2. What degree(s) did I earn?
3. What are the dates during which I attended?
4. What was my major? minor?
5. What was my grade-point average overall? in my major? in my minor?
6. What advanced seminars or research projects have I taken that are related to the job(s) for which I am applying?
7. What academic honors did I earn?
8. What professional organizations did I join? What offices or committee memberships did I hold? When? What were the responsibilities of each position I held?
9. What social organizations did I join?

Work experience
1. What jobs—including volunteer work—have I held?
2. What were the dates of employment for each job?
3. What was the job title for each position?
4. What was the name of the company for which I worked?
5. Who was my supervisor or boss?
6. What were my responsibilities?

Location of credentials file
1. What is the official title and address of the Placement Office?
2. What is the telephone number of the Placement Office?
3. Which employers and professors should I ask for letters of recommendation? How many letters should I have in my file?
4. How can I judge who will write the most effective letter?
5. What is the correct procedure for requesting a letter?
6. How soon should I check to see whether my file contains all of the necessary letters?
7. What should I do if a letter has not been sent yet?

After the information has been collected, the student should write each section (obviously not all of the information is necessarily included; a low grade-point average, for example, is better omitted), making it complete but concise (*wrote press releases* instead of *my responsibilities included writing press releases*). Then the student should consider the arrangement of the sections on the page. Personal data and references are placed first and last, respectively. Education is usually placed second, but those whose employment experience is stronger than their educational preparation may want to place the employment section second. In any event, the students should experiment with the use of spacing, capitalization, and underlining until they discover a format that adequately emphasizes their strengths.

Only after students have completed their résumés should they attempt a letter of application. Having analyzed their background and that of the company, they can better match their strengths with the requirements listed in the job description.

Like other business letters, the application letter follows a thesis-development-action structure, with the applicant's most persuasive qualifications offered on a single page. The first paragraph tells how the applicant learned of the job and why he or she is qualified for it by education and experience; the central strengths are identified at the outset. The second paragraph develops the education section of the thesis (including, perhaps, any research projects or seminars that are directly related to the position and that may or may not be included on the résumé). The third develops work experiences related to the position or to the qualities desired for the position. The concluding paragraph requests an interview. To discover more about the candidate than the one-page letter allows, the reader then refers to the résumé.

ACTIVITIES

1. Help students understand the characteristics of good literature by providing a few short selections of significantly different quality. For example, you can choose a sentimental story from a popular magazine and pair it with a story on a similar subject or theme by a master storyteller, or you can contrast a great poem about love with a piece of greeting-card verse.

2. Ask students to keep a journal in which they record their impressions of literature, including not only the ideas and feelings that their reading inspires but also any questions that occur to them. Point out that a nagging question can often lead to a good essay resolving the problem at issue.

3. Before asking students to read the sample essay on *Frankenstein,* ask what associations they have with that title. Show how memories of films and cartoons may have little relevance to Shelley's text by providing them with the following plot summary:

   Using the letters of an English explorer named Robert Walton, the novel tells the story of an idealistic student named Victor Frankenstein who discovers the secret of imparting life. The creature made by Frankenstein is supernaturally strong and frightening in appearance, but he is also lonely and unhappy, especially after Frankenstein refuses to create a female counterpart for him. The creature eventually turns upon his creator, murdering Frankenstein's brother, friend, and bride. Frankenstein pursues the creature to the Arctic but dies in the pursuit after telling his story to Walton. The creature then disappears to end his own life.

4. Help prepare students for the paper on "Tulips" by providing them with background information on Sylvia Plath (1932–1963):

The child of an autocratic biology professor (whose early death from diabetes was brought on, in part, by his own stubbornness), Plath began writing poetry when she was very young, publishing her first poem when she was only eight. By the time she was a student at Smith College, from which she graduated summa cum laude, Plath was already publishing in *Mademoiselle* and *Seventeen*. While in college, she won a summer internship as a guest editor at *Mademoiselle*. *The Bell Jar,* her only novel, draws upon this experience, but its primary focus is upon the depression of its protagonist, who, like Plath, receives electric-shock therapy after attempting suicide.

Diagnosed as a manic-depressive, Plath was emotionally unstable for most of her short life. Her poetry is best known for its exploration of psychic pain—and also for its rage, much of which is directed against men. *The Colossus,* her first volume of poems, was published in 1960, four years after her marriage to British poet Ted Hughes, whom she had met in England while completing her M.A. at Cambridge University. Badly hurt by her husband's infidelity and their subsequent separation, Plath took her own life (by kitchen gas) during the unusually harsh winter of 1963.

Much of her best poetry, including "Tulips," was written during the last two years of her life. Although *The Colossus* had won high praise, Plath's critical reputation was established by her three posthumous volumes: *Ariel* (1966), *Crossing the Water* (1971), and *Winter Trees* (1972). Feminists have responded to Plath's focus, in these works, upon the pain a woman suffers in marriage and childbearing—and in struggling to assert her own identity. But Plath's success as a poet is also related to the originality and power with which she wrote.

5. Provide students with copies of "Tulips" and discuss the poem in class. Then build upon this discussion by providing copies of either other Plath poems (such as "Daddy" and "Lady Lazarus") or other short poems appropriate for your class.

Tulips
Sylvia Plath

The tulips are too excitable, it is winter here.   1
Look how white everything is, how quiet, how snowed-in.
I am learning peacefulness, lying by myself quietly
As the light lies on these white walls, this bed, these hands.
I am nobody; I have nothing to do with explosions.
I have given my name and my day-clothes up to the nurses
And my history to the anesthetist and my body to surgeons.

They have propped my head between the pillow and the sheet-cuff   8
Like an eye between two white lids that will not shut.
Stupid pupil, it has to take everything in.
The nurses pass and pass, they are no trouble,
They pass the way gulls pass inland in their white caps,
Doing things with their hands, one just the same as another,
So it is impossible to tell how many there are.

My body is a pebble to them, they tend it as water   15
Tends to the pebbles it must run over, smoothing them gently.
They bring me numbness in their bright needles, they bring me sleep.

Now I have lost myself I am sick of baggage—
My patent leather overnight case like a black pillbox,
My husand and child smiling out of the family photo;
Their smiles catch onto my skin, little smiling hooks.

I have let things slip, a thirty-year-old cargo boat   22
Stubbornly hanging on to my name and address.
They have swabbed me clear of my loving associations.
Scared and bare on the green plastic-pillowed trolley
I watched my teaset, my bureaus of linen, my books
Sink out of sight, and the water went over my head.
I am a nun now, I have never been so pure.

I didn't want any flowers, I only wanted   29
To lie with my hands turned up and be utterly empty.
How free it is, you have no idea how free—
The peacefulness is so big it dazes you,
And it asks nothing, a name tag, a few trinkets.
It is what the dead close on, finally; I imagine them
Shutting their mouths on it, like a Communion tablet.

The tulips are too red in the first place, they hurt me.   36
Even through the gift paper I could hear them breathe
Lightly, through their white swaddlings, like an awful baby.
Their redness talks to my wound, it corresponds.
They are subtle: they seem to float, though they weigh me down,
Upsetting me with their sudden tongues and their color,
A dozen red lead sinkers round my neck.

Nobody watched me before, now I am watched.   43
The tulips turn to me, and the window behind me
Where once a day the light slowly widens and slowly thins,
And I see myself, flat, ridiculous, a cut-paper shadow
Between the eye of the sun and the eyes of the tulips,
And I have no face, I have wanted to efface myself.
The vivid tulips eat my oxygen.

Before they came the air was calm enough,   50
Coming and going, breath by breath, without any fuss.
Then the tulips filled it up like a loud noise.
Now the air snags and eddies round them the way a river
Snags and eddies round a sunken rust-red engine.
They concentrate my attention, that was happy
Playing and resting without committing itself.

The walls, also, seem to be warming themselves.   57
The tulips should be behind bars like dangerous animals;
They are opening like the mouth of some great African cat,
And I am aware of my heart: it opens and closes
Its bowl of red blooms out of sheer love of me.
The water I taste is warm and salt, like the sea,
And comes from a country far away as health.

6. Help students understand the model essay on *King Lear* by providing them with the following plot summary:

> Tired after a reign of many years, Lear decides to divide his kingdom among his three daughters: Goneril, Regan, and Cordelia. Before relinquishing his wealth and authority to them, he asks each to proclaim their love for him. Prompted by greed, Goneril and Regan declare their love in lavish and flattering terms. But Cordelia, the youngest daughter, is disgusted by her sisters' insincerity and refuses to prove her love through words. Enraged by her response ("I love your Majesty / According to my bond, no more or less"), Lear disinherits Cordelia and divides his kingdom between Goneril and Regan. Cordelia's honesty appeals to the King of France, who marries her although she is without a dowry, and they disappear until the final act.
>
> Goneril and Regan conspire to humiliate the now-powerless Lear, and they are supported by Edmund, the bastard son of the Earl of Gloucester. At first their conspiracy succeeds. Lear is left to wander helplessly in a terrible storm, Gloucester's eyes are plucked out by Regan's husband (the Duke of Cornwall), and Edmund becomes commander-in-chief of the English army. But Gloucester is rescued by Edgar, his legitimate son; Lear is cared for by the faithful Earl of Kent, and Cordelia returns to England with an army to rescue her father.
>
> Her army is defeated, however, and the play ends with a series of deaths. Goneril poisons Regan out of jealousy and then kills herself after being exposed for plotting to kill her husband. Cordelia is executed upon orders from Edmund, who subsequently dies in combat with Edgar, and Lear dies broken-hearted.

▲ **Note:** *Lear* teaches well, even in freshman English, and you should consider assigning the play if time allows. Although students may be too young to understand Lear's anguish and the isolation of old age, they are usually quick to understand the hypocrisy, hatred, greed, and lust that are so powerfully portrayed in this great play.

7. Ask students to bring to class two business letters and two memos. Students may use ones they have received or, with permission, ones from their jobs. Have them work in small groups to analyze the format (the placement of the parts), the structure (thesis, development, action), spelling, and neatness of each. Ask students how their analyses affect their opinions of the company.

8. Help students understand the role of audience and purpose in business writing by asking them to write two memos evaluating the same employee. The first memo should be directed to a subordinate with the purpose of motivating improvement; the second should be directed to a superior who has requested a survey of all personnel prior to making cuts in staff.

9. Suggest that students attend any résumé or interviewing workshop held by the Placement Office.

10. Ask someone from the Placement Office to talk to the class about the résumés students in the class have written. The instructor should submit

copies well in advance so that the speaker can plan his or her comments and arrange for any necessary visual aids.

11. Ask students to write a letter requesting a letter of recommendation.

12. Invite the person in charge of hiring for a local business to share suggestions for an effective résumé.

13. Have students interview employers to discover the essentials of good writing as far as that company is concerned.

ANSWERS TO EXERCISES

■ Exercise 1 (pp. 520–21) Analyzing the paper

Thesis:	Shelley's characterization of Walton and Frankenstein shows that the desire to attain the unachievable can have serious results.
Development of Comparison:	Part by part in paragraph 2 followed by unit by unit.
References to text:	*Answers will vary.*
Symbols:	Frankenstein's study of authors whose works are scorned is a symbol for his creation of a monster who is abhorred. Walton's journey symbolizes his search for knowledge.

■ Exercise 2 (p. 529) Analyzing the poem

Literal meaning:	One clings to life and love as one grows older. The persona is an older person who is recognizing his own mortality.
Three images:	(1) The fall of the year when tree limbs are bare with only a few yellow leaves still clinging to them. (2) Sunset and the end of the day. (3) A dying fire.

■ Exercise 3 (p. 536) Analyzing a dramatization

Answers will vary.

■ Exercise 4 (p. 550) Writing various letters

Answers will vary.

Part Three
Biographical Data on Writers Cited
in the *Harbrace College Handbook*:
A Partial Listing

ADLER, MORTIMER J. A Ph.D. who never graduated from high school, Mortimer Adler (b. 1902) is the associate editor for the 54-volume *Great Books of the Western World,* published by *Encyclopaedia Britannica.* Convinced that great books contain universal truths, he has advanced his views in numerous books on philosophy and education, including *Art and Prudence* (1937), *Philosopher at Large* (1971), and *Aristotle for Everybody* (1978).

BAKER, RUSSELL Best known for his syndicated column, "The Observer," Russell Baker (b. 1925) is a Pulitzer Prize–winning journalist who specializes in humorous commentary. He is also respected for his 1982 autobiography, *Growing Up,* and its sequel, *The Good Times (1989).*

BARZUN, JACQUES An eminent historian and critic of culture, Jacques Barzun (b. 1907) has taught at Columbia Univerity since 1929. The author of books on such diverse nineteenth-century figures as Berlioz, Darwin, Goethe, Lincoln, and William James, Barzun is also the author of two books on writing: *On Writing, Editing, and Publishing* (1971); and *Simple and Direct: A Rhetoric for Writers* (1975).

BOORSTIN, DANIEL A former Librarian of Congress and director of the National Museum of History and Technology, Daniel Boorstin (b. 1914) is a conservative historian who has taught at Harvard, the University of Chicago, and the Sorbonne, where he was the first occupant of the chair in American history. His many books include *The Decline of Radicalism* (1969), and *The Americans: The Democratic Experience,* for which he won the 1974 Pulitzer Prize for history.

BRONOWSKI, JACOB Born in Poland and trained as a mathematician, Jacob Bronowski (1908–1974) came to the United States in 1964. His many works on science include *Science and Human Values* (1956), which is considered his best work, but he is also known to the general public through *The Ascent of Man,* a series he narrated for PBS (and from which came a collection of essays published in 1974). A highly cultivated and unusually diverse writer, Bronowski also published several books on poetry.

CARSON, RACHEL Best known for *The Silent Spring* (1962), her controversial study of the effects of pesticides and chemical fertilizers upon the environment, Rachel Carson (1907–1964) was a zoologist whose clear prose won her a large popular audience. Among her other books are *Under the Sea Wind* (1941), *The Sea around Us* (1951), and *The Edge of the Sea* (1955).

CATTON, BRUCE A popular historian of the Civil War, Bruce Catton (1899–1978) won both a Pulitzer Prize and a National Book Award for *A Stillness at Appomattox* (1953). His other works include *Mr. Lincoln's Army* (1951), *The Hallowed Ground* (1956), and *Gettysburg: The Final Fury* (1974).

CHESTERTON, G. K. Known to mystery lovers as the author of the Father Brown series of short stories, Gilbert Keith Chesterton (1874–1936) also wrote several books of literary criticism and many volumes of essays on politics and religion.

COUSINS, NORMAN The editor of the *Saturday Review* for over thirty years, Norman Cousins (b. 1915) is the author of several books of nonfiction, the most recent of which are *Anatomy of an Illness* (1979), *Human Options* (1981), *Healing and Belief* (1982), and *The Healing Heart* (1983).

CROSS, AMANDA Amanda Cross is the pen name of Carolyn Heilbrun (b. 1926), a feminist scholar who is a professor of English at Columbia University. Her scholarly works include *Toward a Recognition of Androgyny* (1973), *Reinventing Womanhood* (1979), and *Writing A Woman's Life* (1988). As Amanda Cross, Heilbrun writes mysteries such as *In the Last Analysis* (1964), *The Question of Max* (1976), and *A Trap for Fools* (1989).

DIDION, JOAN A novelist, journalist, and screenwriter, Didion (b. 1934) is best known for her novel *A Book of Common Prayer* (1977). Her nonfiction includes *The White Album* (1979), *Salvador* (1983), and *Miami* (1987) and her essays appear in such periodicals as *Esquire* and the *New York Review of Books.*

EPSTEIN, JOSEPH The editor of the *American Scholar* and a contributor to such magazines as *Commentary* and *Harper's,* Joseph Epstein (b. 1937) teaches English at Northwestern University. His books include *Ambition* (1981) and *Plausible Prejudices* (1985).

FLEMING, WILLIAM Born in 1909, Fleming is a concert pianist who taught at Syracuse University for more than twenty years. His books include *Understanding Music* (1958) and *Art, Music, and Ideas* (1970).

GOLDING, WILLIAM The 1983 winner of the Nobel Prize for literature, William Golding (b. 1911) is an English novelist whose best-known work is a study of evil in children, *The Lord of the Flies* (1954). His other novels include *The Scorpion God* (1971), *Darkness Visible* (1979), and *Paper Work* (1984).

GOULD, STEPHEN JAY A paleontologist who teaches at Harvard University, Stephen Jay Gould (b. 1941) contributes regularly to *Natural History.* His essays for general readers have been collected in *Ever Since Darwin* (1977), *The Panda's Thumb* (1980), *Hen's Teeth and Horse's Toes* (1983), and *The Flamingo's Smile* (1985).

HERSEY, JOHN Born in China of missionary parents, John Hersey (b. 1914) is a former correspondent for *Time* who once served as secretary to Sinclair Lewis. In addition to being the author of several volumes of nonfiction, including *Hiroshima* (1946) and *The Algiers Motel Incident* (1968), Hersey has published such novels as *A Bell for Adano* (1944), *The Wall* (1950), and *The Child Buyer* (1960).

HOFFER, ERIC A self-educated prospector, migrant farm worker, and longshoreman, Eric Hoffer (1902–1983) was the author of several works of nonfiction, the best known of which is *The True Believer* (1951), a study of mass movements.

HOFFMANN, BANESH A mathematician educated at Oxford and Princeton, Banesh Hoffmann (1906–1986) wrote, among other books, three memoirs of Albert Einstein, with whom he worked as a fellow member of Princeton's Institute for Advanced Study in the 1930s.

KIRK, RUSSELL The author of more than twenty books, Russell Kirk (b. 1918) is best known for his nonfiction, which includes *The Conservative Mind* (1953) and *Decadence and Renewal in Higher Learning* (1978). But he is also the author of a book on T. S. Eliot, two collections of supernatural tales, and two gothic novels: *Old House of Fear* (1961) and *Lord of the Dark Hollow* (1979).

LEE, LAURIE The author of several screenplays and travel books, Laurie Lee (b. 1914) is an English writer who has written eloquently about his childhood in a Gloucestershire village in

Cider with Rosie (1959). He has also published three volumes of poetry, much of which is about the richness of the natural world: *The Sun My Monument* (1944), *The Bloom of Candles* (1947), and *My Many-Coated Man* (1955).

LUKAS, JAY ANTHONY A former correspondent for the *New York Times,* Jay Anthony Lukas (b. 1933) is the author of *Common Ground* (1985), a highly acclaimed nonfiction study of three Boston families. His essays appear in such periodicals as *Esquire, New Republic,* and the *American Scholar.*

MATTHIESSEN, PETER An important and graceful writer about the wilderness, Peter Matthiessen (b. 1927) is a Yale graduate who worked as a commercial fisherman while establishing himself as a writer. Of this experience, he reports: "I don't think that I could have done my writing without the fishing. I needed something physical, something non-intellectual." The cofounder of *Paris Review,* his books include *Wildlife in America* (1959), *The Snow Leopard* (1978), *Indian Country* (1984), and *Nine-Headed Dragon River* (1986).

MEAD, MARGARET An anthropologist who taught at Columbia University and served for many years as curator of anthropology at the American Museum of Natural History in New York, Mead (1901–1978) is best known for a pioneering study of life in the South Pacific, *Coming of Age in Samoa* (1928). Her many other books include *Growing Up in New Guinea* (1930) and *Culture and Commitment* (1970).

MOMADAY, N. SCOTT A Ph.D. from Stanford University where he once taught English, N. Scott Momaday (b. 1934) won a Pulitzer Prize in 1969 for his novel, *House Made of Dawn.* He is also known for *The Way to Rainy Mountain* (1969), a collection of tales and legends of his people, the Kiowas, "a lordly and dangerous society," in his words, "of fighters and thieves, hunters and priests of the sun."

MURRAY, DONALD M. A former editor of *Time* magazine, and winner of a Pulitzer Prize in 1954, Donald M. Murray (b. 1924) now teaches writing at the University of New Hampshire. His textbooks for college composition—which include *A Writer Teaches Writing* (1968), *Write to Learn* (1984), and *Read to Write* (1985)—emphasize that writing is a process and that writers learn through writing. He is also the author of a novel, *The Man Who Had Everything* (1964).

PALEY, GRACE The daughter of Russian immigrants, Grace Paley (b. 1922) is the author of two collections of ironic and often plotless short stories about the lives of ordinary people: *The Little Disturbances of Man* (1959) and *Enormous Changes at the Last Minute* (1974). A feminist and antiwar activist, Paley teaches fiction at Sarah Lawrence. When asked how much she revises, she responded: "A lot. I work very hard on that. That's because my first drafts are terrible."

RODRIQUEZ, RICHARD Born in 1944, Richard Rodriquez is an essayist and journalist best known for *Hunger of Memory* (1982), his memoir of growing up in California as the son of Spanish-speaking Mexican-Americans. Of this experience he writes, "I lived in a magical world, surrounded by sounds both pleasing and fearful."

SAGAN, CARL A professor of astronomy at Cornell University, Carl Sagan (b. 1934) has won a national audience by writing about science in terms that can be understood by nonscientists. His books include *The Dragons of Eden* (1977), which won a Pulitzer Prize for literature; *Broca's Brain* (1979; and *Cosmos* (1980).

SHADBOLT, MAURICE A free-lance writer and novelist from New Zealand, Maurice Shadbolt (b. 1932) contributes regularly to such periodicals as *National Geographic,* the *New Yorker,* and *Reader's Digest.* His books include *Danger Zone* (1975) and *Lovelock Version* (1981).

STARR, ROGER A member of the editorial board of the *New York Times,* Roger Starr (b. 1918) is the author of several books on housing and urban problems, including *America's Housing Challenge* (1978) and *The Rise and Fall of New York City* (1985).

STEGNER, WALLACE A winner of both a Pulitzer Prize for fiction and a National Book Award, Wallace Stegner (b. 1909) is the author of such novels as *The Big Rock Candy Mountain* (1943) and *Angle of Repose* (1971). His many volumes of nonfiction include *Mormon Country* (1942) and *One Way to Spell a Man* (1982), a collection of essays.

THOMAS, LEWIS A distinguished physician who is the author of more than two hundred articles for scholarly journals and medical textbooks, Lewis Thomas (b. 1913) is also known as a graceful stylist thanks to his column in the *New England Journal of Medicine,* "Notes of a Biology Watcher." His essays have been collected in several volumes, one of which, *The Lives of a Cell,* won a National Book Award in 1974.

THURBER, JAMES The author of many stories, including "The Secret Life of Walter Mitty," James Thurber (1894–1961) was also a talented cartoonist on the staff of the *New Yorker* for many years. A melancholy humorist, and the author of more than a dozen books, Thurber defined humor as "emotional chaos told about calmly and quietly in retrospect." His books include "*Is Sex Necessary?* (1929), *My Life and Hard Times* (1933), and *The Middle-Aged Man on the Flying Trapeze* (1935).

TOFFLER, ALVIN A former correspondent and editor at *Fortune,* Alvin Toffler (b. 1928) won a large popular audience through such works as *Future Shock* (1970), *The Third Wave* (1980), and *The Adaptive Corporation* (1984), all of which advise preparing for the future as Toffler envisions it.

VIDAL, GORE The grandson of a U.S. Senator from Oklahoma, and the son of an instructor at West Point, Gore Vidal (b. 1925) published his first novel, *Williwaw* (1946), when he was only twenty-one. The author of such best-sellers as *Burr* (1976) and *Lincoln* (1984), Vidal is also a frequent contributor to the *New York Review of Books* and is well known for the readiness with which he will engage in critical dispute.

WALKER, ALICE Best known for her novel *The Color Purple* (1982), which won both an American Book Award and a Pulitzer Prize, Alice Walker (b. 1944) has also published several volumes of poetry and short stories, as well as three other novels, *The Third Life of Grange Copeland* (1970); *Meridian* (1976); and, most recently, *Temple of My Familiar* (1989).

WHITE, E. B. Long affiliated with the *New Yorker,* Elwyn Brooks White (1899–1988) is widely considered one of the best stylists of modern American prose. In addition to his many essays, including the much-anthologized "Once More to the Lake," White is also remembered for *Charlotte's Web* (1952), and *The Elements of Style,* the celebrated book on writing by a Cornell University English teacher named William Strunk, Jr., that White brought to national attention in 1957.

WILL, GEORGE F. An influential conservative columnist, George Will (b. 1941) has been a contributing editor of *Newsweek* since 1975. A 1967 Ph.D. from Princeton, Will has also taught political science at Michigan State University and the University of Toronto.

WOLFE, TOM Born in 1931, Wolfe is widely recognized as a satirist with a gift for incisive prose. His books include *The Electric Kool-Aid Acid Test* (1965), *The Right Stuff* (1979), *From Bauhaus to Our House* (1981), and *The Bonfire of the Vanities* (1985).

ZINSSER, WILLIAM A journalist, critic, and teacher who is the author of more than ten books, William K. Zinsser (b. 1922) is best known for two fine guides to writing nonfiction, *On Writing Well* (1980) and *Writing to Learn* (1988). "Writing is hard work," according to Zinsser. "A clear sentence is no accident. Very few sentences come out right the first time, or the third."

Appendix

SAMPLE SYLLABI

Effective teachers of composition respond to the particular needs of each writing class. Without seeming to shift direction or evaluation criteria, they will modify their syllabus whenever problems with pacing or signs of confusion (or particular interest) signal that a change would be in the best interest of the class. Shape the following syllabi to suit the length and emphasis of your course. (To ensure flexibility, many writing instructors prefer not to distribute a detailed syllabus to their students. You might use the following syllabi to plan your course and then distribute to students a course outline that simply defines the goals of your course, the text that will be used, and the approximate amount of writing that will be required.

One-Semester Composition Course: Language Emphasis

Week One	Sentence structure. Sections **1–3**. Exercises in sentence combining designed to eliminate unintentional fragments. Short writing assignment made.
Week Two	Subordination and coordination. Discuss section **24**. Short writing assignment due.
Week Three	Sentence variety. Section **30**. Return first writing assignment with at least one positive comment on each paper. Give each student appropriate direction for revision, emphasizing skill in sentence structure and variety.
Week Four	Unity and agreement. Sections **6, 23, 27**. Assign exercises in the Handbook. Discuss appropriate topics for a paragraph. Return revisions and exercises.
Week Five	Writing paragraphs. Section **32**. After a discussion of paragraph unity, coherence, and development, ask students to write a paragraph in class, assigning a specific rhetorical mode.
Week Six	Introductory and body paragraphs. Assign section **33**. Discuss audience, purpose, and invention. Assign a two-

223

paragraph sequence: an introductory paragraph and one body paragraph on a topic appropriate for an essay.

Week Seven	Planning an essay. Review **33d, 33e,** and **33f**. Writing assignment due. Respond by next class, providing advice for development in the whole composition. Assign two body paragraphs that demonstrate different methods of development.
Week Eight	Individual conferences to assist in shaping the first essay. Discussion of conclusions in class. Assign essay.
Week Nine	Begin discussion of style. Assign sections **20** and **21**. First essay due. Respond with advice for revision.
Week Ten	Review punctuation and mechanics, emphasizing sections **8** and **12**. Revised essay due.
Week Eleven	Logical thinking. Section **31**. Assign new essay, a short argument.
Week Twelve	Review areas where most students seem to encounter difficulty. New essay due.
Week Thirteen	Discuss sections **26** and **29**. Revised argument due, incorporating lessons on parallelism and emphasis.
Week Fourteen	Provide overview of sections **34** and **35** for future reference. Discuss figurative language. Assign essay.
Week Fifteen	Assign **33i** to help students with exams. Last essay due. Review major characteristics of good writing.

One-Semester Composition Course: Essay Emphasis

This approach usually requires the purchase of a reader as well as a Handbook, but many instructors are able to use model student essays from previous semesters. When you read a good student essay, ask if you can keep a copy to help future students.

Week One	The writing process. Assign section **33** for discussion in class.
Week Two	Methods of development. Assign section **32**. Emphasize description or narration. Assign an expressive essay, incorporating one of these modes.
Week Three	Eliminating wordiness. Assign section **21**. Review Reviser's Checklist in section **33**. First essays due.
Week Four	Review importance of revision. Return papers with advice for improvement. Assign section **8** on manuscript form.
Week Five	Review punctuation and mechanics. First revision due. Read model essays of comparison/contrast. Assign new essay.

Week Six	Peer editing in class. Second essay due. Read model essays of classification, definition, or cause and effect in preparation for writing an informative essay.
Week Seven	Return student essays and assign informative essay. Conferences with students to discuss writing habits and performance.
Week Eight	Informative essay due. Assign section **31**. Do exercises in logic in class. Discuss elements of argument and persuasion.
Week Nine	Examine model essays and assign a persuasive essay. Peer editing in class.
Week Ten	Persuasive essays due. Assign section **34**. Emphasize finding a topic for the research paper and provide introduction to library resources.
Week Eleven	Paraphrase, summary, and direct quotation. Help students avoid plagiarism through advice on careful note taking and exercises in paraphrase and documentation. Assign working bibliography.
Week Twelve	Continue discussion of documentation. Provide examples of well-integrated source material. Working bibliography due.
Week Thirteen	Organizing and drafting a research paper. Discuss model essays in section **34**. Schedule conferences at which students must explain the purpose and thesis of their research paper and show their plan.
Week Fourteen	Research paper due. Assign section **35**. Discuss writing across the curriculum.
Week Fifteen	Return research papers. Review the writing process and **33i** on exam writing. Urge students to keep on writing and provide information on other writing courses from which they might benefit.